PRACTICE & THEORY IN SELF–DIRECTED LEARNING

Huey B. Long & Associates

Motorola University Press

ISBN 1-56946-056-6

CONSULTING EDITORS

The manuscripts selected for inclusions in this volume were reviewed by a panel of reputational consulting editors with expertise in self-directed learning. Appreciation is expressed to each of the following for their timely assistance.

TABLE OF CONTENTS

List of Tables

List of Figures

PREFACE

This is the 13th volume on self-directed learning published as a follow-up to the 1999 meeting of the International Self-Directed Learning Symposium. Each of the symposia has produced an interesting and different set of issues concerning self-direction in learning. But as has been observed the more things change, the more they remain the same! The reader who has studied some of the previous books will recognize some of the topics explored in earlier volumes, but the conversation has moved further. It may not have moved as far as some would expect or desire. Nevertheless, I think that our understanding of what is meant by self-direction in learning and self-directed learning is either growing deeper, or at the least changing.

Some of the issues that persist across the volumes include the means of characterizing individuals as self-directed learners. The focus upon Guglilielmino's Self-Directed Learning Readiness Scale (SDLRS) is not as great here as in previously published volumes. Different measurement of individual self-directed learning propensities are found in the work of Jane Pilling-Cormick. Jane and her colleagues report early work based on the use of her instrument. Ponton, Carr and Confessore report what may be the first of several investigations into learning conation. The question of the relationship between self-directed learning attitudes/behaviors and personality is revisited. Even though the reported findings fail to support the hypothetical association between personality and self-directed learning, the findings are preliminary. The research designs leave adequate room for the suggestion of alternative interpretations or explanations of findings. Further research is needed before we can conclude there is no relationship between self-directed learning and personality. Elsewhere, I have suggested that a tendency to be self-directed in learning may be associated with a psychological syndrome. As such, several psychological elements that may or may not be associated with personality and conation may combine in self-direction or other-direction. Existing instruments may not be sufficiently robust to identify the various elements.

The reader will find a variety of topics and style in the following chapters.

As is customary in these publications, I have the pleasure of introducing and attempting to further explicate our knowledge and understanding of self-directed learning. Chapter One identifies some of the things we believe, or as I have stated, what we think we know about self-directed learning. Chapter Two is designed for the novice in the self-directed learning literature as well as the practitioner who limits the concept to the learning of a socially independent or isolated learner or to an educational technique or method. Some have suggested that self-directed learning cannot occur in a group such as a class or even in an independently chosen and voluntarily attended lecture. I have attempted, once again, in Chapter Two to identify those psychological and cognitive phenomena that hypothetically the learner can influence, or direct. I hope the chapter will be helpful to readers such as I often encounter in my university classes who are occasionally frustrated by the lack of agreement about the definition of self-directed learning. Some seem to want someone to require all writers to define self-directed learning in a singular and simple way. These readers are unaware of intra-discipline conflicts over such commonly used terms as intelligence; or the debate about the nature and purposes of history.

Other chapters in this volume include papers that are hortatory or philosophically based as well as chapters based on qualitative and quantitative research. A few comments about some of the chapters will communicate the nature of the volume.

There are a total of 21 chapters. Seven chapters, according to my interpretation deal with psychological questions: Confessore and Park (learning orientation), Hoban and Sersland (self-efficacy), Nuckles (personality), Plowman (motivation), Ponton, Carr and Confessore (conation) Kreber, Cranton and Allen (self-directed learning readiness, psychological type, learning style, creativity and logic), Yoo, Cheong and Cheong (deomgraphic and psychological determinants). Four are concerned with a new instrument, Jane Pilling-Cormick's Self-Directed Learning Perception Scale (Plling-Cormick, Pilling-Cormick and Bullik, and two chapters by Pilling-Cormick and Kops).

The remaining nine chapters are distributed across several topics. They include the two chapters by Long mentioned above, a chapter describing an example of situated cognition by Boham, and six chapters dealing with teaching, techniques and methods. Barnes and Morris report on teacher perceptions and student nurses SDLR scores; Beitler discusses the use of learning contracts. Bulik and Hanor turn their attention to learning in a digital age, Kreber reflects on self-direction in professional development (university professor). Two chapters (Guglielminoe and Knutson, and Urban) examine self-directed learning and development of teachers and school improvement. Zomorrodian explores a framework for an additional instrument.

Two of the above chapters may be useful in improved understanding of cross-cultural aspects of self-direction in learning. Despite your expectations, only one of the two deals with a culture beyond the United States. Yoo, Cheong and Cheong continue previous studies of Korean youth. Bohnam's inquiry into situated cognition draws from an American folk culture to reveal how roles and skills are developed.

Over the past 13 years a number of individuals have made important contributions to the success and vitality of the International Self-Directed Learning Symposium. The contributions of the following are gratefully acknowledged: Gary Confessore, George Washington University, Richard Durr, Motorola; Godon Eisenman, Palm Beach Atlantic College, and Lucy and Paul Guflielmino, Florida Atlantic University. Others have helped give the various symposia a truly international dimension. They include Philippe Carre, Chija Kim Cheong, and Ji Woong Cheong, Roland Focher, and Gerald Straka. A special thanks and appreciation goes to my wife, Marie for her assistance with registration, and various related tasks. She makes my job easier.

Huey B. Long
Norman, OK
January 1, 2000

CHAPTER ONE

WHAT WE THINK WE KNOW ABOUT
SELF–DIRECTED LEARNING

Huey B. Long

Please note this topic is not what we **know** to be true about self-directed learning, instead it is what we **think** we know. I have purposely selected this rather awkward title because history reveals that it is not infrequent for what is believed by some at some time to later be accepted as being incorrect. For example, our great grandparents believed that nutrition was in some way related to brain function, that is, fish was brain food. A later generation scoffed at such arcane and uninformed folklore. Currently, our great grandparents' beliefs on the general matter of a relationship between mental function and food is once again in vogue. A related example is found in the area of faculty psychology. That once popular notion concerned the belief that one increased cognitive function via mental activity. Faculty psychology was dismissed about fifty years ago as meaningless. Therefore it may be a surprise to learn that current brain theory envisions mental structures as plastic phenomena that are modifiable by stimulation. Until very recently it was generally accepted that almost all cells in the human body could be renewed, or that we could generate new cells, in almost every organ except the brain. Current research findings now suggest that certain kinds of cells in certain locations of the brain are renewable. If you are interested in identifying other beliefs that later were challenged see Morgan and Langford's (1981) humorous book entitled <u>Facts and Fallacies: A Book of Definitive Mistakes and Misguided Predictions</u>. Given the former observations, you may assume that I am not 100 per cent certain that some of my comments that follow will not be challenged by future theory and research findings. It is assumed, however, that I have some reasonable positions to share concerning what self-directed learning is about. This chapter is divided into two major subsections; part one is comprised of a discussion of the obvious aspects of self-directed learning; the first part refers to beliefs about which a consensus exists. Part two identifies and discusses more uncertain ideas and findings about the meaning and nature of self-directed learning.

POINTS OF AGREEMENT

While, there may be a greater number of points of agreement among self-directed learning theorists and practitioners, here are at least six major topics on which general agreement seems likely. The following six findings are of such common acceptance, it does not seem necessary to document them. Yet, should any doubt the substance of this assertion, support is readily available in Confessore and Long (1992), Long and Confessore (1992), and Long and Redding (1991) and selected annual publications based on the International Self-Directed Learning Symposium.

Little disagreement concerns the following six topics:

1. There is an extensive body of literature on the topic of self-directed learning.
2. There are numerous definitions and at least four important conceptualizations of self-directed learning.
3. A significant amount of the empirical research is based on the Guglielmino Self-directed Learning Readiness Scale.
4. Scores on Guglielmino's Self-directed Learning Readiness Scale (SDLRS) roughly form a normal distribution curve.
5. The mean adult SDLRS score, Form E, is approximately 215; baccalaureate graduates usually report the highest scores.
6. Managers and professionals usually report scores above 210.

It is desirable to briefly comment on each of the above. Perhaps the first of the three areas of agreement is the most obvious to anyone who has done any kind of literature search for self-directed learning. Gary Confessore and I identified 544 citations of works concerning self-directed learning published between 1966 and 1991. It is obvious to those who read in this topical area that publication of articles, books and chapters concerning self-directed learning has not ceased. Probably at least 200 additional publications of research and theory have been added in the past six years.

Unfortunately, for theory development and communication, the number of important conceptualizations of self-directed learning has not declined. On the other hand, I don't think the number has increased. We continue to be aware of the same four conceptual frameworks that have existed for the past twenty years. They are as described below. Self-directed learning conceptualized according to social criteria, that is, self-directed learning is a highly individual activity wherein the learner is mostly free of any kind of role subordination to some powerful other. Or, self-directed learning conceptualized as a technique employed by some powerful other, usually a teacher, to encourage learners to assume and discharge greater personal responsibility for their learning. Or, self-directed learning conceptualized as a distance modality where the learner is separated from the teacher by distance, and where the relationship is facilitated by prepared media. Finally, the fourth and most powerful conceptualization is the psychological one where self-directed learning is conceptualized according to cognitive choice, control and focus directed by the learner. See chapter two for related discussion.

The fourth conceptualization as described above appears to be necessary and sufficient to explain self-directed in any of the first three conceptualizations. If learners lack the discipline, control and motivation to learn, it is unlikely they will engage successfully in learning associated with the other three conceptualizations. Hence, the personal psychological conceptualization must, in some way, be considered when discussing and planning self-directed learning.

As is noted later, even though recognition that psychological phenomena may be critical to the understanding of self-directed learning, questions remain. Too few inquiries have focused on the psychological characteristics of individuals who engage success-fully in self-directed learning. Issues related to the origins, devel-opment and consequence of the psychological set that may account for self-direction in learning are numerous. See Yoo, Cheong and Cheong in this volume.

The third area of agreement concerns the importance of the Guglielmino Self-Directed Learning Readiness Scale. Even though at least ten other scales and measurement instruments designed to produce some information about self-directed learning according to one of the four conceptualizations mentioned above exists, the Guglielmino SDLRS has been used more often that any other one instrument. It is possible that it may have been used more fre-quently than any other two scales combined. Confessore and Long (1992) noted that 33 of the 242 publications they identified were based on the SDLRS. The nearest second place instrument was the Oddi Continuing Learning Inventory which was reported in five works. Long and Redding (1991) noted that 27% of the self-directed learning dissertations they studied, reported between 1977 and 1991, were based on the SDLRS. See Guglielmino and Knut-son in this volume for an informative review of the scale's use.

Findings associated with agreement areas four, five and six ob-viously flow from the research based on the SDLRS and their accu-racy ultimately depend upon the validity and reliability of the in-strument. While a few investigators have raised serious questions of the validity and reliability of the SDLRS, supportive results far exceed them. As long as research findings, which depend on the validity of the SDLRS, are reported the instrument will be a topic of study. Given the nature of education research it is unlikely that anyone will be successful in absolutely proving that the SDLRS is either valid or invalid. Sample characteristics, statistical concerns, scale constructive theory, personal biases and other variables are likely to keep the issue alive until other instruments are preferred and used. Then those instruments will be the topic of debate and study. See chapter five in this volume based on Jane Pilling-Cormick's new instrument, the Self-Directed Learning Perception Scale (SDLPS).

AREAS OF UNCERTAINTY

Unfortunately there are more areas of uncertainty about self-directed learning than topics about which beliefs concur. Time and space do not permit a complete enumeration of the areas of uncertainty, therefore, the following comments address what I think are the some of the most important topics about which we have some debatable positions.

First, the varied definitions and conceptualizations reflect the uncertainty about the very fundamental nature of the construct. By defining self-directed learning solely as a set of teaching strategies and activities, or by the social isolation of the learner, I think we begin in the middle of the paradigm of self-directed learning. Perhaps it would be best if we began at the beginning, that is with the distinctiveness of the name that has been accorded to the construct. The term, self-directed learning, must have some significance that requires it to be referred to in that way. The term is composed of an adjective and a noun, or two adjectives and a noun according to use and preference. Self-directed describes a specific kind of mental process that we have named learning. By using the adjective form we imply that learning may be described in more than one way, or there is little usefulness in the adjective. For example, to say that a flower is beautiful would be redundant if all flowers were beautiful. In other words, devising and using the term <u>self-directed learning</u> it is self-evident that we believe there is some other learning that does not merit or need the additional phrase, self-directed. As I discussed a few years ago, if the use of the term self-directed is to have meaning or usefulness, it must refer to one kind of learning that may be distinguished from some other kind of learning. We are not required to know if there are three or more kinds of learning—but we must agree that there are at least two kinds of learning, self-directed and some other kind. If not, we should stop using the term and merely refer to learning. The greatest logical support for ceasing to use the term self-directed learning is found in the argument of those who insist that all learning is self-directed; hence to place self-directed sequentially ahead of learning is redundant. To logically discount the assertion that all learning is self-directed we must only be able to identify one thing that has been learned that was accomplished through some agency of something other than intentional activity of the learner. For example, if there is such a thing as unintentional learning, a topic we find in the literature, then we have two types of learning: self-directed (which is purposive and intentional) and unintentional (which by its label, refers to coincidental or casual learning. If we can demonstrate that some learning, that is, the acceptance of a belief or some kind of behavioral modification, can be traced to acquiescence, coercion, indoctrination, or propaganda, it would seem that we have once again demonstrated that there is some other kind of learning at a psychocognitive level that differs from intentional, reasoned critically based learning.

The next topic about which uncertainty exists concerns the proposition that people differ on the propensity to be self-directed in learning, and if so why? This issue is important because it is concerned with the very important dimension of human nature. It encourages thought about questions of self-direction in learning as a trait or state phenomenon. It also stimulates our awareness of the possibility that people may be different in the strength of the characteristic. If we assume that there are differences among people on self-direction we are then challenged to explain what causes the difference. Is the explanation to be found in personal differences, or is it in the situational contingencies? If we believe that self-direction in learning is primarily a state phenomenon, we need to identify the conditions that elicit or give rise to it. Are the conditions social, environmental, or what? If we believe that self-direction in learning is fundamentally a state condition, then we may favor the technique conceptualization of self-directed learning. We, thus, assert, that differences are really not explained by

6

the individual variance as much as it is by how the learning environment is structured. On the other hand, if we believe that differences among individuals on self-direction in learning arise from a trait, we imply that there is something in the nature of the individuals, rather than the environment that explains the difference. But it also is possible that some kind of interaction may occur between state and trait phenomena. Regardless, of the position we take on the state/trait hypothesis the need for additional answers persist. Scholars cannot dismiss the problem simply by characterizing self-directed learning as a trait, a state or interactive. We must be concerned with obtaining answers to support our belief. If we subscribe to the belief that self-directed learning is a state characteristic, we are challenged to identify the nature of the conditions that universally facilitate or inhibit self-direction. If we assume that self-directed learning is explained solely by state conditions, we must believe that the same conditions are equally effective for all learners in every situation. But, I don't think we really believe in the universality of conditions. Those of us who have taught more than two classes of students are aware that there are very few, if any, classroom activities that work equally well with all students. We, also, face an equally fascinating set of problems if we accept the hypothesis that self-directed learning is a trait phenomenon. If we believe this, we must explain how one individual manifests self-direction differently across situations, or explain any differences among situations. It is likely that individuals may manifest some differences in learning behavior under different conditions. If so we are challenged to be informed of the interaction between the trait and the environment. The trait argument, does not assert that the self-directing learning behavior is equally powerful in all circumstances. If we assume that self-directed learning is a trait phenomenon that exists to <u>some</u> degree across all situations, we can analyze the interaction to locate the facilitating or inhibiting elements. See Long (1990, 1991) for additional comments on the state/trait and situational issues.

A second problem arising from the trait hypotheses concerns the nature of the trait. For example, is self-directed learning a cognitive phenomenon or a personality characteristic? The research available on this topic suggests that it may be a combination. Until we have more sensitive instruments with which to measure and discriminate between cognitive and personality dimensions, I am satisfied with the hypotheses that self-directed learning is explained by a combination of cognitive and personality phenomena; that is, it is a psychological construct. Unfortunately, my position is not without its problems. While there is psychological theory that defines personality as the soil in which cognitive behavior resides, we are aware that personality does not completely explain cognitive behavior. Neither can we confirm that every aspect of personality is universally potent. See Yoo, Cheong and Cheong, Kreber and Allen, and Ponton, Carr and Confessore in this volume.

A third problem, thus, flows from the second one as discussed immediately above. What causes the self-directed learning trait, either as a cognitive or personality phenomenon. If it exists we should have some ideas about its origin. But at this point, we are not sure. It seems that nature and nurture are both important. It also seems that while the strength of the phenomenon, as measured by the Guglielmino Self-Directed Learning Readiness Scale differs across individuals, it does increase in childhood to young adulthood. There is some evidence to support the importance of teacher developed opportunities for learners to practice or apply self-direction in learning. That is, practice in being self-directed appears to increase SDLRS scores. Yet, we do not yet know if the aggregate change in SDLRS score of someone who scores low on the scale will equal the change of someone who scores high. Given results of other tests of human development such as IQ, I would hypothesize that the answer is no.

SUMMARY AND CONCLUSIONS

My comments have addressed two different kinds of beliefs concerning self-directed learning. The first set of beliefs includes three topics about which there is consensus:

1. There is an extensive body of literature on the topic of self-directed learning.

2. There are numerous definitions and at least four important conceptualizations of self-directed learning.

3. A significant amount of the empirical research is based on the Guglielmino Self-directed Learning Readiness Scale.

4. Scores on Guglielmino's Self-directed Learning Readiness Scale (SDLRS) roughly form a normal distribution curve.

5. The mean adult SDLRS score, Form E, is approximately 215; baccalaureate graduates usually report the highest scores.

6. Managers and professionals usually report scores above 210.

We noted that the level of agreement on the final three topics depends on acceptance of the SDLRS. The validity and reliability, hence the usefulness of the SDLRS likely will remain a topic of inquiry as long as it is the dominant research instrument in self-directed learning. Future instruments should receive similar scouting.

The second set of beliefs concern topics about which we are less certain. There seems to some chronic uncertainty about the nature of self-directed learning. Some have proposed that all learning is self-directed. We also seem to be uncomfortable with efforts to explain self-directed learning either as a state or trait phenomenon. Uncertainties about the former contribute to questions about the importance of conditions and psychological traits. As a further consequence we cannot adequately explain why some conditions seem to support self-directed learning for some and not for others. We have not been consistent in differentiating between self-directed learning as a process and between self-directed learning as conditions that affect the process. Furthermore, we must deal with hypotheses about the origins of self-directed learning in order to be able to definitively explain them. We do have some data that suggests that self-directed learning attitudes increase with age among children and young adults. But our-beliefs about why this may be true are difficult to defend.

In some ways, I conclude these comments in much the same way as I have done at previous meetings of the International Self-Directed Learning Symposium. The opportunities for theory development and empirical research are great. As I look back over the 32 years that I have been concerned with self-directed learning, I realize that while some of the questions have changed, many remain the same.

REFERENCES

Confessore, G.J., & Long, H.B. (1992). Abstracts of literature in self-directed learning, 1983-1992. Norman, OK: Oklahoma Research Center for Continuing Professional and Higher Education, University of Oklahoma.

Long, H.B. (1990). Changing concepts of self-direction in learning. In H.B. Long & Associates, Advances in research and practice in self-directed learning (pp.1-8). Norman, OK: Oklahoma Research Center for Continuing Professional and Higher Education, University of Oklahoma.

Long, H.B. (1991). Challenges in the study and practice of self-directed learning. In H.B. Long & Associates, Self-directed learning: Concensus and conflict (pp. 11-28). Norman, OK: Oklahoma Research Center for Continuing Professional and Higher Education, University of Oklahoma.

Long, H.B., & Confessore, G.J. (1992). Abstracts of literature in self-directed learning, 1966-1982. Norman, OK: Oklahoma Research Center for Continuing Professional and Higher Education, University of Oklahoma.

Long, H.B., & Redding, T.R. (1991). Self-directed learning dissertation abstracts, 1966-1991. Norman, OK: Oklahoma Research Center for Continuing Professional and Higher Education, University of Oklahoma.

Morgan, C., & Langford, D. (1981). Facts and fallacies: A book of definitive mistakes and misguided predictions. New York, NY: St. Martin's Press.

CHAPTER TWO

UNDERSTANDING SELF–DIRECTION IN LEARNING

Huey B. Long

Reams of paper have been used over the past 30 years to attempt to explicate and understand self-direction in learning. A wide of variety of terms have been used to try to communicate the essence of the activity. Terms designed to connote self-direction in learning include autodidaxy, self-education, self-learning, self-regulated learning and so forth. Definitions are too numerous to list. Two illustrative definitions are given below:

> Elsewhere (Long, 1987 p.3), I defined self-directed learning as follows:
> ...a personally directed purposive mental process usually accompanied and supported by behavioral activities involved in the identification and searching out of information.

Knowles (1975, p..18) provided one of the first definitions of self-directed learning as follows:

> In its broadest meaning "self-directed learning" describes a process by which individuals take the initiative , with or without the assistance of others, in diagnosing their learning needs, formulating learning goals, identifying human and material resources for learning, choosing and implementing appropriate learning strategies, and evaluating learning outcomes.

The purpose of this contribution, however, is not to revisit the numerous definitions. The awareness of definitions is merely instrumental to the attainment of the ultimate goal of the discussion, that is to contribute to an understanding of self-direction in learning. In order to achieve the purpose of this discussion, the remaining comments are organized as follows: (a) explication of four conceptualizations of self-directed learning; (b) identification and discussion of three primary dimensions of self-direction in learning; (c) commentary on four secondary dimensions of self-direction in learning; (d) implications; and (e) a summary. Yet, before addressing the aforementioned topics it is desirable to explain the focus of this chapter – that is, self-direction in learning.

Many two-part terms pose challenges for definers, because we must try to define both terms in their relationship to the other. If both terms are used inconsistently or are used by individuals to refer to different phenomena, the problem is greater. That is one of the sources of difficulty in defining and understanding self-direction in learning. Even though it seems as if almost every psychologist and educator has a special definition for learning, we seem to accept that practice more easily than we accept the variety of definitions and meaning for self-direction. Our position is that everybody should know what direction means, but less certainty applies to definitions of self. Here the hyphenated word seems to confuse us. That is because even if we understand self-direction in normal discourse what does it mean as a theoretical construct that is a part of another theoretical construct, learning? For example, some think that all learning is directed by the self. What does that mean? How does learning occur that is not self-directed (Long, 1997, 1998)? Is indoctrination self-directed? Is compulsive behavior, including learning, self-directed in the sense of being under control of the compulsive individual (Shapiro, 1981). Since our purpose is to try to clarify rather than confuse we will define the last part of the term first. Then the rest of the chapter addresses the parts of the learning process in which humans may exert influence and direction so that the result is self-direction in learning.

Learning has as many meanings and definitions as does self-direction. It is, therefore, important that you be aware of how I am using the word. Learning is a psycho-neurological and personological process whereby various sensory and innate phenom-

12

ena are perceived, transmitted and encoded in the autonomic and central nervous systems resulting in a change in neural mass and structure that affects an individual's awareness, memory, recognition, understanding, and muscular control. The above definition means that the human being brings psychological as well as neurological substance to bear upon the environment, real or symbolic, (including themselves) to explain, understand and act upon it. Self-direction of that process means that the individual is conscious of at least some of the important parts of the process and is able to apply the self (consciousness) to those elements for purposes of controlling the process. Some of the areas in which the learner may exert control for the purpose of learning should become clear later, if clarity is lacking here.

Note that my earlier definition and Knowles' definition provide limited insights into the learning process. Both definitions comment upon the use of resources for learning, and both emphasize the purpose and initiation of the activity by the learner. This paper seeks to add to the understanding of the learning process.

FOUR CONCEPTUALIZATIONS

Various conceptualizations have been designed to organize the definitions of self-directed learning. My preferred conceptualizations are as follows, in order of their appearance in the literature:

1. The sociological concept based on Tough's definition and research into adults' learning projects
2. The technique concept based on Knowles' ideas about teaching formats
3. The methodological concept, based on the distance method of delivering instruction
4. The psychological concept based on my ideas of self control over the cognitive process of learning.

A few more comments about relationships and distinctions among the four conceptualizations are useful to the understanding of self-direction in learning, or learning through self-direction.

Sociological Conceptualization

The sociological conceptualization emphasizes the solitary learner. The original problem in Tough's learning project inquiry was to understand how the individual conducted the process of learning. Tough was concerned with the organizational and interpersonal relationships more than the intra-personal process. The main features of Tough's intra-personal dimensions were formulating the questions to be addressed, identifying the resources (including possible mentors) to be used, and determining when and where to "learn." Tough (n.d.) actually lists 26 decisions steps that the adult takes in preparation for learning projects, but few of these help us to understand the learning process as defined above, and as discussed later in this chapter. I often have referred to the sociological conceptualization as the Lone Ranger or Robinson Crusoe concept. As the Lone Ranger and Robinson Crusoe are represented as being mostly isolated or independent in their activities, they both had side-kicks or subordinates in Tonto and Friday, respectively. In the sociological conceptualization, the mentors, teachers, experts, or however the other humans recruited to assist in the learning process are identified, they are not superordinate to the learner. Their influence is limited to their content or skill competence and are expendable when they have served their purpose.

Technique Conceptualization

In contrast to the socially independent learning characterized by the sociological conceptualization, the technique conceptualization, following Knowles, focuses on humans learning in groups. The technique conceptualization, therefore, is founded upon ideas of the role of a leader, teacher, tutor, mentor, or facilitator in designing a format in which learners can effectively direct their learning. In this conceptualization, the teacher-facilitator maintains some social relationship with the learner, and usually the relationship is influenced by the facilitator's authority as well as competence. Note how this relationship contrasts with the facilitator's relationship with the learner according to the sociological conceptualization. According to the technique conceptualization, the facilitator/

planner/teacher/coordinator is expected to be competent and skillful in designing and organizing the social events of the teaching-learning environment as well as fostering and supporting the individual learning activities among the group members. Knowles was recognized for his use of two different techniques to facilitate self-direction in learning. The first of the techniques is a small group discussion technique wherein the groups are provided very little information or instruction other than to discuss X. The small groups then work through their various ideas and agendas related to X. The learning contract is the second technique, espoused by Knowles. According to the learning contract technique learners negotiate their individual learning goals, procedures and evaluation with the facilitator at the beginning of the learning activity.

Methodological Conceptualization
The methodological conceptualization has a few of the elements similar to each of the above. The methodological conceptualization is based on the ideas and processes underlying distance education. The variety of distance methods and media contribute to a wide range of opportunities for self-direction in learning. In some instances the learner may be alone and physically isolated from the teacher/facilitator and other learners; in other situations learners may make use of distance methods while in groups. Furthermore, the amount of learner choice and control, two important ideas to be discussed later, may vary greatly among distance designs. In distance education many of the planning decisions found in Tough's work are performed by someone other than the learner. In some designs the learner's options are extremely limited by a very tight structure based on stimulus-response theory and programmed instruction. Other designs may incorporate student choice options and learning contracts similar to those found in face-to-face techniques used by Knowles.

Psychological
The psychological conceptualization is the most recent among the various efforts to organize and understand self-direction in learn-

ing. The psychological conceptualization flows, at least in part, from my work in the early 1980s. It became obvious that the first three conceptualizations addressed the symptoms, or external manifestations of self-direction in learning rather than the internal processes. Effective and/or successful self-direction in learning among the first three conceptualizations is not probable, and likely not possible, without the psychological processes that foster self-direction in cognition. Please note that it is here where self-direction in learning is focused. I believe that the human self (conscious awareness) can and does influence cognitive processes that result in learning. Three primary dimensions of the psychological conceptualization include metacognition, motivation, and self-regulation. Secondary aspects of the psychological include the four Cs of choice, competence, control, and confidence.

I am increasingly convinced that in order to understand self-direction in learning we must have improved knowledge of the above seven primary and secondary dimensions of the critical psychological processes. Therefore, the rest of this essay reflects my current beliefs and ideas about the former. The following discussion is divided into two major divisions: the first examines the three primary dimensions of motivation, metacognition and self-regulation in that order; the second treats choice, control, competence, and confidence in the order listed.

THREE PRIMARY DIMENSIONS

Motivation

Elsewhere, I have suggested that we can't understand how or why an individual would manifest self-direction in learning without having some awareness of the role of motivation(Long, 1987). Motivation is defined here as energy, drive, or desire that encourages, impels, stimulates, or sustains an individual to accomplish a goal or task. Learning is a high energy activity because of the requirements of mental activity. Without focus, mental activity like physical exertion devolves to entropy and exhaustion (Csikzentmihalyi, 1990). Therefore, self-direction in learning needs a focus in order to be sustained over time. Hence, it is difficult to understand (including planning for) self-direction in learning without accounting for motivation.

Following Deci and Ryan (1985), we note three types of the motivation construct: amotivation (meaning no motivation), extrinsic motivation, and intrinsic motivation. While it is not impossible to have self-direction in learning in an extrinsically motivated situation, persistence and efficacy are less likely than in an intrinsically motivated state. Extrinsic motivated learning is defined as motivation that emerges from a desire for a goal or reward beyond the learning itself. For example, when someone makes an effort to learn something primarily because of recognition, reward, avoidance of punishment, and so forth it is believed that eventually the efforts expended will diminish, or the quality of the effort will be limited to merely satisfying the external conditions.

Intrinsic motivation, in contrast to extrinsic motivation, comes from the individual's interest in the learning process itself. Intrinsic motivation often is associated with curiosity. Learning is the reward! It need not have any consequence for the learner beyond the activity itself. The intrinsically motivated learner enjoys the learning activity for itself. The process is a source of pleasure and satisfaction. It may resolve a dilemma, answer a question, satisfy a paradox, and so forth, but the results are not sought to obtain recognition or reward. It is hypothesized that when someone engages in intrinsically motivated learning, self-direction will be more intense, be of a higher quality, and be more persistent.

Amotivation is not likely to lead to self-direction in learning until it is changed to either extrinsic or intrinsic motivation. From the above, my preference for intrinsic motivation should be obvious. But please observe, it is not absolutely necessary. Therefore, extrinsic motivation is preferred to amotivation. Facilitators are challenged to identify learner interest as a step toward helping the amotivated learner move to a motivated state. John Dewey's (1913) classic <u>Interest and effort in education</u> is an informative source.

Metacognition

Metacognition is a useful theoretical concept to help understand self-direction in learning. Simply stated, metacognition is thinking about thinking. Stated another way, it is being conscious or aware of how or what one is thinking. Metacognition includes a hypothetical construct referred to a as executive control. Executive control monitors the individual's thinking. For example, executive control alerts a reader when he or she is reading without attending to what he or she is reading. The process by which this occurs may vary among individuals and is weakly or strongly developed across a sample. Another example of metacognition is found in one's awareness of failed versus successful problem solving procedures. A few years ago I observed, in two different studies, subjects who repeatedly employed identical unsuccessful attempts to solve two different kind of problems. In each instance the unsuccessful subjects had one approach that they employed repeatedly without stopping to try to analyze what they had done or why their efforts had been unsuccessful. The aforementioned experiences are even more amazing inasmuch as the subjects talked about their procedures as they performed them.

Gagne' (1985, p.79) provides some helpful comments on the executive control function.

> It is apparent... that learning and remembering cannot be fully accounted for in terms of a simple diagram of information flow. There must also be processes by which the learner selects the nature of processing at each of the stages... How the attention of the learner is directed, how the information is encoded, how it is retrieved, and how it is expressed in organized responses are all matters that require a choice of strategies. This choice is the function of the executive control processes, including expectancies established before the learning is undertaken. The processes have the effect of making the learner a truly intelligent being—one who can learn to learn, and therefore one who can engage in a large scale measure of self-instruction.

It is proposed that self-direction is learning is improved when the learner engages executive control along with other metacognitive processes. It is hypothesized that self-direction requires a conscious awareness of important aspects of the cognitive processes employed in learning. For example, in self-direction learners may note, either on paper or in memory, the steps or activities conducted along with the consequences, i.e., what worked and what didn't. Furthermore, self-direction would suggest that the learner would attempt to develop an explanation for failure and success. In contrast, the learner who desires to learn via other direction rather than self-direction may prefer to wait for someone else, a teacher or supervisor, to point out the salient aspects of the experience that relate to success or failure. In seeking to understand self-direction in learning it appears to be difficult to overlook the role of metacognition. Thus, it is posited that when someone is engaged in self-direction in learning they are actively resorting to metacognition.

Self-Regulation

Self-regulation is a critical element in self-direction that flows naturally from the former discussion of metacogntion. While the two topics are concerned with similar phenomena they are not the same. It is not difficult to argue that self-regulation cannot occur without metacognition. Thus, while self-regulation may be made possible by metacognition it is not the same thing. For example, the elements sodium and chlorine are necessary for the compound sodium chloride, but the compound is different from the two elements. Self-regulation in learning, as is true of self-direction, has multiple definitions that reflect the psychological orientation of the definer (Zimmerman and Schunk,1989).

Self-regulation assumes that before a learner can engage in self-regulated behavior, he or she must be able to manifest self-control. Someone who is pathologically compulsive may lack the control mechanisms that permit self-regulation. While the above may appear to be circular, it is critical because the observation reflects a philosophy of the human being. Namely, the healthy human is capable of assuming self-control rather than being an automaton who is controlled by external stimulation or conditions. Compare the observation with the comment regarding compulsive behavior. Our logic goes something like this, the human being is a thinking (cognitive) being who can be aware of certain cognitive processes. If, the human being can think, and be aware of his or her thinking, then the human being can control (regulate) thinking in some way.

Some of the salient aspects of self-regulation include the following: (a) making choices between alternatives; (b) attributing values to consequences of the chosen alternative; and (c) choosing between immediate and delayed consequences. Let us look at the above building blocks of self-regulation. Assume that most of the time individuals may be faced with choosing to do a, b, or c. Assume that a, b, and c have different consequences. A may result in joyful satisfaction. B may result in the completion of a task. C may result in immediate pleasure, but pain may be a long term outcome. Given the possible consequences, choice among them may be influenced by the immediacy of the consequences.

Given the above model of human control and choice there are some sub-processes at work in self-regulation. They are as follows: (a) self-monitoring; (b) self-instruction; (c) self-reinforcement; (d) goal setting; (e) self-planning; (f) self-selection of strategies; and (g) self-evaluation. Other aspects of self-regulation include self-system development that is concerned with a variety of phenomenological elements such as achievement motivation, self-esteem, self-efficacy, and so forth. It should be apparent that success and quality of self-direction in learning are associated with most, if not all, of the processes of self-regulation.

FOUR SECONDARY DIMENSIONS

Four secondary dimensions of self-direction learning that I have labeled as the four cs include choice, competence, control, and confidence. It is not surprising that the secondary elements are found among the three primary dimensions discussed above. A few additional comments are appropriate, however. Whether the learner is engaged in isolated autodidactic learning, voluntarily attending a lecture, or participating in learning via a class, training group or distance education, choice is an important variable.

Choice

Choice may be manifested in many ways. First, how much choice does the learner have to participate at any level? Is participation the result of some kind of coercion, or is participation completely voluntary? If voluntary, what other opportunities or activities have been ignored in favor of this activity? Second, what choices are available within the learning format? Are different activities possible? Are different resources available from which to choose? Are alternative social interactions possible. Can the learning be evaluated in different ways, and can the learner chose among them? Being able to make choices in learning contribute to the learner's awareness of control or lack of control as discussed later in this section.

Competence

The results of self-direction in learning are directly related to the competence of the learner. Competence may manifested in different ways. First, is the learner competent in the fundamental knowledge and skill elements of the subject or task? For example, it is unlikely that someone can engage in self-direction in learning calculus without having competence in math. It is not likely that one would be able to compare French authors with English authors without being able to read both languages. The learner may be free to engage in self-direction, but not be able to do so until the critical fundamentals are mastered. So, if learners without math competence wish to be self-directed in learning calculus they must begin at their level of incompetence.

Control

Control is closely associated with choice. Some might say they are negative and positive expressions of the same phenomena. I think, however, that they relate to subtle, but important psychological differences. Making a choice is the consequence of control. Even though the teaching-learning situation may contain many possible options, none of them are real until the learner has manifested control and selected from among the alternatives. Furthermore, control may have a proactive or assertive dimension that distinguishes it from choice. That is, choice may be provided by the circumstances. Control may change the circumstances.

Confidence

Confidence in one's ability to do anything is perhaps the beginning of effort. Desire without confidence that one will be successful in attaining the object of desire limits the strength to initiate or continue an effort. A learner who has expectations of success is more likely to make an effort to learn than one who expects to fail. Confidence is believed to be developmental except possibly among the compulsive. Confidence as reflected in self-efficacy is found among the phenomenologically inspired lists of self-regulatory variables. It is often associated with competence and self-efficacy. Success with self-direction in learning contributes to feelings of competence and confidence.

IMPLICATIONS

The above comments are designed to contribute to understanding of self-direction in learning, frequently referred to as self-directed learning. Because self-directed learning is a term that is used often to refer to the socially independent or isolated learner, to distance education methods, and to the techniques employed as well as the psychological process, I have chosen to use the term self-direction in learning here. The discourse on the sociological, technique and methodological concepts should be helpful in distinguishing among the various ways that self-directed learning has been discussed. It is not difficult, when the four conceptualizations are placed before us, to become aware of the important differences among them. It, also, should be reasonably clear that despite the technique, the method, or independent status of the learner, self-direction in learning is most directly related to, and explained by, the psychological conceptualization. In other words, the socially independent learner as well as the learner in a group setting must employ psychological processes to engage in self-direction in learning.

This essay, therefore, has identified and discussed some of the more critical psychological constructs and processes that contribute to self-direction in learning. Three primary dimensions of self-direction in learning were identified as motivation, metacognition, and self-regulation. The thesis underlying the above is that motivation is crucial to self-direction in learning. Somehow, the amotivated state must be changed. Preferably, intrinsic motivation will prevail in order for the learner to extend learning to higher quality levels. Metacognition is important in that it is a resource the learner can use to increase efficacy of self-direction. Finally, self-regulation includes important processes that can be implemented by the self-directed learner.

Four secondary dimensions of self-directed learning flow from the three primary ones mentioned in the above paragraph. They are discussed as the four cs as each begins with the letter c: choice, competence, control, and confidence. The four secondary elements are highly interactive. They supplement and reinforce each other to contribute to the most positive outcomes of self-direction in learning.

Given the above framework for understanding self-direction in learning there are some steps that can be taken by the learner when occurs in an independent mode and some steps for the facilitator when the learning occurs as a part of instruction and training. When the learning primarily is in the independent mode the learner assumes a greater responsibility for remaining motivated, therefore, if the learning produces some satisfaction as a result of the process, it is likely to be continued. The learner, also, must constantly employ executive control to keep on task.. Finally, the four cs need to be implemented.

When self-direction in learning occurs within a group based activity under the leadership of a teacher, trainer, or facilitator the leader should be knowledgeable of the three primary and four secondary dimensions of self-direction identified herein. Forearmed with knowledge about motivation, metacognition, self-regulation, choice, competence, control and confidence the leader can work more successfully with individual learners to assist them to develop their self-regulatory system..

SUMMARY

The purpose of this discussion of self-direction in learning was to contribute to an understanding of self-direction in learning. In order to accomplish our purpose , the four major conceptualizations of self-direction in learning were identified and explicated. Three of the four conceptualizations principally refer to modes of learning and teaching. The fourth, which I believe to be the critical distinction of self-directed learning, is the psychological conceptualization. The psychological conceptualization draws from a wide array of psychological schools and theory. Accordingly, self-direction in learning is comprised of at least seven phenomena: three primary and four secondary. Each of the seven phenomena was discussed. Finally, some implications of the explication were discussed.

REFERENCES

Csikzentmihalyi, M. (1990). Flow: The psychology of optimal experience. New York: Harper Perennial.

Deci, E., & Ryan, R. (1985). Intrinsic motivation and self-determination in human behavior. New York: Plenum.

Dewey, J. (1913). Interest and effort in education. New York: Houghton Mifflin Co.

Gagne', R. (1985) The condition of learning and the theory of . instruction (4th edition). New York: Holt, Rnehart and Winston.

Knowles, M. (1975). Self-directed learning: A guide for teachers. Chicago: Association Press.

Long, H. (1987). Self-directed learning and learning theory . Unpublished paper presented at the Conference of the Commission of Professors of Adult Education. Washington, D.C.

Long, H.B. (1997). Self-directed learning: Smoke and mirrors? In H.B. Long & Associates, Expanding horizons in self-directed learning (pp. 1-12). Norman, OK: Pubic Managers Center, University of Oklahoma.

Long, H.B. (1998). Some provocative comments concerning self-directed learning. In H.B. Long & Associates, Contemporary ideas and practices in self-directed learning (pp. 1-16). Norman, OK: Public Managers Center, University of Oklahoma.

Shapiro, D. (1981). Autonomy and rigid character. New York: Basic Books.

Tough, A. (n.d). The adult's learning projects. Ontario: The Ontario Institute for Studies in Education.

Zimmerman, B., & Schunk, D. (1989). Self-regulated learning and academic achievement. New York: Springer-Verlag

CHAPTER THREE

RELATION BETWEEN SELF–DIRECTED LEARNING
AND SITUATED COGNITION AS ILLUSTRATED
IN A SOUTHERN FOLK CULTURE

L. Adrianne Bonham

As Huey Long's opening chapter indicates, there are a number of things we think we know about self-directed learning. One thing is so obvious that we don't even state it: Self-directed learning involves the individual learner. We may make the caveat that the individual learner does not have to work in isolation from other persons in order to be self-directed. What we usually mean, though, is that the individual learns *from* other persons, rather than that the individual learns *with* other persons.

Perhaps it is time to consider how the individual can be self-directed while learning in a social environment and while constructing meaning along with other persons in that environment. This study combines the individual and social construction of meaning as it is manifested in the Southern folk culture of Sacred Harp singing.

DEFINITIONS

Seven key phrases help define concepts related to the culture, self-directed learning, and various concepts related to situated learning.

Sacred Harp Singing

In the South of the 19th century, there was a recreational and relig-
ious tradition of the community gathering to sing. Over time, certain
groups adopted the name of the book that they used. One of those
books was Sacred Harp (B.F. White Sacred Harp, 1992; The Sacred
Harp, 1991). Although this tradition remains rooted in the South,
singings take place throughout the United States.

This culture is both casual and sharply defined. The atmosphere
is relaxed, friendly, and emotionally expressive; the group is accept-
ing of new members and visitors. At the same time, most procedures
for conducting the singing and related activities are closely prescribed and are taken for granted by oldtimers. This study deals with
how newcomers learn to be part of this culture.

Self-directed Learning (SDL)

Reading my description of Sacred Harp singing, one might wonder
whether any of the commonly agreed upon definitions of SDL
(Long, chapter 1) describe the learning in that culture. I believe that
two of the definitions do fit. Perhaps, because they fit in unusual
senses, this discussion will add depth to our understanding.

The first of Long's definitions seems appropriate for this study.
"Self-directed learning is a highly individual activity wherein the
learner is free of any kind of role subordination to some powerful
other." A person learning to participate in the Sacred Harp culture is
learning from the group, but that group does not act as a powerful
other.

The fourth of Long's definitions also seems to describe the way
individuals learn Sacred Harp culture. "Self-directed learning is
conceptualized according to cognitive choice, control, and focus
directed by the learner." In this culture, the group does not usually
call attention to what the learner should learn. It is up to the individual to detect the salient features of the culture and make them part of
her or his thinking and actions.

Situated Learning

All learning—in fact, all cognition—is situated within some particular setting, which both shapes learning and becomes an integral part of what is learned. There is a wholeness to the lived and learned experience; the knowledge is concrete rather than being abstract or generalized (Kirshner & Whitson, 1997; Lave & Wenger, 1991).

Apprenticeship

An apprenticeship is a particular kind of learning experience in which the learner operates within an authentic setting, to learn the wholeness of a role or task. Some crafts, such as plumbing, are taught through apprenticeships. The concept of apprenticeship is a crucial element in understanding the situatedness of learning. Trades such as plumbing require apprenticeship in order to enter the trade. Other occupational groups call apprenticeships by names such as clinical training or internships or residencies. Apprenticeships are avenues of access to communities of practice.

Community of Practice

A group engaged in a common activity, often an occupation, is known as a community of practice. Certain language, values, and ways of operating are shared by the persons who participate in such a community. Medicine constitutes a community of practice with numerous roles (doctor, nurse, technician—and patient).

Full Participation

The purpose of apprenticeship in a community of practice is to enter into full participation. Even when someone can be said to have attained full participation, learning still occurs. Learning is, in fact, a part of full participation.

Legitimate Peripheral Participation (LPP)

The pattern of activity that leads an apprentice to learn a role within a community of practice has been called legitimate peripheral participation (Lave & Wenger, 1991). The phrase assumes that, within the total task, there are roles central to the practice and roles peripheral to the practice. Even though some roles are peripheral and require less skill, they are authentic (legitimate), in that they must also be accomplished as part of the work of the community.

> This central concept denotes the particular mode of engagement of a learner who partici-
> pates in the actual practice of an expert, but only to a limited degree and with limited re-
> sponsibility for the ultimate product as a whole. (Hanks, 1991, p.14)

A plumber's apprentice, for instance, is sent to bring tools and supplies to the master plumber. In the medical field, nurses-to-be have clinical experiences; a modern trend in their education is to place them in clinicals from the beginning, so that they will learn the entire role of nurses.

LINKING SDL AND LPP

The task of an apprentice within a community of practice is ulti-mately self-directed. While the master assigns and oversees the roles, the apprentice must take the initiative to learn from the assigned tasks in order to make sense of what (s)he sees, hears, touches, and feels of body movement. The apprentice must watch the master and the more-advanced apprentices to learn how to do the assigned task, because a characteristic of this kind of learning often is that the master specifies the task but does not specify how the task is to be done. The apprentice also must see the range of tasks that go into the community's practice and must create a whole understanding of the practice.

> Apprentices gradually come to be master practitioners. Apprentices learn to think, argue, act,
> and interact in increasingly knowledgeable ways, with people who do something well, by
> doing it with them as legitimate, peripheral participants. (Lave, 1997, p.19).

Thus, the apprentice is a self-directed learner, deciding what actions and words to make into resources for learning, and making sense of the barrage of stimuli that are present in the authentic environment.

EXAMPLES OF LPP

In their classic text on LPP, Lave and Wenger (1991) identify five examples drawn from their research and that of others. Apprentices work under masters—in the usual sense—in tailor shops in Liberia; butchers in the United States and quartermasters in the U.S. navy do the same. Some Yucatec Mayan girls grow up in families in which the grandmothers are midwives; they absorb the skills and later feel a calling to the task. In Alcoholics Anonymous, nondrinking alcoholics learn a 12-step program but also learn how to tell the story of their alcoholism; thus, they move from the culture of alcoholism to the culture of AA.

Lave is the researcher who studied tailors in Liberia (Lave & Wenger, 1991). She found that the order of learning tasks was governed by the skills of the apprentice and the needs of the master—not by the chronological order of the tailoring process. She also found that, at a certain stage of the apprenticeship, the apprentice had learned the essentials that went into producing a garment. Then he stayed behind when the shop closed at night and guided his own skill development by making garments. The price that a customer was willing to pay for one of his garments was a natural test of the apprentice's skills.

MY EXAMPLE OF A COMMUNITY OF PRACTICE AND ITS LPP

I have witnessed another example of a culture that continues to exist because it has a strong pattern of involving newcomers in LPP—although the relationship of the participation to the total activity is different than in the examples mentioned above.

My example is the Southern folk activity of Sacred Harp singing. The name comes from the songbook used, and refers to the human voice as a sacred musical instrument. The original songbook was published in 1844; today there are two versions (The B.F. White Sacred Harp, 1992; The Sacred Harp, 1991), which have gone through different revision histories. But well-trained singers have no trouble switching between the two. Singings are held on weekends all over the United States and in places beyond. But the culture has been maintained longest in the rural South.

Participants sing a cappella for a total of four hours a day, with dinner on the grounds in the middle of the day. Locations and dates of singings are traditional, and there is usually little publicity about the events outside of the sources that circulate among singers. What little publicity there is usually indicates which of the two songbooks will be used. Each singer provides his/her own songbook.

A good facility for singing has a low ceiling and hard, sound-reflecting surfaces. At least some of the chairs or benches must be moveable, because of the required room arrangement. The chairs/benches are always arranged in the same way: facing the center of a hollow square. The larger the crowd, the smaller the space in the square, where each song leader must stand. Tenors always have their backs to the main entrance to the room, with altos facing them, basses to their left, and trebles to their right. Both men and women sing tenor and treble—an octave apart. Only men sing bass; only women sing alto. Anyone who comes just to listen sits behind the tenor section; but the only place to get the full effect of the sound is in the hollow square.

Full Participation

To understand how people learn the culture, it is appropriate to consider first what it means to participate fully in the culture. I describe the most basic part of this experience in first person.

I am in my chosen seat at the exact starting time, because that is when the chairperson will lead the first song. I have my book ready to find the first page number when the leader calls it, and I will follow that pattern intensely: The average time between ending one song and beginning the next is about 25 seconds!

The first sound of singing is someone on the front row of tenors who gives pitches for the various parts. The leader begins to mark time with one hand as the whole group begins to sing—not with the first verse but with something not written in the book.

The book has what are called shaped notes, with the head of each note taking a particular shape—triangle, oval, square, or diamond.

Experienced singers are able to decode the shapes, pronouncing the syllable that relates to each shape—no matter how fast the tempo or how many notes there are per measure. It is this practice of singing the notes that gives the singing its other name—fasola—because the names of the shapes are fa, sol, la, and mi. The original intention for this form of notation was to teach people in Colonial America how to sing when there was no other form of music education. (The memory of this educational intent is retained in calling the group a *class* and one song a *lesson*.) Now the notation is a major hurdle for a new person who tries to become part of the culture. Being able to sight-read music in the present conventional sense does little to help a newcomer sing the fasolas.

The singing begins vigorously—and loudly. There is not the timidity usually found in church congregational hymn-singing. Every person sings as loudly as possible. If a person does not sing well, or is unfamiliar with a particular hymn, any mistakes will be masked by the volume of sound. But generally the singers follow the music well, even though it can be complex. Many of the tunes are fuguing tunes, meaning that the different sections of singers enter the music at different points and sing different words at the same time.

One reason people are drawn to Sacred Harp singing is that there is a strong emotional response that the group makes to and through the music. At the end of a song, there may be exclamations of enjoyment aimed either at the leader or at one's inner satisfaction— but really at both.

As one leader completes the leading of the first song and takes his/her seat, someone sitting behind the alto section calls the name of the next leader: "John Smith, followed by Mary Jones." John, having been warned in advance, rises quickly and announces the number of his chosen song as he moves into the hollow square and faces the tenor section. Several people repeat the page number so that all can find the music. Immediately the leader raises a hand, the pitch is sounded, and the group launches into the fasolas. A new leader is called for each song, and anyone present can choose to lead. The wording of the leader's announcement is almost always the same: "Number 45, on the top; first verse only, no repeats on the notes," meaning that on page 45 there are two songs and the group will sing the one that begins at the top of the page; no repeats that appear in the music will be sung as we do the fasolas, and only the first verse will be sung.

If a leader calls a song that has already been sung that day, the general cry goes up: "Been used." The leader must quickly choose a different number, or receive help from the group in identifying one that hasn't been used. There are always a few old hands who can remember, by page number and name, every song that has been sung so far that day. They call out, "Been used" even before the arranging committee (the person or persons sitting behind the alto section) can check the minutes it is creating, a list of songs and song leaders.

After an hour of singing, there is a brief recess, followed by another hour of singing, then dinner on the grounds and two more periods of singing.

LPP in Sacred Harp Singing

I did not grow up singing Sacred Harp, as many people of all ages did. Thus I'm acutely aware of what it takes to become a skilled participant. First, I have to learn when and where singings will be held. I do that by obtaining a book of minutes published for singings throughout the United States. Besides recording the names and page numbers for every participant at a singing, this book gives dates of singings for the next year.

My first act on arrival is to find my place. I sing tenor, so I look for the section with its back to the door I've just entered. I know not to try for a seat on the first row; that one is reserved for the strongest tenor singers, usually including the person(s) chosen to pitch each song. While I don't choose the first row, I don't want to get too far back—among the spectators. The greatest dynamic exists in the hollow square and the first row of seats in each section. So I want to be as close as possible to that, without violating my position as a novice.

I learn the order of opening events: a song led by the chairperson of the singing, a prayer led by one of the men regularly called on for that, a song led by the vice-chair, and then songs led by persons called by the arranging committee. Only experienced leaders are called for the first few songs, so as to start the event strongly. The arranging committee is always sensitive to call on visitors, with the word being defined only as insiders understand it. Other than that distinction, none is made. There is a mix of men and women, children and adults. Sometimes people lead together, especially if one is inexperienced. This is often the way children begin leading, although they can become full participants in leading while still preschoolers and unable to read the book they hold.

The fact that I participate as a novice isn't a problem; the singing can go on as the culture dictates, so long as a large portion of singers are experienced. I may not know the fasolas or even be able to keep up with the words when the fuguing tune is complex. I may not know the tune and may sing it poorly. But I experience all the satisfaction of singing as part of a group.

My chief way of learning to sing the notes has been to attend singings and to participate to the extent I could, with experienced persons carrying on the heart of the activity.

LPP in Leading Sacred Harp Singing

While apprenticeship and legitimate peripheral participation can be seen in terms of singing, they are even clearer in terms of leading the group in a song. I attended many singings before I tried to lead, although other persons begin the first time they attend a singing, because they already know how to lead singing.

When I lead, I depend on the person giving the pitch for the group, even though experienced singers sometimes give their own pitches for the songs they lead. I choose a person to watch in the front row of tenors—someone I know. I depend on him to help me begin the singing and keep the beat. Some other people always keep the beat for themselves, even when they are seated. But when an inexperienced adult or child is leading, even more people keep the beat. Thus, it is easy to sense all around the leader what the beat should be.

If I have inadvertently chosen a fuguing tune, I'm in trouble. The leader is supposed to turn and point to each group as it enters the song. The person I'm watching—and probably the whole first row of tenors—leans out of the chair and makes exaggerated gestures toward the group that should be entering the music. I follow their motions as I'm able.

If I have forgotten to specify which verses to sing and none of the tenors has thought to ask me before the singing begins, the person I'm watching makes the decision and either ends the song after the first verse or launches into other verses, taking me along. I once heard a teenager talking to his mentor about what had just happened when the teenager led a song. The mentor said, "Yes, if they see any hesitation on your part, they'll take it away from you." This was one of those cases in which the front-row tenors didn't know the teenager's skill level. Maybe they read natural timidity for lack of skill in leading, and they took over in order to fill in the gap and keep the singing at full force.

Differences in LPP as Seen in Sacred Harp Singing

Thus far I have pointed out commonalities between LPP as defined by Lave and LPP as illustrated in Sacred Harp singing. There is a difference, however. In Lave's conceptualization, the apprentice is assigned discrete tasks and does them alongside others who are doing other tasks that are part of the total enterprise. A tailor's apprentice, for instance, hems pants. Beside him, the master is cutting cloth for the next pair.

In Sacred Harp singing, however, the basic tasks of singing and leading are done by everyone. The peripherality experienced by the apprentice singer is not in being assigned a different task but in how well (s)he performs the task. The lack shown by the novice is compensated by the whole group, which actually serves as the master. An individual singer or leader does as much as that person knows how to do; the group provides everything that is missing. The visual image I have is that the performance of the novice is an irregularly shaped rock dropped into a bucket. The experienced singers are water that flows around the rock and fills the bucket to a smooth, full level. The masters take whatever shape and volume are needed in order to accomplish a whole performance.

34

RELATION OF CONCEPTS OF SDL AND
SOCIAL CONSTRUCTION OF KNOWLEDGE

Although it is easy to see that the culture of Sacred Harp singing illustrates the social-construction-of-knowledge concepts of *community of practice, apprenticeship,* and *legitimate peripheral participation*, it is more difficult—so far—to see how the culture illustrates the use of self-directed learning.

Long's first definition (chapter 1) focuses on the learner's autonomy in the learning process. In what sense is a learner autonomous in learning the carefully defined culture of Sacred Harp? Obviously, the learner decides to become involved in this activity. To be a regular participant, the individual must rearrange priorities related to how she or he spends time on weekends. There must also be a commitment to considerable travel in order to get to the widely separated places where singings are held.

The newcomer may also arrange to attend practice sessions or singing schools. Singing schools are held occasionally, usually with a noted singer teaching fundamentals of singing. Traditionally, singing schools were held in rural communities for a week or two during the summer and were designed chiefly for children in Sacred Harp families. Children met with the teacher during the day, and local adults came at night for singings, in which children led songs they had practiced during the day.

Besides being self-directing in deciding to be involved in the culture and to learn it through practices and singing schools, newcomers decide how much they will question the oldtimers about the customs of the culture. And they decide how much risk they are willing to take in standing before the group to practice leading. Some, for instance, will lead only in very small groups, where time will be taken to help them and where their weak performance will not hold back a lively singing. Others show no timidity, regardless of their experience with leading other kinds of music.

While Long's first definition (chapter 1) can be illustrated in Sacred Harp culture, his fourth definition is even more interesting. "Cognitive choice, control, and focus" are exercised by the learner as he or she decides what to give his or her attention to, during the singings. Some learners attune themselves to the culture by being sensitive to events and patterns. Others are oblivious to the rules of the culture.

The latter kind of newcomer was illustrated to me the first time I attended a singing. I saw a child lead a song in which the group began singing the first verse and did not sing the fasolas. Sometime later, a man got up to lead, saying this was his first time to attend a singing. The way he launched into keeping the beat and beginning to sing made it clear that he had had some experience in leading music. But the group wasn't with him. They started singing the fasolas and he was singing the words of the first verse. As they realized what he was doing, they switched to the words; nothing was said to him afterward, so far as I could hear. Several weeks later, the same man was at another singing convention, and he did the same thing in leading his song. He had not attended to what was happening around him. He had failed to notice what children or inexperienced adults said when they wanted to skip the fasolas: "Number 45 on the top; the words only."

Some persons are more skilled than others at recognizing unfamiliar actions or word patterns and learning what the actions or words mean in the culture. When they realize unfamiliar patterns, they use a variety of ways to learn what they need to know. At singings, a good time to quiz oldtimers is lunchtime. They are eager to share the culture but have no way to know what is unfamiliar to an individual unless that person asks questions.

Observant newcomers can also learn just by watching a number of leaders or seeing patterns in the ways songs are sung or listening to the people singing the same part around them. In order to answer their own questions, it is necessary for newcomers to draw back from participation, and listen and watch. That was how I knew what the man mentioned above should have done if he didn't want to sing the fasolas.

One gets a new perspective on, and appreciation for, the exuberance of a lively singing when, instead of watching the book, he or she watches movements of an oldtimer who moves around the hollow square, bring in the various parts in a lively fuging song. Seventy-five years of practice may have led to that event.

One characteristic of the music is that there are many repeats. Even a person who reads music, however, has to give close attention to how the written music differs from the singing. Oldtimers sing repeats that aren't written and omit ones that are. For instance, it is customary to sing repeats only on the last verse of a song. Part of a leader's instructions may tell how the group is to repeat: "Number 45 on the top; verses 1 and 2; repeat on the notes and the last verse."

The leader may even give instructions to sing "the unwritten verse," meaning that custom has attached a verse which everyone supposedly knows even though it is not written on that page.

In summary, there are ways in which a newcomer is self-directed in deciding how to become a member of the culture (Long's first definition) and in focusing attention (Long's fourth definition) on the unfamiliar in order to make it familiar.

CONCLUSION

If learning is defined as making meaning out of experience, is that a process to be studied in terms of the individual (SDL) or in terms of social constructions (communities of practice)? This is a question that does not require a choice; it can be both. Taking this dual perspective opens new avenues of thought for those who seek to understand learning in all of its manifestations.

REFERENCES

The B.F. White Sacred Harp: Revised Cooper Edition. (1992). Samson, AL: Sacred Harp Book Co., Inc.

Hanks, W.F. (1991). Foreword by William F. Hanks. In J. Lave & E. Wenger, Situated learning: Legitimate peripheral participation (pp.13-24). New York: Cambridge University Press.

Kirshner, D., & Whitson, J.A. (1997). Editors' introduction to Situated cognition: Social, semiotic, and psychological perspectives. In D. Kirshner & J.A. Whitson (Eds.), Situated cognition: Social, semiotic, and psychological perspectives (pp.1-16). Mahwah, NJ: Lawrence Erlbaum Associates.

Lave, J. (1997). The culture of acquisition and the practice of understanding. In D. Kirshner & J.A. Whitson (Eds.), <u>Situated cognition: Social, semiotic, and psychological perspectives</u> (pp.17-35). Mahwah, NJ: Lawrence Erlbaum Associates.

Lave, J., & Wenger, E. (1991). <u>Situated learning: Legitimate peripheral participation</u>. New York: Cambridge University Press.

<u>The Sacred Harp, 1991 Revision: The best collection of sacred songs, hymns, odes, and anthems ever offered the singing public for general use</u>. (1991). Carrollton, GA: Sacred Harp Publishing Company, Inc.

CHAPTER FOUR

THE DISTRIBUTION OF HOULE'S LEARNER
ORIENTATION TYPOLOGY AMONG
BACCALAUREATE STUDENTS:
A COMPARATIVE STUDY OF TRADITIONAL AND
NON–TRADITIONAL STUDENTS IN KOREA
AND THE UNITED STATES

Gary J. Confessore & Eunmi Park

It has been four decades since Houle conducted the research that
led to the 1961 publication of his concept of learner orientation in
The Inquiring Mind. In that work, he built his adult learning construct around two major objectives: first, he set out to develop a
typology of reasons for participating in adult education activities;
and second, to place the self-education efforts of adult learners into
the explanatory context afforded by this typology.

Houle was interested in learner orientation as a framework with
which to understand the expectations and aspirations that individuals bring to learning situations. He labeled these "learner orientations." At least two subsequent studies of adult learning activities
(Cross, Valley & Associate, 1974; Johnstone & Rivera, 1965) took
note of the distribution of this typology in their populations. In the
present study, knowledge of learner orientation is viewed as fundamental to understanding the motivation to learn in a variety of
contexts, including self-directed learning.

Houle (1961) described three categories into which he was able to place most adult learning activities of an American population. These are: (1) activity-oriented learning—"The activity-oriented take part in learning primarily for reasons unrelated to the purposes or content of the activities in which they engage" (p.19). He asserts, the person "who takes courses simply for the credits themselves or for the diplomas, certificates, or degrees which may eventually be won by piling up the proper number of credits," is an activity-oriented learner (p.21). (2) Goal-oriented learners—He explains, "… are the easiest to understand, chiefly because their views accord so well with the usual beliefs about education. Knowledge is to be put to use, and, if it is not, why bother to pursue it?" (p.16.) "The continuing education of the goal-oriented is in episodes, each of which begins with the realization of a need or the identification of an interest" (p.18). "The need or interest appears and they satisfy it by taking a course, or joining a group, or reading a book, or going on a trip" (p.18). (3) Learning-oriented adults are those who are involved for the sheer pleasure of learning something new. What they do has continuity, a flow, and a spread that establish the basic nature of their participation in continuing education. For the most part, "they are avid readers and have been since childhood: they join groups and classes and organizations for educational reasons; they select the serious programs on television and radio" (p.24). Houle found this group to be the most homogeneous. "They have goals; they enjoy participation, and they like to learn. Their differences are matters of emphasis" (p.29).

Recently, Confessore and Barron (1997) investigated whether the distribution of learner orientations in "baby boomers" (people born in the United States between 1946 and 1966) differed from people born before 1946 (pre-boomers) or after 1966 (post-boomers). Their study was prompted by the observations of Chickering and Havighurst (1981), and of Gerald and Hussar (1995), among others, who had commented on the affect of the observed life-style differences of boomers and post-boomers, with the latter often referred to as "generation X."

Barron's (1999) dissertation studied the relationships among selected demographic characteristics and the distribution of Houle's typology among of college students. Her main purpose was to inform the processes of curriculum development, program marketing and retention efforts at individual universities through an understanding of the distribution of learner orientations in populations served by each school.

PURPOSE

The present study was designed to answer three questions. (1) What is the distribution of learner orientations in Korean baccalaureate students? (2) Does the distribution of learner orientations in Korean baccalaureate students in a traditional program differ significantly from that of students in a low-residence program? (3) Do these distributions differ significantly from the distributions found in similar populations of American baccalaureate students?

METHODOLOGY

Confessore, Kim-Cheong and Park (1997) surveyed volunteers in low-residence and traditional baccalaureate programs in Seoul, Korea and compared their findings to those of Confessore and Herrmann (1997), who surveyed students in low-residence and traditional baccalaureate programs in the United States. Within each program equal numbers of males and females were surveyed, as were equal numbers of beginning freshmen, ending sophomores and ending seniors. Data were gathered using the Learning Profiles Questionnaire (Confessore & Confessore, 1994) in formal classes, program meetings, libraries, snack bars, and other common areas on campus. Respondents were invited to complete the survey and return their responses to the researchers within several minutes. The completed surveys were analyzed and learner orientations were assigned using the protocol developed and validated by Confessore and Barron (1997).

Each investigator assigned a learner orientation category to each respondent and the results were then compared. Differences were reconciled after review of the reference protocol. Since both the learning-orientation and the school / class data are categorical, descriptive statistics and non-parametric independent group comparisons were used to assess the three issues under investigation.

FINDINGS

One hundred and two usable responses were gathered in each program for a total of 204 Korean students and 204 American students. In each program the sample was limited to 17 males and 17 females representing each of the freshmen, sophomore and senior classes.

Chi square analysis was conducted with reference to the distribution of learner orientations in Korean baccalaureate students. The results of that analysis are presented in Table 4.1 which reveals, Korean freshmen tend to begin their academic careers as either learning- (41.2%) or goal- oriented (36.8%). By the end of the sophomore year Korean students tend to be activity- (41.2%) or goal-oriented (38.2%) and by the end of the senior year even more are activity-oriented (48.5%). This "migration" seems to involve a steady decline in the percentage of students who are learning-oriented as they move from 41.2% as beginning freshmen, through 20.6% as ending sophomores, to 17.6% as ending seniors. The observed distribution is significantly different than expected (p = 0.004).

The results of chi square analysis of the learner orientation and school year of all the American students surveyed are presented in Table 4.2, which reveals that the observed distribution of learner orientation among American students does not differ significantly from that expected (p = 0.327).

The results of chi square analysis of the learner orientation and school year of Korean students in a traditional program are presented in Table 4.3. This Table reveals that Korean students in a

Table 4.1.   Learner Orientation and School Year for All the Korean Respondents

	Activity	Goal	Learning	Total
Freshmen	15 (22.0%)	25 (36.8%)	28 (41.2%)	68
Sophomores	28 (41.2%)	26 (38.2%)	14 (30.6%)	68
Seniors	33 (48.5%)	23 (33.8%)	12 (17.6%)	68
TOTAL	76 (37.2%)	74 (36.3%)	54 (26.5%)	204
X^2 = 15.449	p = 0.004			

Table 4.2.   Learner Orientation and School Year for All the American Respondents

	Activity	Goal	Learning	Total
Freshmen	23 (33.8%)	27 (39.7%)	18 (26.5%)	68
Sophmores	26 (38.2%)	20 (29.4%)	22 (32.4%)	68
Seniors	25 (36.8%)	23 (33.8%)	20 (29.4%)	68
TOTAL	74 (36.3%)	70 (34.3%)	60 (29.4%)	204
X^2 = 2.235	p = 0.327			

traditional program tend to begin their freshman year as learner-oriented (50.0%) or goal-oriented (32.4%). Between the beginning of the freshman year and the end of the sophomore year there is a "migration" to activity-orientation (47.1%) and goal-oriented (35.3%). These proportions remain essentially unchanged through the end of the senior year. The observed distribution of learner orientation in this population differs significantly from expected (p = 0.016).

Table 4.3.   Learner Orientation and School Year for Korean Respondents in a Traditional Program

	Activity	Goal	Learning	Total
Freshmen	6 (17.6%)	11 (32.4%)	17 (50.0%)	34
Sophmores	16 (47.1%)	12 (35.3%)	6 (17.6%)	34
Seniors	15 (44.1%)	12 (35.3%)	7 (20.6%)	34
TOTAL	37 (36.3%)	35 (34.3%)	30 (29.4%)	102
X^2 = 12.376	p = 0.016			

The results of chi square analysis of the learner orientation and school year of American respondents in a traditional program are presented in Table 4.4. This table reveals that these students tend to begin their academic careers as activity- (44.1%) or goal-oriented (41.2%) and the distribution does not change significantly over the college careers of this group (p = 0.585).

Table 4.4.   **Learner Orientation and School Year for American Respondents in a Traditional Program**

	Activity	Goal	Learning	Total
Freshmen	15 (44.1%)	14 (41.2%)	5 (14.7%)	34
Sophmores	18 (52.9%)	8 (23.5%)	8 (23.5%)	34
Seniors	18 (52.9%)	10 (29.4%)	6 (17.6%)	34
TOTAL	51 (50.0%)	32 (31.4%)	19 (18.6%)	102
$X^2 = 2.840$	p = 0.585			

The results of chi square analysis of the learner orientation and school year of Korean students in a low residence program are presented in Table 4.5. This Table reveals that these students tend to begin their academic careers as goal- (41.2%) or learning-oriented (32.4%) and the distribution does not change significantly over the college careers of this group (p = 0.205).

Table 4.5.   **Learner Orientation and School Year for Korean Respondents in a Low Residence Program**

	Activity	Goal	Learning	Total
Freshmen	9 (26.5%)	14 (41.2%)	11 (32.4%)	34
Sophmores	12 (35.3%)	14 (41.2%)	8 (23.5%)	34
Seniors	18 (52.9%)	11 (32.4%)	5 (14.7%)	34
TOTAL	39 (38.2%)	39 (38.2%)	24 (23.5%)	102
$X^2 = 5.942$	p = 0.205			

The results of chi square analysis of the learner orientation and school year of American students in a low residence program are presented in Table X.6. This Table reveals that these students tend to begin their college careers as goal- or learning-oriented and remain so throughout their undergraduate years. The observed distribution does not differ significantly from expected (p = 0.069).

Table 4.6   **Learner Orientation and School Year for American Respondents in a Low Residence Program**

	Activity	Goal	Learning	Total
Freshmen	8 (23.5%)	13 (38.2%)	13 (38.2%)	34
Sophmores	8 (23.5%)	12 (35.3%)	14 (41.2%)	34
Seniors	7 (20.6%)	13 (38.2%)	14 (41.2%)	34
TOTAL	23 (22.5%)	38 (37.2%)	41 (40.2%)	102
$X^2 = 5.353$	p = 0.069			

DISCUSSION AND CONCLUSIONS

The observed distribution of learner orientations of all the Korean respondents is significantly different than the expected distribution (see Table 4.1). When compared to the observed distribution of all the American respondents, it appears that the Korean students tend to experience a change in learner orientation that is not observed among the American students (see Table 4.2). However, comparisons that separate the respondents in traditional programs from those in low residence programs yield some interesting insights.

Examination of Table 4.3 and 4.5 reveals that the tendency to change learner orientation is much higher among the respondents in the Korean traditional program than for those in low residence program. There is a substantial migration from learning-oriented among the Korean traditional students during the freshman and sophomore years (see Table 4.3) that is not observed in the Korean low residence population (see Table 4.5). Indeed, it appears that the source of most of the change noted among Korean students resides in the traditional respondents (p = 0.016).

Tables 4.2, 4.4, and 4.6 reveal what appears to be a high degree of stability in learning-orientation among both traditional and low residence American students. It is interesting to note that American students in traditional programs tend to be activity-oriented (50.0%), while only 22.5% of the Americans in low residence programs tend to be activity-oriented. Conversely, 18.6% of the traditional American students are learning-oriented and 40.2% of the American low residence students are learning-oriented. Given the cross-sectional method used in this study, one should be careful not to assume that these migrations are unidirectional. For example, a net increase of one in any category should not be treated as the migration of a single individual. The actual complexity of the migrations can only be resolved by further study using a longitudinal model. Yet, the data indicate clear differences in the distribution of learner orientations among the four groups surveyed in this study.

These results seem to provide insight into a phenomenon reported by Confessore, Kim-Cheong and Park (1997). Their study noted that American traditional students exhibited no significant change over the period of their college careers in the self-perception that they possess characteristics often associated with learner autonomy. They also found that American low residence students exhibited a significant increase in such perceptions over the period of their freshman and sophomore years and again when surveyed at the end of their senior year. In the same study, Korean low residence students exhibited the same pattern of increases in these perceptions at the same points in their college careers, as did their American counterparts. However, the Korean traditional students exhibited a significant decrease in these perceptions between the beginning of the freshman year and the end of the sophomore year. While these perceptions increased during the junior and senior years, the change was not significant. Nor did the perceptions return to the high level reported by beginning freshmen.

Confessore, Kim-Cheong and Park (1997) could only note the data seemed to indicate that something occurs during the first two years of college that lowers the perceptions traditional Korean students have of their capacity to function as autonomous learners. The present study may provide some insight into the earlier observation.

The American low residence group contains a higher portion of learning-oriented students than any other group studied. Also, it did not undergo significant migration to alternate learner orientations. Yet, their perception that they possess characteristics often associated with autonomous learning increased significantly throughout the college years.

Taken together, these findings led to the conjecture that relative stability in learner orientation may contribute to increases in self-perceptions associated with learner autonomy. In the alternative, one might conjecture that changes in learner orientation detract from these self-perceptions. For example, a person who enters school with the primary goal of becoming a skilled business manager upon graduation would be viewed as a goal-oriented learner. However, if this same student were to lose sight of the external goal in favor of simply enjoying the social life of college, he or she would then be viewed as an activity-oriented learner. One could infer from the findings of this study that such a shift in orientation might be associated with lower scores on the LPQ, which is a measure of self-perception as an autonomous learner.

The findings of Confessore and Touchstone (1998) may have laid a foundation for confirmation of this conjecture. Their longitudinal study compared the LPQ scores of doctoral students in a staged self-directed learning program to those of students in the same program, but without staging of their learning experiences. The staged self-directed program was designed in accordance with Grow's (1991) model for systematically moving students from highly directed to highly autonomous learning activities. This model is difficult to implement in non-cohort programs because students often take courses in different sequences from one another and therefore, staging cannot be assured.

The LPQ scores of the cohort students increased significantly form the beginning of the program to the mid-point and again from the mid-point to the end of course work. There was no significant difference at either point for the non-cohort students. Confessore and Touchstone concluded that the cohort students had become more autonomous as learners during their doctoral studies while the non-cohort students show no significant change in that regard. This was taken to be an indicator that the cohort students had acquired self-perceptions that might facilitate completion of the autonomous work associated with the doctoral dissertation. However, they made no attempt to assign their respondents to categories within Houle's typology.

Given the results of the present study, those of the Confessore, Kim-Cheong & Park (1997) and the Confessore & Touchstone (1998) studies, it would seem appropriate to conduct further research specifically designed to test hypotheses about the relationships of the stability of learner orientation to self-perceptions associated with autonomous learning. Indeed, Houle's typology should be applied to the raw data from the Confessore & Touchstone study to learn whether any meaningful relationships exit between changes in LPQ scores and changes in learner orientation for those populations.

During the course of this investigation we became concerned that Houle's activity-oriented category might be more meaningful if it were divided into three separate categories. Houle included in this category individuals who undertake learning projects for "social reasons," those who are simply "collecting required credits," and those "seeking degrees or certificates." Analysis of responses gathered in this study led us to speculate that these are sufficiently different orientations to warrant separate categories. At first, it seemed that "credit-oriented" would be a reasonable label for individuals who undertake a particular learning activity simply because it is a required part of a program (collecting required credits), but not primarily as a means to an external end (goal-oriented). This might accommodate those who cannot articulate a clear learning goal for taking a course other than the fact that it is required for the degree or certificate.

To be sure, one could argue that the goal in some cases is to acquire the degree or certificate for which the course is required. Yet, that argument does not capture the true expectations and aspirations of individuals who report that there seems to be no value or purpose in taking some courses <u>except</u> that it is required.

There is evidence that these individuals represent a type that is different from those who are seeking degrees or certificates. Analysis of over 1800 responses to the LPQ reveals that when asked to select one of three conditions related to initiation of the learning the project described by the respondent, 12% selected, "I have been **directed or required** to undertake this learning project. **I do not believe** that completion of this project will contribute directly to my own learning objectives." While the goal of such persons might be to avoid the sanctions of an employer or other authority, we suggest that this hardly represents a learning goal. As such, it warrants a separate category that might be called "requirement-oriented."

We propose to interpret reasons such as pursuit of a degree or certificate as goal-orientation rather than as activity-orientated or as we first though, credit-oriented. We also propose that a new category, "social-oriented." This category would be limited to those who undertake a learning activity primarily because of the social contacts or human interaction associated with the learning project. We would then dispense with the use of the "activity-oriented" category.

The proposed changes in the typology are represented in Figure 4.1.

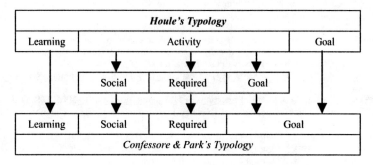

Figure 4.1.   **Proposed Changes in Houle's Typology**

Note: The cells in this figure are not intended to be proportional. Neither Houle nor we assert that the various orientations do not overlap.

It would be interesting to apply this new typology to the raw data collected in recent studies such as Confessore a Barron (1997), Confessore and Touchstone (1998), and the present study as an initial test of how the changes proposed would affect the outcome of studies already in the literature.

REFERENCES

Barron, D.L. (1999). The Distribution of Houle's Learner Orientation Typology Across A Selected Population of College Students. Unpublished Doctoral Dissertation. The George Washington University.

Chickering, A.W., & Havighurst, R.J. (1981). The life cycle. In A.W. Chickering & Associates, The modern American college, pp.16-50. San Francisco, CA: Jossey Bass.

Confessore, G.J., & Barron, D.L. (1997). Learner orientations among baby boomers: Is there more self-directed learning in the future of higher education. In H.B. Long & Associates, Expanding horizons in self-directed learning. Norman, OK: Public Managers Center of The University of Oklahoma.

Confessore, S.J., & Confessore, G.J. (1994). Learner profiles: A cross-sectional study of selected factors associated with self-directed learning. In H.B. Long & Associates, New ideas about self-directed learning. Norman, OK: Oklahoma Research Center for Continuing Professional and Higher Education of the University of Oklahoma, pp.201-27.

Confessore, G.J., & Herrmann, R. (1997). Developing self-efficacy among baccalaureate students: Pygmalion revisited. In H.B. Long & Associates, Expanding horizons in self-directed learning. Norman, OK: Public Managers Center of The University of Oklahoma.

Confessore, G.J., Kim-Cheong, C., & Park, E. (1997). Assessing the potential for lifelong learning in baccalaureate students: A comparative study of traditional and non-traditional students in Korea and the United States. In P. Baveye, G. Pineau, N.A. Tremblay & R. Foucher (Eds.). Self-directed learning in higher education. Montreal, Canada: Group for Interdisciplinary Research on Autonomy and Training.

Confessore, G.J., & Touchstone, D.A. (1998). A longitudinal study of doctoral students in a staged self-directed learning program: Enhancing potential for completion of the dissertation. In H.B. Long & Associates, Developing paradigms for self-directed learning. Norman, OK: Public Managers Center of the University of Oklahoma, pp.125-36.

Cross, P.K., Valley, J.R. & Associates. (1974). Planning non-traditional programs. San Francisco: Jossey-Bass.

Gerald, D.E., & Hussar, W.J. (1995). Projections of Educational Statistics to 2005. U.S. Department of Education, Office of Educational Research and Improvement, Report number NCES 95-169.

Grow, G. (1991). The staged self-directed learning model. In H.B. Long & Associates. Self-directed learning: Consensus & Conflict. Norman, OK: Oklahoma Research Center for Continuing Professional and Higher Education of the University of Oklahoma, pp.199-226.

Houle, C.O. (1961). The inquiring mind: A study of the adult who continues to learn. Madison, WI: University of Wisconsin Press.

Johnstone, J.W.C., & Rivera, R.J. (1965). Volunteers for learning. Chicago, IL: Alpine Publishing.

CHAPTER FIVE

DEMOGRAPHIC AND PSYCHOLOGICAL DETERMINANTS OF SELF–DIRECTED LEARNING READINESS OF KOREAN ADULT LEARNERS

Kwi-Ok Yoo, Ji Woong Cheong & Chija Kim Cheong

INTRODUCTION

A series of studies have been conducted to identify variables related to adults' self-directed learning. Few studies, however, have been conducted to identify determinant variables between demographic variables and psychological variables in South Korea. The objectives of this study were (a) to measure the level of self-directed learning readiness of Korean adult learners, (b) to identify its related demographic variables and psychological determinant variables, and (c) to draw implications for providing better self-directed learning environments for adult learners in South Korea.

In order to measure adults' self-direction in learning, the Korean Self-Directed Learning Readiness Questionnaire(SDLRQ) was developed for this study with 32 items based on Guglielmino's Self-directed learning readiness scale (SDLRS) and related studies. The questionnaire also included seven demographic items and 37 psychological items (15 locus of control items modified from Rotter's locus, control instrument, 12 self-esteem items modified from Coopersmith's Self-Esteem Inventory-B (SEI-B) form, 10 life satisfaction items abstracted from Jin Yun's elderly life satisfaction scale and Kozma/Stones' MUNSH (The Measurement of Happiness), 19 items of educational participation motives modified from Boshier's EPS, and 4 items related to learners' experience and on-going activities.

Cheong et al's exploratory study in South Korea (1995) was used to develop the instrument for this study. Cheong et al's study standardized the SDLRS in a Korean version that considers cultural differences. The number of items and the Cronbach Alpha reliability coefficients of each factor of the instrument for this study are reported in Table 5.1.

Table 5.1. The Reliability (Cronbach Alpha) of Coefficients of Each Factor of SDLRS

Factor Domain	Number of items	Reliability coefficient
Love of learning	8	0.88
Self-confidence as a learner	8	0.77
Openness to challenge	8	0.60
Inquisitive nature	4	0.61
Self understanding	2	0.69
Acceptance of responsibility for learning	2	0.73
Total	32	0.73

The instrument also included seven demographic variables—gender, age, marital status, years of schooling, occupation, level of income and residential area- and five psychological variables including locus of control, self-esteem, life satisfaction, motivational orientations of adult education participants, and the number of participation activities in adult education programs. For measuring locus of control, 15 items of the instrument originally developed by Rotter (1971) and modified by Cha et al in a Korean version with 21 items (1975) were used, its Cronbach's alpha reliability coefficient was 0.63 with the samples for this study.

To measure self-esteem twelve items of the instrument were developed based on the Coopersmith's SEI consisted of 25 items which were translated into the Korean version and used by Kang (1989); its Cronbach's alpha reliability coefficient was 0.56. The life satisfaction was quantitatively measured with 10 items based on the life satisfaction scale for the elderly developed by Yoon (1992) and the MUNSH developed by Kozma and Stone (1980). Its reliability score was 0.67.

To measure motivational orientations of adult education participants, 19 items in five domains were developed as an exploratory instrument based on the EPS(Educational Participation Scale) developed by Bosher (1971, 1977) consisting of 48 items in seven domains. The number of items and the reliability coefficient of each domain of this instrument were as follows:

Table 5.2. The Reliability(Cronbach Alpha) of Coefficient of Educational Participation Motives

Educational Participation Motives	Number of items	Reliability of coefficient
Cognitive interest	4	0.74
Self-development	4	0.80
Career development	4	0.73
Community service	4	0.73
Affiliation (participation)	3	0.85
Total	19	0.77

A total of 292 Korean adults who had participated in various continuing education courses offered in the year of 1996 by the four universities located in metro Seoul as well as the local area were asked to respond to the questionnaires. 217 responses(74%) were analyzed for this study after data cleaning. The SPSS (Statistical Package for Social Sciences) 1997 for Windows 95 Version for the personal computer was used to analyze the data. Statistics such as t-test, F-test, multiple regression analysis, and LSD test for a post-hoc interpretation were employed with a significance level of .05.

RESULTS OF THE STUDY

Level of Self-direction in Learning

The mean score of the Korean adult learners' self-directed learning readiness was 115.78 (209 equivalent to Guglielmino's SDLRS) with the range from 88 to 154 and a standard deviation of 13.69. The mean item score was 3.61 (possible maximum score: 5), which revealed a mean score similar to a Korean study (Chija Kim Cheong 1996). The mean score was lower than that of an American study of adult learners (mean SDLRS score was 213 and mean item score was 3.68 Redding's study 1991: 163).

Table 5.3.   Average Item Scores of Six Factor Domains of Adult Learners' Self-Directed Learning

SDL Factor Domain	Average item score
Love of learning	3.96
Self-confidence as learner	3.51
Openness to challenge	3.31
Inquisitive nature	3.55
Self-understanding	3.71
Acceptance of responsibility for learning	3.81

The mean item score of each factor domain ranged from 3.31 (openness to challenge) to 3.96 (love of learning).

Demographic & Socio-economic Variables
Related to Self-Directed Learning Readiness

Four of seven demographic characteristics—age, schooling years, income level and residential area—were observed to be closely related to SDLR in the Korean sample. Individuals in their 20s and 30s reported higher mean scores than those of 40s and 50s or older. Adults who had graduated from institutes of higher learning (16 or longer years of schooling) reported the highest mean score among the respondents.

The wealthier subjects, earning three million won or more per month, reported higher mean scores than the relatively poorer subjects, earning less than three million won. The residential area was

Table 5.4. **Demographic Variables Associated with Self-Direction in Learning Readiness**

Variables	Classification	n	%	Mean	SD	t/F value	df(t) or LSD(F)
Gender	Male	79	31.8	116.51	13.12	t = .60	df=171.70
	Female	138	68.2	115.37	14.04		
Age	1) 19—29	54	28.9	116.50	13.16		1) 2) 3) 4)
	2) 30—39	103	47.5	117.88	13.07	3.10*	1)
	3) 40 -49	49	22.6	110.84	14.07		2)
	4) 50 or older	11	5.0	114.64	16.46		3) * *
							4)
Marital Status	unmarried	37	12.5	116.19	12.48	.21	df = 56.14
	married	180	87.5	115.70	13.96		
Years of Schooling	1) 12 or less	121	55.8	116.07	13.60		1) 2) 3)
	2) 13-15	40	18.4	111.35	14.01	3.15*	1)
	3) 16 or more	56	25.8	118.32	13.13		2)
							3) *
Occupation	1)prof'l tech.	35	16.1	117.97	14.05		
	2)manag't	23	10.6	111.48	11.74		
	3)sale/service	34	15.7	113.56	13.46	2.29	
	4)agriculture	36	16.6	12064	13.09		NS
	5)jobless	89	41.0	114.92	13.94		
Level of Income (monthly)	1) < 2m. won	78	35.9	112.72	13.29		1) 2) 3) 4)
	2)2—3m. won	80	36.0	115.64	13.40	3.31*	1)
	3)3—4m. won	32	14.8	120.22	13.89		2)
	4) > 4m. won	27	12.4	119.81	13.76		3) *
							4) *
Residence Area	1) metropol.	78	36.0	109.81	11.49		1) 2) 3)
	2) urban	81	37.3	118.49	14.37	13.14***	1)
	3) rural	58	26.7	120.03	12.82		2) *
							3) *
	Total	217	100.0	115.78	13.69		

*p < .05, *** < .001

the most crucial variable related to the respondents' self-direction in learning. Individuals in the rural areas reported higher mean score than those in the urban areas.

This result was different from that of Peter and Gordon's research, which showed that individuals in rural areas had fewer self-learning planning and implementation experiences than those in urban area. The reason that Korean rural adult learners were more self-directed than urban ones was not investigated in this study. It is speculated that the rural adults who had participated in the continuing education courses were highly motivated to learn and more self-directed in learning, however.

Psychological Variables Associated with Self-direction in Learning

Regarding to the psychological variables, five determinants were identified: locus of control, self-esteem, life satisfaction, motivational orientations of continuing education participants, and the participation frequencies in education programs.

1. **Locus of Control.** The adult learners who had internal control showed higher mean score than the externally controlled learners. A t-test showed that there was close relationship between locus of control (external or internal) and self-direction in learning (see Table 5.5).

Table 5.5. Self-Directed Learning Score by Internal and External Locus of Control

Classification	f	%	Mean	SD	t value	df
External (3-9pt.)	100	46	110.27	12.91	5.89**	208.00
Internal (10-15pt.)	117	54	120.50	12.58	*	
Total	217	100	115.78	13.69		

***P<.001

The mean score of the internal control group (120.50) was higher than that of external group(110.27). This result coincided with Skaggs' study(1981) and supported Long and Agyekum's results (1988) which found that locus of control was an important factor in determining self-direction in learning. Subject's who were more self-directed and more responsible in learning believed that their success and failure were dependent on the internal locus of control such as efforts and ability.

2. **Self-esteem.** Those with a high level of self-esteem produced relatively high self-directed learning readiness score. There was a significant difference in self-directed learning readiness score by the level of self-esteem (Table 5.6). This result supported the conclusion of Sabbaghian's (1980), Savoie's (1980) and McCune's (1989) studies.

3. **Life Satisfaction.** The respondents with high satisfaction mean score had higher self-directed learning readiness score. The LSD analysis indicate that there was a significant difference between high and low life satisfaction groups in their SDL readiness scores (Table 5.7). This finding is supportive of the results of Brockett (1983) and Curry (1983)'s studies.

Table 5.6. **Self-Directed Learning Score by the Level of Self-Esteem**

Classification Self-esteem	··	~	:▯↦	▯λ	▯ ↦ℓ↵	···▯λ
Low [4 pts. or below] (1)	55	25.3	109.49	11.77		(1)
Middle [5▯7 pts.] (2)	111	51.2	115.91	12.43	12.85***	(2) ▯
High [8 pts. or more] (3)	51	23.5	122.29	15.28		(3) ▯▯
Total	217	100.0	115.78	13.69		

*** p <. 001

Table 5.7. **Self-Directed Learning Scores by the Level of Life Satisfaction and Self-Direction in Learning**

Classification Life satisfaction	▯	~	:▯↦▯	▯λ	▯ ↦ℓ↵	···▯λ
Low [29 pts. or below] (1)	67	30.9	111.61	12.47	18.78***	(1)
Middle [30-▯ pts.] (2)	99	45.6	113.78	12.73		(2)
High [8 pts. or more] (3)	51	23.5	122.29	15.28		(3) ▯▯
Total	217	100.0	115.78	13.69		

*** p <. 001

4. **Motivational Orientations of Adult Education Participation.** Out of five motivational orientation factors (cognitive interest, self-development, advancement in job, community service, and social contact), self-development was the most determinant one, while the social contact was the least useful to determine the self-directed learning readiness levels. (Table 5.8)

Table 5.8. **Motivational Orientations Scores of Adult Education**

Classification	Possible Max Score	Mean	SD	Ma5.	Min.	Range
Cognitive interest	20	13.52	5.3	20	7	13
Self-development	20	14.12	9.19	20	5	15
Advancement in job	20	13.44	13.14	20	4	16
Community service	20	12.54	9.47	20	4	16
Social contact	15	8.25	6.50	14	3	11

The analyses of variances of motivational factors (Table 5.9) revealed:

1. The mean SDLR scores of low and middle level of cognitive interest groups were 111.95 and 111.46 respectively. The mean score of the high level of cognition interest group was 127.80.

Table 5.9.   Self-Directed Learning Score by Adult Education Motivational Factors

Classification	Level	n	%	Mean	SD	F value	LSD
Cognitive interest	Low [11 pts. or below] (1)	41	18.9	113.71	15.24		(1)
	Middle [12-1□ pts.] (2)	132	60.8	114.60	12.84	4.65*	(2)
	High [16-20 pts.] (3)	44	20.3	121.27	13.58		(3)□
Self-development	Low [11 pts. or below] (1)	37	17.1	111.95	13.25		(1)
	Middle [12-1□ pts.] (2)	111	51.1	11.46	11.89	27.28*	(2)
	High [16-20 pts.] (3)	69	31.8	127.80	12.37		(3)□
Advancement in job	Low [11 pts. or below] (1)	64	29.5	112.33	13.07		(1)
	Middle [12-□ pts.] (2)	911	42.0	112.64	12.55	17.95***`	(2)
	High [16-20 pts.] (3)	62	28.5	123.97	12.64		(3)□
Community service	Low [10 pts. or below] (1)	49	22.6	112.20	12.72		(1)
	Middle [11-14 pts.] (2)	110	60.8	114.31	13.75	8.04***	(2)
	High [15-20 pts.] (3)	58	16.6	121.60	12.77		(3)□
Social contact	Low [11 pts. or below] (1)	56	28.5	120.41	13.83		(1)
	Middle [7-10 pts.] (2)	114	52.5	113.39	12.63	5.13***	(2) *
	High [11-14 pts.] (3)	47	21.7	116.06	14.82		(3)
	Total	217	100.0	115.78	13.69		

* p<.05, ** p<.01, *** p<.001

2. For the motivational orientation in job advancement, results were very similar to the above two factors showing the mean scores of three groups 111.95, 111.46, and 127.8, respectively.

3. Low, middle, and high level of motivational orientation groups in their community services reported the mean SDLR scores of 112.20, 114.31 and 121.60, respectively.

4. Low level of motivational orientation group in their social contact aspect reported higher mean SDLR score(120.41) than the other two groups(middle and high social contact groups) whose mean scores were 113.39 and 116.06, respectively.

The LSD analysis showed that the difference between the low and high contact groups was not significant. There was a significant difference between the low and the middle contact groups in their mean SDLR scores, however. (Table 5.9)

5. **Degree of Participation in Adult Education Programs.** The learners who participated in adult education programs reported the highest mean SDLR score, and those who did not participate at all showed the lowest mean score. There was a significant relationship between frequent participation group and non-participant group at .001 level of significance. Individuals without any experience of adult education reported lower scores than those with experience. The more experienced did, the higher SDLR score they had.

Table 5.10. **Self-Directed Learning Score by the Number of Adult Education Participation**

Classification No. of participation	▯	˜	∶▯↦▯	▯λ	▯ ↦ℓ▯	···▯λ
0 (1)	129	59.4	113.17	13.02		(1)
1-2 (2)	39	18.0	118.08	14.28		(2) *
3-4 (3)	24	11.1	114.83	10.87	7.85***	(3)
5 or more (4)	25	11.5	126.60	13.41		(4) ▯▯▯
Total	217	100.0	115.78	13.69		

*** p <. 001

6. **Number of Experiences of Self-learning Planning and Implementation.** The learners who had more self-planned and self-implemented learning experiences showed higher SDLR score than who did not. (Table 5.11)

Table 5.11. **Self-Directed Learning Score by the Number of Experiences of Self-Planned Learning**

Classification Number	n	%	Mean	SD	F value	LSD (1) (2) (3) (4)
0 (1)	91	41.9	110.81	12.10		(1)
1 (2)	36	16.6	116.25	12.05		(2) *
2 (3)	49	22.6	118.49	14.57	9.67***	(3) *
3 or more (4)	41	18.9	123.17	13.42		(4) **
Total	217	100.0	115.78	13.69		

*** p <. 001

Table 5.12.   Correlation Between Self-Direction in Learning and All the 15 Variables

	SDLR	v2	v3	v4	v5	v6	v7	v8	v9	v10	v11	v12	v13	v1	v15	v16
SDLR	1.00															
v2	.431**	1.00														
v3	.146**	.255**	1.00													
v4	.347**	.369**	.501**	1.00												
v5	.220**	-.021	-.009	.220**	1.00											
v6	.176**	.010	.089	.057	.295**	1.00										
v7	.371**	.047	.006	.242**	.216**	.145**	1.00									
v8	-.128*	-.133	-.080	-.066	-.001	.337**	.645**	1.00								
v9	.274**	.008	.030	.056	.183**	-.001	-.047	-.183**	1.00							
v10	-.139*	-.008	-.031	-.031	.087	.145*	-.134*	.131	-.183**	1.00						
v11	.002	.078	.008	.005	.043	.337**	.007	.060	-.037	.472**	1.00					
v12	-.000	-.001	-.140*	-.182*	-.022	.183*	-.005	-.181*	-.060	-.037	-.087	1.00				
v13	-.014	.078	.322	.031	.176	-.237*	.011	.071	.169*	.150*	.154*	-.142*	1.00			
v14	.168**	.141*	.141*	.099	.060	.176	-.124	.108	-.175*	.060	-.069	-.217**	-.006	1.00		
v15	.217**	.121	.009	.012	.035	-.073	-.122	-.181*	.150*	.142*	-.088	-.217**	.093	.155*	1.00	
v16	.254**	.241**	.229**	.107	-.018	.035	.064	.128	-.047	.061	.175*	-.144*	-.133	.131	.465**	1.00

v1) SDLR Score
v2) locus of control
v3) self-esteem
v4) life-satisfaction
v5) cognitive interest motivation
v6) community service motivation
v7) self-development motivation
v8) social contact motivation,

v9) Advancement in job
v10) age
v11) schooling year
v12) gender
v13) marital status
v14) income
v15) number of participation in Adult Education
v16) number of experiences of self-learning planning and implementation

Comparison of Variables Affecting Self-Direction Learning Readiness
The correlation between SDLR scores and the 10 variables the locus of control, self-esteem, life satisfaction, cognitive interest, self-development, advancement in job, community services, income, number of participation in adult education, and independent planning and implementation of learning -showed positive correlation. The correlation between SDLR scores and four variables motivational orientation of social contact, schooling year, gender and marital status – did not show significant correlation and only one (age) showed negative correlation (Table 5.12).

The result of multiple regression analysis revealed that the five determinant variables- locus of control, motivational orientation of self-development, self-esteem, age, and income- explained 37.7% of adult learners' self-directed learning readiness. The psychological determinants explained 34.8% of total SDLRQ readiness scores. Especially, the motivational orientation of self-development and age were found to be the two most powerful determinant variables in this study. The individuals with internal locus of control, higher life satisfaction, higher motivational orientation of self-development, more participation in adult education programs, and relatively young age (30's) were highly self-directed in learning.

CONCLUSIONS

This study identified four demographic variables (age, level of income, residential area, and schooling year) out of seven variables and five psychological variables (locus of control, self-esteem, life satisfaction, motivational orientations of adult education participants, and the number of participation in adult education programs) as determining variables of the adult learners' self-directed learning readiness. In analyzing correlations among SDLR, all the 15 sub-variables, and 10 variables (locus of control, self-esteem, life satisfaction, motivational orientation of cognitive interest, self-development, advancement in job, community services, income, the number of participation in adult education, independent learning planning and implementation) showed positive correlation. One variable (age) showed negative correlation, and four (motivational orientation of social contact, schooling year, gender and marital status) did not show significant correlation.

The psychological variables of adult learners were more determinant than demographic variables in the learners self-directed learning readiness. In order to have better self-directed learning environments for adults, therefore, step-wise and various self-directed learning strategies need to be provided based on individual differences in self-directed learning readiness. Further studies need to be conducted focusing on learning situations and processes in self-directed learning, on educators' role in facilitating the self-directed learning, and on development of more culturally valid instruments for measuring self-direction in learning.

REFERENCE

Boshier, R.W. (1971). "Motivational orientations of adult education participants: A factor analytic exploration of Houle's typology" Adult Education, 21(2), pp.3-26.

Boshier, R.W. (1991). "Psychometric properties of the alternative form of the education participation scale," Adult Education, 41(3), pp.150-167.

Brockett, R.G. (1983). "Self-directed learning readiness and life satisfaction among older adults." (Doctoral dissertation, Syracuse University, 1982). Dissertation Abstracts International, 44, 42A.

Brockett, R.G., & Hiemstra, R. (1991). Self-direction in adult learning. New York: Routledge.

Cheong, C.K., Lee, C.K., & Long, H.B.,(1995). "Self-directed learning readiness and some related variables: A study of self-educated people in Korea." In H.B. Long & Associates, New dimensions in self-directed learning (pp.267-276). Public Managers Center, Educational Leadership and Policy Studies, Department College of Education, Univ. of Oklahoma.

Confessore, G.J., Confessore, S.J. (1992). "In search of consensus in the study of self-directed learning." In H.B. Long & Associates, Research and application in self-directed learning (pp.25-46). Norman: Oklahoma Research Center for continuing Professional and Higher Education.

Confessore, G. J., Long, H.B., & Redding, T.R. (1993). "The status of self-directed learning literature, 1996-1991," Emerging perspectives of Self-directed Learning, Oklahoma Research Center for Continuing Professional and Higher Education of the Univ. of Oklahoma.

Curry, M.A. (1983). "The analysis of self-directed learning readiness characteristics in older adults engaged in formal learning activities in two settings" (Doctoral dissertation, Kansas State University, 1983). Dissertation Abstracts International 44, 1293A.

Guglielmino, L.M. (1977). "Development of the self-directed learning readiness scale." (Doctoral dissertation, University of Georgia, 1977). Dissertation Abstracts International, 38, 6467A.

Guglielmino, P.J., Guglielmino, L.M., & Long, H.B.(1987). "Self-directed learning readiness and performance in the workplace." Higher Education, 16, pp.303-317.

Kozma, A., & Stones, M.J. (1980). "The measurement of happiness: MUNSH," Journal of Gerontology, 35(6).

Long, H.B (1994). "Challenging some myths about self-directed learning research." In H.B. Long & Associates, New ideas about self-directed learning (pp.1-14). Oklahoma Research Center for Continuing Professional and Higher Education of the University of Oklahoma.

McCune, S., Gugielmino, L.M., & Garcia Jr., G. (1990). "Adult self-direction in learning: A meta-analytic study of research using the self directed learning readiness scale." In H.B. Long & Associates, Advances in research and practice in self-directed learning (pp.145-156). Norman : Oklahoma Research Center for Continuing Professional and Higher Education of the University of Oklahoma.

Redding, T.R. (1991). "Spark gap to space: A study in self-directed learning." In H.B. Long & Associates, Self-directed learning: Consensus & conflict. Oklahoma Research Center for Continuing Professional and Higher Education of the University of Oklahoma.

Sabbaghian, A.S. (1980). "Adult self-directness and self-concept : An exploration of relationships" (Doctoral dissertation, Iowa State University, 1979). Dissertation Abstracts International, 40, pp.50-52.

Savoie, M.M. (1980). "Continuing education for nurses : Predictors of success in courses requiring a degree of learner self-direction" (Doctoral dissertation, University of Toronto, 1979). Dissertation Abstracts International, 40, 6114A.

Skaggs, B.J. (1981). "The relationship between involvement of professional nurses in self-directed learning activities, locus of control, and readiness for self-directed learning measures"(Doctoral dissertation, The University of Texas, Austin, 1981). Dissertation Abstracts International, 42,1906A.

Torrance, E.P., & Mourad, S.(1978). "Some creativity and style of learning and thinking correlates of Guglielmino's self-directed learning readiness scale," Psychological Reports, 43, pp.1167-1171.

West, R.F., & Bentley, E.L. (1990). Structural analysis of the self-directed learning readiness scale: A confirmatory factor analysis using lisrel modeling. In H.B. Long & Associates, Advances in research and practice in self-directed learning. Norman: Oklahoma Research Center for Continuing Professional and Higher Education of the University of Oklahoma.

CHAPTER SIX

LEARNING CONATION: A PSYCHOLOGICAL PERSPECTIVE OF PERSONAL INITIATIVE AND RESOURCEFULNESS

Michael K. Ponton, Paul B. Carr & Gary J. Confessore

In 1987 Oddi pointed to a major dilemma within the field of self-directed learning (SDL) noting that the definition of SDL varied subtly or considerably from one researcher to another. For over a decade others in the field echoed her concern. However, Long's (1998) assertion that most conceptualizations of SDL can be categorized under one of four major paradigms: sociological, teaching technique, methodological, and psychological seems to have been accepted by most active SDL researchers. Long concluded that each paradigm has a requisite set of implications and assumptions. Moreover, he asserts that of these four paradigms, only "the *psychological conceptualization* is both necessary and sufficient to explain SDL" (p.10). He states:

> The psychological conceptualization implies that fundamentally learning is a self-initiated, self-directed, and self-regulated cognitive process whereby the learner can choose to ignore instruction, to merely absorb it by casual attention, to carefully memorize without critical reflection, or to seek to change or create an understanding of information. (p.9)

Confessore (1992) states that in order for a self-directed learning activity to result in a personally satisfying experience, a learner must exhibit the conative factors of desire, personal initiative, resourcefulness and persistence. The purpose of this thesis is to present a psychological perspective on the development of intentional behaviors and the role of conation as they relate to personal initiative and resourcefulness. Note that SDL represents only a subset of the behavioral activities in which an individual may engage. The model developed by Fishbein and Ajzen (1975) explains the process from belief formulation to intentional behaviors. It forms the foundation of the present discussion. Selected psychological literature concerning the characteristics of the conative factors of personal initiative and resourcefulness are also presented in this discussion.

THE MODEL OF FISHBEIN AND AJZEN

Fishbein and Ajzen (1975, p.15) provide a general model that indicates the relationship between beliefs, attitudes, behavioral intentions, and behaviors:

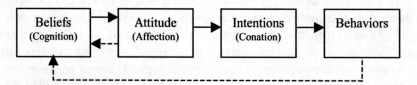

Within this model, beliefs represent the cognitive process of assigning attributes to objects where "the terms 'object' and 'attribute' are used in a generic sense, and they refer to any discriminable aspect of the individual's world" (Fishbein & Ajzen, 1975, p.12). They further assert: "the object of a belief may be a person, a group of people, an institution, a behavior, a policy, an event, etc., and the associated attribute may be any object, trait, property, quality, characteristic, outcome, or event" (p.12).

Such object-attribute assignments are developed via personal experience or observational modeling. Observational modeling refers to the learning acquired through vicarious experiences (Bandura, 1965; Bandura, 1977). Beliefs provide the informational foundation that influences (solid arrows in the figure) the development of one's attitudes, behavioral intentions, and intentions (Fishbein & Ajzen, 1975). Quite simply, beliefs represent the cognitive process through which a person *knows* the world. (Note that *know* does not necessitate the acquisition of factual information—if one assigns completely erroneous attributes to a given object but this person truly believes that the assignments are valid, then these object-attribute assignments are part of this individual's belief structure.)

A person may assign many attributes to any given object. Each attribute can be subjectively interpreted as either a positive or negative belief. Hence, the plural form of belief is used in the model to represent multiple attributive assignments to a given object. Based upon these assignments, a total affect is developed. Attitude is this total affect and "can be described as *a learned predisposition to respond in a consistently favorable or unfavorable manner with respect to a given object*" (Fishbein & Ajzen, 1975, p.6). Note that the dashed arrow between beliefs and attitude within the model represents a feedback process. An attitude with respect to a given object can influence the development of new object-attribute assignments that may in turn influence one's total affect.

Behavioral intentions with respect to an object are influenced by one's attitude toward the object. Behavioral intentions are the personal determinations to perform specific behaviors. However, one's attitude is only a "*general* predisposition" (Fishbein & Ajzen, 1975, p.15) that cannot predict a specific intention and subsequent behavior. "Rather, it [attitude] leads to a set of intentions that indicate a certain amount of affect toward the object in question" (p.15). Fishbein and Ajzen state that intentions are formulated based upon the perceived valence of behavioral outcomes and the influence of social norms with respect to the intended behavior.

Behavioral intentions are described as conations where conation refers to "an instinctually motivated biological striving that may appear ... in behavior as action tendencies" (Gove, 1976, p.468). Fishbein and Ajzen (1975) state three factors that influence the level of correlation between intentions and resultant behaviors:

"the degree to which intention and behavior correspond in their levels of specificity; stability of the intention; and the degree to which carrying out the intention is completely under the person's volitional control" (p.369). Provided these three factors are present to sufficient degrees, intentional behaviors with respect to the object are performed.

The behaviorists' perspective is that "an activity, to qualify as a behavior, must be directly observable and measurable" (Wolman et al., 1973, p.41); hence the commonly used juxtaposition *overt behavior*. But this definition does not limit observable actions solely to ocular detection. As Barrett, Johnston and Pennypacker (1986) assert:

> The epidermis need not be a barrier to [determine what constitutes an overt] behavior. Thus, both visible actions and intraorganism activities such as muscle potential changes and heartbeats qualify. The movement requirement [of an overt action] provides for detection by means of public responses or by instruments that convert response occurrences into measurable changes in some aspect of the environment. Thus, gross displacement of objects by some act of the behavior as well as amplified transduction that deflects a needle or changes a display on a monitoring screen both exemplify the movement that makes various forms of behavior accessible to standard scientific measurement. Private events externalized via publicly observable responses are no exception [to being classified as behaviors]. (p.164)

Therefore, an action is deemed an overt behavior if the action results in some environmental change. Such behaviors can be completely internal to a person but made observable (i.e., overt) by measurement methodologies.

As an example, consider goal-directed behavior. According to action theory, "human behavior ... is directed toward the accomplishment of goals" (Frese & Sabini, 1985, p.xxiii). However, the establishment of goals may not be observable per se. But, through the use of a valid psychological instrument, intraorganism goal formulation is translated to an observable event in the environment (i.e., the subject's response) and is measurable via the instrumentation.

Within the figure of Fishbein and Ajzen's (1975) model, the dashed arrow that extends from behaviors to beliefs represents another feedback process that activates an additional iteration through the model. As Chapman and Skinner (1985) assert:

> The basic premise of action theory is that human beings interpret their own and others' behavior in terms of action-related concepts such as goals, plans, intentions, and beliefs and that their actions are in part determined by those reflexive interpretations. (p.201)

Thus, action theory describes the process in which one acts on the environment and the results of these actions provide feedback information that shapes one's belief structure. Such actions also incorporate observational modeling. These beliefs influence future attitudes, intentions, and behaviors.

This model is consistent with social cognitive theory that posits that human agency (i.e., intentional actions) is predicated on the triadic reciprocal interaction between personal behavior, internal personal factors (i.e., one's cognitive, biological, and affective characteristics), and the environment (i.e., everything external to the individual) (Bandura, 1997). However, triadic reciprocal causation provides for additional mechanisms of influence. For example, while the environment can affect behaviors, the environment can also be affected by behaviors. The reciprocity of influence varies in magnitude dependent upon the context of application.

CONATIVE FACTORS IMPORTANT TO LEARNING

The recent work of Ponton and Confessore (1998), and Carr and Confessore (1998) suggests that both personal initiative and resourcefulness can be described as behavioral syndromes, i.e., co-occurring behaviors. Confessore (1992) posits these two conative factors as critical to a satisfying self-directed learning activity. They are referred to as conative factors because personal initiative and resourcefulness are intentional actions induced by an internal learning motivation.

I. Personal Initiative

The recent work of Hoehne (1990), Frese, Kring, Soose, and Zempel (1996), and Frohman (1997) indicates that personal initiative can be viewed as a behavioral syndrome. Based upon this research, Ponton and Confessore (1998) suggest that the behaviors of importance to self-directed learning are goal-directedness, action-orientation, overcoming obstacles, active-approach, and self-starting. The following a description of each of these behaviors and the relevant literature that highlights their salient features.

1. *Goal-Directedness*

Goal-directedness refers to the behavior of establishing goals that serve as motivators for action. Thus, there are two characteristics associated with goal-directed behavior: establishing goals and working toward the accomplishment of the goals. However, these two aspects are closely related because the nature of the goals that are created must satisfy specific theoretical criteria in order to serve as incentives to engage in actions directed toward goal accomplishment.

According to goal theory (Bandura, 1997), "the capacity to exercise self-influence by personal challenge and evaluate reaction to one's own performances provides a major cognitive mechanism of motivation and self-directedness" (p.128). Bandura and Cervone (1983) state that "when people commit themselves to explicit standards or goals, perceived negative discrepancies between what they do and what they seek to achieve creates self-dissatisfactions that serve as motivational inducements for enhanced effort" (p.1017). Thus, goal-directed behavior refers to establishing clearly defined goals and working to accomplish these goals whereby personal motivation is induced through a comparison between current and desired future states. Therefore, for maximum learning motivation clear learning goals must be created.

70

Heckhausen and Kuhl (1985) "define [a] goal as the molar endstate whose attainment requires actions by the individual pursuing it" (pp.137-138). They further assert that "goals rest on three levels of endstates with an ascending hierarchical order" (p.138) and are described as follows:

> On the first-order level the endstates are the activities themselves: the interest in, or the enjoyment of, doing something repetitively or continuously, because it provides excitement... . On a second-order level the endstate is an action outcome with characteristics that are required or preset and that are inherently valuable. Finally, at the third-order level, the endstate refers to desirable consequences that might arise from an achieved outcome. (p.138)

This indicates that learning goals can be: (a) the creation of interesting, enjoyable, or exciting learning activities; (b) required or self-valued learning outcomes; or (c) a desirable consequence of such outcomes.

Frese, Fay, Hilburger, Leng, and Tag (1997) state that a *"longer time frame* with its long-term goals is a prerequisite of initiative" (p.140) whereby the activities one chooses to engage in have benefits that extend over long time periods. The purpose of a long-term focus is due to the proactive aspect of initiative whereby a person solves problems presently that will likely reappear in the future (Frese et al., 1996). Thus, a learner with initiative who identifies a learning need with long-term implications works to satisfy this need presently rather than wait until the need resurfaces at a later time.

Chapman and Skinner (1985) indicate that goals are selected based upon their subjective probability of successful accomplishment. They further assert that success probabilities are a function of plan selection; thus, "goal selection and plan selection will function concurrently" (Chapman & Skinner, 1985, p.202). Frese et al. (1996) state, "initiative implies good planning" (p.40). Therefore, planning is integral to a goal-directed behavior.

Bandura (1986) states that people will exert more effort and receive more satisfaction if goals are challenging (i.e., not too easy) provided the goals are not unrealistically difficult and perceived to be beyond reach. In addition, Bandura (1997) asserts:

> Superordinate distal goals give purpose to a domain of activity and serve a general directive function, but subgoals are better suited to serve as the proximal determinants of the specified choice of activities and how much effort is devoted to them. (p.134)

This indicates that intermediate sub-goals should be formulated to enhance the self-motivation required to accomplish the larger, challenging learning goal.

2. *Action-Orientation*

Action-orientation describes the behavior of translating intentions quickly into actions. Chapman and Skinner (1985) state that "the intentionality of action implies a differentiation of ends and means ... [whereby] the action is performed *in order* to bring about a certain goal" (p.201). Thus, a person with initiative will be both goal-directed and action-oriented (Frese et al., 1996).

"Long-term goals only have an impact if they are translated into actions ... Action-oriented people do not think about the problems and advantages of their goals; rather they translate these goals quickly into actions" (Frese et al., 1996, p.39). Note that Frese et al. use the term goal, in this context, synonymously with intention. Bandura (1997) also likens intentions to proximal goals. For a learner, action-orientation refers to a behavior in which the learner establishes an intention to engage in a learning activity and then quickly engages in the activity.

Chapman and Skinner (1985) state that goal-setting and planning are action-related concepts. But while a plan may be completed while acting, Frese and Sabini (1985) assert, "according to action theory, there must be at least a general notion of a goal and a general plan before one is able to act at all" (p.xx). For example, if a learner desires to learn about pyramids (i.e., outcome goal), s/he must at least develop a performance goal (e.g., read a book that contains information about pyramids) and a plan (e.g., acquire a book that contains information about pyramids) before any action (e.g., reading) can occur. Thus, an action-oriented learner will quickly develop "at least a general notion of a goal and a general plan" (Frese & Sabini, 1985, p.xx) after establishing a learning desire.

If the learner is confronted with two or more behavioral intentions of comparable value, then a decision must be made concerning which action to engage in. Heckhausen and Kuhl (1985) indicate that a change in setting or "reflecting on the positive aspects of goal attainment" (p.153) may help in prioritizing one intention over another. To facilitate transforming a learning intention into a behavior, the learner may seek an environment conducive to learning or consider the anticipated positive consequences of accomplishing learning goals.

Additionally, Blankenship (1985) states:

> The initial activities associated with the dominance of an intentional action tendency would be characterized as the OTIUM [opportunity, time, importance, urgency, means] checks that would either result in the repeated inhibition and immediate decrease of the ongoing action tendency, if OTIUM criteria were not met, or result in the additional instigation of the action tendency and withdrawal of previous inhibitory force, if the OTIUM criteria were met. (p.168)

Thus, the presence of opportunity, time, importance, urgency, and means are also salient contributors to action tendencies.

3. *Overcoming Obstacles*

Frese et al. (1997) assert: "if one does not overcome ... difficulties, if one gives up quickly in face of barriers, [then] there is no initiative" (p.141). Thus, overcoming obstacles refers to the behavior of continuing action in spite of the presence of barriers that attempt to inhibit action. Frohman (1997) asserts, "if there is one element that describes those who successfully take personal initiative, it is their dogged sense of purpose, commitment to keep going, and understanding that it takes time" (p.47).

The deterrents to adult continual learning may come in many forms some of which are a lack of learner confidence, a lack of relevant courses, time constraints, low priority of learning as compared to other activities, monetary costs, and personal problems (Darkenwald & Valentine, 1985). These impediments can be categorized within the framework of social cognitive theory under three types of barriers: cognitive, situational, and structural (Bandura, 1997). Bandura asserts that cognitive barriers take the form of perceived self-inefficacy and structural barriers are of the form of inadequate resources. Personal problems "reflect situational difficulties related to child care, family problems, and personal health problems or handicaps" (Darkenwald & Valentine, 1985, pp.184-185). In addition, Houle (1961) states that another major deterrent to continual learning is the opposition, not merely apathy, from the family and friends of the person who desires to engage in a learning activity.

4. *Active-Approach*

An active-approach refers to the behavior of taking the responsibility for the development of solution strategies to one's own problems. "Initiative ... implies that one will deal with ... obstacles actively and persistently [emphasis removed]" (Frese et al., 1997, p.141).

To overcome the obstacles that are confronted in the pursuit of a goal, solution strategies must be developed. "A search for a solution can be delegated to somebody else ... or actively pursued [by] oneself" (Frese et al., 1996, p.48). Thus, when one pursues solutions to his/her own problems, one is exhibiting an active-approach. This pro-activity is a behavior of personal initiative (Frese et al., 1997).

Several obstacles have already been discussed as impediments to learning: lack of confidence, lack of relevant courses, lack of time, low learning priority, lack of money, perceived self-inefficacy, lack of resources, and personal problems associated with child care, family problems, and personal health. For a desired learning activity to continue in spite of these obstacles, a learner exhibiting an active-approach behavior will develop solutions to overcome the problems associated with these impediments.

5. *Self-Starting*

The characteristics of goals needed to provide maximum intrinsic motivation have already been discussed. But while such characteristics are important, they do not guarantee self-initiated action. A self-starting behavior is the behavior of beginning an activity under one's own volition.

A self-starting behavior is the manifestation of the intrinsic motivation associated with desire (Ponton & Confessore, 1998). "Such [intrinsic] motivation emerges spontaneously from internal tendencies and can motivate behavior even without the aid of extrinsic rewards of environmental controls" (Deci & Ryan, 1985, p.43). A person with initiative exhibits a self-starting behavior (Frese et al., 1996; Hoehne, 1990) and begins the chosen activity via personal agency. Additionally, for a person with a high level of initiative the beginning of a learning activity will incorporate goal formulation and planning. A self-starter is intrinsically motivated to do both without relying on the motivation induced by others.

A self-starting behavior is not restricted to the initial beginning of a learning activity. A learning endeavor may transpire over a long time-period with multiple opportunities for inactivity. Self-starters will initiate learning activities after periods of inactivity without the need for extrinsic motivational processes.

II. Resourcefulness

Rosenbaum (1989) defines learned resourcefulness as "a behavioral repertoire of self-control skills necessary for ... self-control" (p.249). Essentially, he states that successful coping with stressful events involves self-regulation. For the learner, stress can manifest itself from the onset of the learning endeavor. Carr and Confessore (1998) postulate that if learned resourcefulness and a high degree of self-efficacy are combined at the beginning and during a self-directed learning activity, the conative factor of resourcefulness constitutes a syndrome of self-control behaviors. These resourceful behaviors are prioritizing values, delaying immediate gratification, anticipating future rewards, and problem solving.

1. *Prioritizing Values*

Rokeach (1979) defines values as "standards that are to a large extent derived, learned, and internalized from society and its institutions" (p.6). Further, Bandura (1997) states, "human adaptation and change are rooted in social systems. Therefore, personal agency operates within a broad network of sociostructural influences. In agentic transactions, people are both producers and products of social structures" (p.6).

Values are important because they "are used in making selections of objects and actions, resolving conflicts, invoking social sanctions, and coping with needs or claims for social and psychological defenses of choices made or proposed" (Rokeach, 1979, p.20). However, a learner must do more than prioritize values—the learner must value learning over other things if s/he is to prioritize learning activities over other activities. Such a valuation is influenced by the values expressed by family members, peers, and society.

Values can also be formulated by assessing the basis for past behaviors. Rokeach (1979) states, "values are components in the guidance of anticipatory and goal-directed behavior; but they are also backward-looking in frequent service to justify or explain past behavior" (p.20).

Bandura (1997) states, "people also motivate themselves and guide their actions anticipatorily by the outcomes they expect to flow from given courses of behavior" (p.125). He also writes that "the expectancy-value theory predicts that the higher the expectancy that certain behavior can secure specific outcomes and the more highly those outcomes are valued, the greater is the motivation to perform the activity" (p.125). Thus, values that are attributed to behavioral outcomes, rather than the behaviors themselves, can also serve as motivators for action.

Bandura (1997) states:

> Development of capabilities for self-directedness enables individuals not only to continue their intellectual growth beyond their formal education but to advance the nature and quality of life pursuits. Changing realities are placing a premium on the capability for self-directed learning throughout the life span ... Self-development with age partly determines whether the expanded life span is lived self-fulfillingly or apathetically. (p.227)

Thus, to be resourceful, lifelong learners must value learning throughout their lives.

2. *Delaying Immediate Gratification*

Rosenbaum (1989) argues that "whereas redressive self-control attempts to resume normal functions that were disrupted, reformative self-control attempts to break ineffective or harmful habits in order to adopt new, better behavior ... this includes the ability to delay immediate gratification" (p.250). Mischel, Shoda, and Peake (1988) assert, "perhaps the ability to delay immediate gratification effectively for the sake of larger goals may itself play an increasingly powerful and pervasive role in cognitive and social coping" (p.694). They also assert, "indeed, earlier analyses of self-regulation have contrasted this type of delay ability or competence with the motivational preference for delayed larger versus immediate, smaller gratification" (p.694). A resourceful learner will choose to engage in a learning activity presently due to the anticipated distal gratification even though another non-learning activity may provide an immediate gratification.

It should be noted that highly resourceful autonomous learners might not have to delay immediate gratification when it comes to learning activities. This scenario is appropriate to seasoned autonomous learners who gain immediate gratification from the learning endeavor itself by essentially practicing redressive self-control behaviors.

3. *Anticipating Future Rewards*
   Bandura (1986) argues that:

> In social cognitive theory, intention plays a prominent role in the self-regulation of behavior. An intention is defined as the determination to perform certain activities or to bring about a certain future state of affairs. Intentional regulation of behavior operates principally through two cognitively based sources of motivation, both relying on cognitive representational mechanisms. One form operates anticipatorily through the exercise of forethought. We saw earlier that the capacity to represent future consequences in thought provides a necessary condition for one cognitive source of motivation. Through cognitive representation of future outcomes individuals can generate current motivators for courses of action that are instrumental in attaining the outcomes they value. A second cognitively based source of motivation relies on goal setting ... Intentions, whether expressed in determination to engage in a specific course of action or to attain certain levels of performance, increase the likelihood that sought futures will be realized. (p.467)

Rosenbaum (1989) asserts that "in most cases, redressive self-control is rewarded immediately by relief from unpleasant feelings. Reformative self-control, in contrast, requires someone to force herself into an unpleasant situation in the hope that her behavioral change will be rewarded in the future" (p.252). In essence, the learner is looking toward the future benefits of the learning that is undertaken in the present to generate the intrinsic motivation required for self-directed learning.

4. *Problem Solving*
    Frese, Stewart, and Hannover (1987) state that:

> Most individuals set goals and develop some plans during the course of a day. When one prefers to plan a course of action while taking a shower or before going to bed, it would be crippling to most people to have this process of goal refinement and planful behavior prevented completely. Actions are determined and guided by goals, plans and feedback. The goals determine the course for the plan, and the feedback from the environment redirects the plan, providing the basis for an assessment of whether a plan will serve a given goal and whether the desired goal has been achieved. Goals and plans are organized hierarchically and include major goals and sub goals, and major plans and sub plans. Although actions are goal oriented, not all goals are specified in detail and not all actions are oriented toward one particular goal. (p.1182)

Kennett (1994) argues that:

> Research has demonstrated that high achievers are very academically resourceful. They set goals, use effective problem-solving strategies, think positively despite academic demands or challenges, rely on information and assistance from both social and non-social sources, keep records, structure their environment to make learning easier, apply self-consequences and review written material. Even when they do poorly on a test or an assignment, they remain optimistic, evaluate reasons for the failure, and restructure study goals and strategies. In short, they are neither likely to give up nor succumb to anxiety. Instead, they look for ways to rectify the problem. (p.295)

In essence, the application of problem solving strategies, such as planning, evaluating alternatives, and anticipating consequences are requisite factors of learned resourcefulness (Carr & Confessore, 1998; Kennett, 1994).

CONCLUDING REMARKS

One's degree of autonomy in learning can be viewed along a continuum. At one extreme, the learner is completely dependent on external factors while on the other extreme the learner is completely independent of all external factors. Both extremes are contrary to the premise of social cognitive theory. As Bandura (1986) asserts:

> Social cognitive theory embraces an interactional model of causation in which environmental events, personal factors, and behavior all operate as interacting determinants of each other. Reciprocal causation provides people with opportunities to exercise some control over their destinies as well as sets limits of self-direction. (p.xi)

Thus, while the conative factors of personal initiative and resourcefulness are manifested as a result of an intrinsic motivation to learn something, such a motivation is not at the exclusion of social influence. Much of human thought and action is influenced by societal norms, but cognized beliefs and attitudes also influence behavioral intentions (i.e., conations) and subsequent behaviors.

Fishbein and Ajzen (1975) assert, "the best predictor of a person's behavior is his intention to perform the behavior" (p.381). Intentions are formulated based upon the perceived valence of behavioral outcomes in conjunction with the influence of social norms. They further suggest, "the most important factor influencing the size of the intention-behavior relation is the degree to which the intention is measured at the same level of specificity as the behavior to be predicted" (p.369). Therefore, to predict the degree to which an individual will exhibit behaviors associated with personal initiative and resourcefulness in their self-directed learning requires an enhanced understanding of learning conation. Such an understanding must incorporate the psychological perspective.

REFERENCES

Bandura, A. (1965). Behavioral modifications through modeling procedures. In L. Krasner & L.P. Ullman (Eds.), Research in behavior modification (pp.310-340). New York: Holt, Rinehart and Winston.

Bandura, A. (1977). Social learning theory. Englewood Cliffs, NJ: Prentice-Hall, Inc.

Bandura, A. (1986). Social foundations of thought and action: A social cognitive theory. Englewood Cliffs, NJ: Prentice-Hall, Inc.

Bandura, A. (1997). Self-efficacy: The exercise of control. New York: W.H. Freeman and Company.

Bandura, A., & Cervone, D. (1983). Self-evaluative and self-efficacy mechanisms governing the motivational effects of goal systems. Journal of Personality and Social Psychology, 45(5), pp.1017-1028.

Barrett, B.H., Johnston, J.M., & Pennypacker, H.S. (1986). Behavior: Its units, dimensions, and measurement. In R.O. Nelson & S.C. Hayes (Eds.), Conceptual foundation of behavioral assessment (pp.156-200). New York: The Guilford Press.

Blankenship, V. (1985). The dynamics of intention. In M. Frese & J. Sabini (Eds.), <u>Goal-directed behavior: The concept of action in psychology</u> (pp.161-170). Hillsdale, NJ: Lawrence Erlbaum Associates.

Carr, P.B., & Confessore, G.J. (1998). Resourcefulness: One of the conative factors associated with self-directed learning. Paper presented at the 12th International Symposium on Self-Directed Learning, Kissimmee, FL. February 19-23, 1998.

Chapman, M., & Skinner, E.A. (1985). Action in development—Development in action. In M. Frese & J. Sabini (Eds.), <u>Goal-directed behavior: The concept of action in psychology</u> (pp.200-213). Hillsdale, NJ: Lawrence Erlbaum Associates.

Confessore, G.J. (1992). An introduction to the study of self-directed learning. In G.J. Confessore & S.J. Confessore (Eds.), <u>Guideposts to self-directed learning: Expert commentary on essential concepts</u> (pp.1-6). King of Prussia, PA: Organization Design and Development, Inc.

Darkenwald, G.G., & Valentine, T. (1985). Factor structure of deterrents to public participation in adult education. <u>Adult Education Quarterly, 35</u>(4), pp.177-193.

Deci, E.L., & Ryan, R.M. (1985). <u>Intrinsic motivation and self-determination in human behavior</u>. New York: Plenum Press.

Fishbein, M., & Ajzen, I. (1975). <u>Belief, attitude, intention, and behavior: An introduction to theory and research</u>. Reading, MA: Addison-Wesley Publishing Company.

Frese, M., Fay, D., Hilburger, T., Leng, K., & Tag, A. (1997). The concept of personal initiative: Operationalization, reliability and validity in two German samples. <u>Journal of Occupational and Organizational Psychology, 70</u>(2), pp.139-161.

Frese, M., Kring, W., Soose, A., & Zempel, J. (1996). Personal initiative at work: Differences between East and West Germany. <u>Academy of Management Journal, 39</u>(2), pp.37-63.

Frese, M., & Sabini, J. (1985). Action theory: An introduction. In M. Frese & J. Sabini (Eds.), <u>Goal directed behavior: The concept of action in psychology</u> (pp.xvii-xxv). Hillsdale, NJ: Lawrence Erlbaum Associates.

Frese, M., Stewart, J., & Hannover, B. (1987). Goal orientation and planfulness: Action styles as personality concepts. <u>Journal of Personality and Social Psychology, 52</u>(6), pp.1182-1194.

Frohman, A.L. (1997). Igniting organizational change from below: The power of personal initiative. <u>Organizational Dynamics, 25</u>(3), pp.39-53.

Gove, P.B. (Ed.). (1976). <u>Webster's third new international dictionary of the English language: Unabridged</u>. Springfield, MA: G. & C. Webster Company.

Heckhausen, H., & Kuhl, J. (1985). From wishes to action: The dead ends and short cuts on the long way to action. In M. Frese & J. Sabini (Eds.), <u>Goal-directed behavior: The concept of action in psychology</u> (pp.134-157). Hillsdale, NJ: Lawrence Erlbaum Associates.

Hoehne, K.A.K. (1990). Initiative-a neglected psychosocial dimension. <u>Social Psychiatry and Psychiatric Epidemiology, 25</u>, pp.101-107.

Houle, C.O. (1961). <u>The inquiring mind: A study of the adult who continues to learn</u>. Madison, WI: The University of Wisconsin Press.

Kennett, D. (1994). Academic self management counseling: Preliminary evidence for the importance of learned resourcefulness. <u>Studies in Higher Education, 19</u>(3), pp.295-307.

Long, H.B. (1998). Theoretical and practical implications of selected paradigms of self-directed learning. In H.B. Long, et al. (Eds.), <u>Developing paradigms for self-directed learning</u> (pp.1-14). Norman, OK: Public Managers Center, College of Education, University of Oklahoma.

Mischel, W., Shoda, Y., & Peake, P. (1988). The nature of adolescent competencies predicted by preschool delay of gratification. <u>Journal of Personality and Social Psychology, 54</u>(4), pp.687-696.

Oddi, L.F. (1987). Perspectives on self-directed learning. <u>Adult Education Quarterly, 38</u>(1), pp.21-31.

Ponton, M.K., & Confessore, G.J. (1998). Characteristic behaviors of personal initiative: A conate associated with self-directed learning. Paper presented at the 12th International Symposium on Self-Directed Learning, Kissimmee, FL. February 19-23, 1998.

Learning Conation

Rokeach, M. (1979). <u>Understanding human values: Individual and societal</u>. New York: The Free Press.

Rosenbaum, M. (1989). Self control under stress: The role of learned resourcefulness. <u>Adverse Behavioral Therapy, 11</u>, pp.109-121.

Wolman, B.B., et al. (Eds.). (1973). <u>Dictionary of behavioral science</u>. New York: Van Nostrand Reinhold Co.

CHAPTER SEVEN

WHY ASSESSING SELF-EFFICACY FOR SELF–DIRECTED LEARNING SHOULD BE USED TO ASSIST ADULT STUDENTS IN BECOMING SELF–DIRECTED LEARNERS

Gary J. Hoban & Claudia J. Sersland

There can be little doubt that interest in the concept and the practices of self-directed learning has soared over the years. A recent check of the Internet using the Excite search engine showed that the topic had received nearly two and a half million hits and the list of entries, with an incredible array of variation in the use of the term "self-directed learning," was staggering, running into the thousands.

The same can be said for the construct of "self-efficacy" and its uses first described by Albert Bandura in 1977. Bandura's construct of self-efficacy, restated, holds that one can execute specific behaviors to produce a desired outcome and that one's self-efficacy or one's confidence that he or she has the ability to complete a specific task successfully relates to performance and perseverance in a variety of endeavors.

Again, a recent search of the Internet showed that there had been close to a million and a quarter "hits" or inquiries and a list of entries numbering over a thousand. In these searches it is true that the topics "self-directed learning" and "self-efficacy" are broadly defined and used to cover a number of concerns. A perusal of the many entries for self-efficacy, for example, shows a melange of considerations including self-esteem, self-regulation, self-health monitoring, self and religion, self-talk, and self help. Despite the broad use of the term, there appears to be an underlying assumption that having a sense of confidence of succeeding in each of these areas, and in others not noted, is a key component of the use of the constructs.

With all of these entries, not to speak of the books and articles written on the subject, one could conclude that about everything that has been said about the subjects has been said before. In fact, the ERIC system used by educational researchers shows that there are 996 entries for self-efficacy and 411 entries for self-directed learning. It is tempting to suggest that additional research and speculation in these areas is redundant. With the rapid movement toward new instructional delivery systems—on-line, distance education, CD ROM, to name but a few—becoming an integral part of higher education, more, rather than less, needs to be known about not only how adult students become self-directed learners but also about how they become *successful* self-directed learners. This need for more knowledge about self-directed learners was underscored in a January 18, 1999, article in *The San Diego Union,* entitled "Online Learning" written by Michele Himmelberg for *The Orange County Register.*

In her article, Himmelberg observes, "Add a new phrase to your career-survival vocabulary: on-line learning. It's virtual instruction, the next-best thing to being in an intimate classroom. It's better than static computer-based training because you can interact with the instructor and students, and it's better than a live video-conference because you can do it anywhere, anytime." According to Himmelberg, citing an article in *Training Magazine,* "the on-line market is expected to grow nine-fold by 2001, ... capturing a bigger share of the $60.7 billion budgeted this year for workplace training." After noting the major increase in on-line instruction, which, of course, must, in the end, involve self-directed learning, Himmelberg acknowledges this concern: "But not everyone is disciplined enough to take advantage of this method."

It is this question of self-discipline to be a successful online learner or, for that matter, any kind of self-directed learner, that needs to be addressed. Proponents of self-directed learning (in this case online learning), especially for industrial training and for specialized graduate programs such as those offered by the University of Phoenix, which reports that about 60 percent of its online students graduate and receive degrees and perform as well or better than students enrolled in its regular programs, still need to be cautious. Himmelberg notes that, "Despite the wondrous potential of online learning, even advocates have expressed concern that it might fall flat on its complex face. The challenge—and the opportunity—will be making this type of education an engaging, user-friendly experience."

Many institutions of higher education have been struggling with the implications of self-directed learning for a number of years. Using a variety of instructional delivery systems, these institutions have debated not only if self-directed approaches should be used but also how and under what constraints they should be used. At National University, a university head-quartered in San Diego with campus centers throughout California and dedicated to serving the working adult learner (average age of 35), these issues have been of significant concern for some time. Since 1993 faculty at National University have been involved with research into self-directed learning in an attempt to determine what are the most productive avenues to pursue as the University ventures more and more into self-directed learning instructional delivery systems. Currently, National University offers nursing programs through distance education utilizing television links throughout California, and has computer on-line programs offering a global master of business administration, an-E-commerce master's degree, the cross cultural and language acquisition and development certificate for teacher education (CLAD), and a new bachelor's in nursing program. It is a goal of the University to have all programs available on-line within the next several years.

One of the questions that has been looked at intently through research at National University has been the challenge of motivation and discipline on the part of the adult learner that Himmelberg noted in her article. The construct that faculty researchers at National University have used to study this aspect of self-directed learning is self-efficacy. They have completed and presented the results of studies dealing with the relationship between self-efficacy and general academic performance, the relationship between self-efficacy and subject specific performance—writing and mathematics—at a variety of educational levels, and, more recently, the relationship between self-efficacy and self-directed learning as measured by Guglielmino's Self-Directed Learning Readiness Scale (SDLRS). The results of these studies have been reported extensively at five international self-directed learning symposia and in the books which have been published subsequent to those symposia.

One of the most interesting findings in the first study, completed by Hoban and Wall in 1993, was that adult students returning to the college classroom after an absence of a number of years tended to rely more heavily on what goes on in the classroom than on outside work, perhaps being quite dependent on their instructors for their learning. In other words, it appeared that it could not and should be assumed that adult learners have a predisposition to being self-directed. This conclusion corresponded well with the thinking of those who believe that self-directed learning is not an all or nothing construct. In many ways it supported the model proposed by Gerald Grow at the 4th International Self-Directed Learning Symposium which suggested 1) there is nothing wrong with being a dependent learner—one who needs to be taught; 2) self-direction can be learned—and it can be taught; and, 3) the ability to be self-directed is situational: one may be self-directed in one subject, a dependent learner in others (Grow, 1991).

The findings by Hoban and Wall led to further research, funded through National University Presidential Research Award grants, to investigate the extent to which self-efficacy was related to self-directed learning. Self-efficacy had been demonstrated in a number of studies to be a powerful predictor of academic and task performance and readiness for self-directed learning, as measured by the Guglielmino instrument, proved to be a strong indicator of an individual's willingness and desire to be a self-directed learner. What appeared to be missing was a direct connection, if any, between self-efficacy and self-directed learning. Further, in light of many studies relating self-efficacy to performance, it would appear that a successful self-directed learner would have a strong self-efficacy to be self-directed.

Wall, Hoban and Sersland (1996) tested the linkage of the constructs in studies examining the correlation of adult learner performance in mathematics with a subject specific self-efficacy instrument they developed and validated and the Self-Directed Learning Readiness Scale (SDLRS) used nationwide. The self-efficacy instruments correlated significantly with subject specific (mathematics) performance but the SDLRS did not. In subsequent years, Hoban and Sersland replicated their work with Wall at middle and high school levels, discovering that not only was there a strong correlation between performance on mathematics tests and scores on the SDLRS, but also strong correlations between scores on the self-efficacy instruments and the SDLRS. They concluded that there is a definite connection between self-efficacy and self-directed learning. The larger question, though, is, "What is that connection?"

In 1998, realizing National University's rapid move toward utilizing new instructional delivery systems predicated on the learner being self-directed, Hoban and Sersland examined the degree to which self-efficacy could predict success in being a self-directed learner. This study tested the hypothesis: *Readiness for self-directed learning is positively correlated with self-efficacy for self-directed learning.* The conclusions of this study (Hoban and Sersland, 1998) were based on the scores of 86 National University, graduate beginning teacher education students who completed a self-efficacy scale for self-directed learning developed and validated by the investigators and on scores on the SDLRS. While a number of variables were considered as part of the study, the results led to the finding that there was a significant relationship between self-efficacy for self-directed learning and readiness for self-directed learning.

The implication of this relationship would support the belief that there is a connection between the two constructs and that this relationship demonstrates that it is possible to predict success at being or becoming a self-directed learner. A high self-efficacy for self-directed learning score attained by an entering student would indicate that he or she is ready to undertake self-directed work and a lower score would indicate probable lack of success as a self-directed learner. Unless steps are taken to deal with the areas identified by the student as ones in which he or she has little confidence in his or her ability to pursue self-directed learning, it would be futile for the student to begin academic work relying heavily on self-directed learning instructional delivery modes. We concur with Grow (1991) that there is nothing wrong with being a dependent learner and self-direction can be learned and it can be taught.

CURRENT RESEARCH

It is the purpose of the research conducted in 1998-1999 to further validate the study concluded in 1998. While the 1998 study dealt exclusively with National University students, the 1999 study was expanded to involve students from three universities—National University, Chapman University, and Point Loma University. All participants in this study are students who are preparing to become school administrators. A description of the study, with attention to data collection, sample, findings, and a discussion of the results follows.

DATA COLLECTION

The hypothesis for this study is: that self-efficacy for self-directed learning can be assessed or, to restate the investigators' 1998 hypothesis, readiness for self-directed learning is positively correlated with self-efficacy for self-directed learning. Once an adult student's self-efficacy for self-directed learning is determined, then appropriate instructional strategies—be they directed by others or self-directed—can be developed. Enhancing an adult student's self-efficacy for self-directed learning will make it possible for the student to gain a greater degree of self-directedness in the university setting and/or in the industrial training milieu.

Two instruments were used for data collection: 10 item Self-Efficacy for Self-Directed Learning Questionnaire developed by Hoban and Sersland, 1998, and the SDLRS developed by Guglielmino, 1988. The internal consistency measure of reliability for the Self-Efficacy for Self-Directed Learning Questionnaire and the SDLRS was evaluated using Cronbach's Alpha. The internal consistency was .89 for the Self-Efficacy for Self-Directed Learning Questionnaire and .79 for the SDLRS.

Since the purpose of this study was to validate the findings of the 1998 study, the sample was not only drawn from students at National University but from two additional universities; Point Loma and Chapman whose student population is primarily made up of adult learners. All students sampled were in the educational administration program. One class from each university was invited to participate in the study. The classes which were invited to participate were at about the same point in their respective programs. The students were told that they were being asked to complete two instruments, a Self-Efficacy for Self-Directed Learning Questionnaire and the SDLRS instrument. Also, the students were being asked to complete a demographic sheet seeking information such as gender, age, language first spoken as a child, years since last degree, and years since attending college. Each of the instruments were identified with a code number to make it possible to do comparison statistical analysis later. All responses were anonymous. Also, all students were assured that their participation was strictly voluntary and they signed a consent form before participating.

SAMPLE

There were 70 students who provided complete responses to the instruments being used. Refer to Table 7.1 for the demographic makeup of the sample.

Forty-three percent of the students were from National University, nineteen percent were from Point Loma University, and thirty-three percent were Chapman University. While language first spoken, years since last degree and years since attending college were not variables being examined, some participants chose to provide that information. Of those who reported their first spoken language, 83 percent reported speaking English first (58); ten percent reported speaking Spanish first (7); and the remaining five students reporting either speaking French, Hindi or Tagalog first. National University students reported an average of 10.41 years since their last degree, Point Loma University students reported an average of 17.46 years, and Chapman University students reported an average of 9.91 years. National University students reported an average of 3.07 years since last attending college, Point Loma University students reported an average of 4 years, and Chapman University students reported an average of 3.32 years.

FINDINGS

Data were transcribed from the Self-Efficacy for Self-Directed Learning Questionnaire, the Self-Directed Learning Readiness Scale, and a demographic self-reporting sheet. The Self-Efficacy for Self-Directed Learning Questionnaire had, as noted above, 10 questions which students responded to on a Likert scale ranging from "0" to "10." Scores could range from "0" to "100", with a score of 100 showing the highest degree of self-efficacy possible as measured by the scale. The SDLRS adult version consists of 58 items with a numerical response for each item being from "1" to "5." Scores could range from a low of "58" to a high of "290" with the higher number indicating strong readiness to be a self-directed learner. Data was transcribed from the questionnaire answer sheets to the Statistical Procedure for the Social Sciences (SPSS) spreadsheet for analysis. (Appreciation is extended to John Stephens, California School of Professional Psychology, Fresno, for his statistical work).

Table 7.1. Summary of Demographic Information for National University (n=30), Point Loma University (n=13) and Chapman University (n=27)

College	N	Mean Age	Years Since Last Degree	Years Since Attending College
National	30	36.63	10.41	3.07
Male	9	38.78	12.75	4.00
Female	21	35.71	9.52	2.67
Point Loma	13	42.08	17.46	4.00
Male	1	26.00	4.00	1.00
Female	12	43.42	18.58	4.25
Chapman	26	33.88	9.91	3.32
Male	11	35.09	9.13	3.30
Female	16[a]	33.00	10.36	3.33

[a]One respondent did not report her age.

Table 7.2. Zero Order Correlation of Sex, Age, SDLRS, and Self-Efficacy for Self-Directed Learning for National University (n=30), Point Loma University (n=13), and Chapman University (n=27) students.

					Correlation
Variable	Alpha	n	2	3	4
1. Sex		70	.03	−.04	.07
2. Age		67	—	.31[*]	.32[**]
3. SDLRS		66		—	.62[***]
4. Self-Efficacy for SD		68			—
		Mean	36.62	208.67	80.44
		SD	8.69	15.37	12.73

[*]p<.05, [**]p<.01, [***]p<.001.

Refer to Table 7.2 for the zero order correlation of sex, age, SDLRS, and Self-Efficacy for Self-Directed Learning scores for the entire sample. This table provides statistics for results one, two,

Table 7.3.   Summary of SDLRS and Self-Efficacy for Self-Directed Learning Scores for National University (n=30), Point Loma University (n=13), and Chapman University (n=27)

School	SDLRS		Self-Efficacy for Self-Directed Learning	
	Mean	SD	Mean	SD
National	213.87[a]	11.39	83.46	10.42
Male	214.78	14.15	80.75	11.16
Female	213.48	10.38	84.55	10.20
Point Loma	215.15	12.10	85.69	7.61
Male[b]	208.00	—	—	—
Female	215.75	12.43	86.08	7.81
Chapman	199.78	16.75	74.78	14.87
Male	206.36	13.82	81.73	10.60
Female	195.25	17.48	70.00	15.77

[a]Two respondents did not complete the Self-Directed Learning Questionnaire.
[b]Only one male respondent available.

and three above. Refer to Table 7.3 for the SDLRS mean scores and the Self-Efficacy for Self-Directed Learning mean scores by university by sex. This table provides statistics for results four and five above.

After the data analysis was completed, the following results emerged:

1. There was a substantial relationship between the SDLRS scores and the Self-Efficacy for Self-Directed Learning scores (r (68) = .62, p<.001. This affirms the hypothesis stated earlier and validates the findings in the 1998 study by Hoban and Sersland. This finding substantiates that the two instruments do validate each other and self-efficacy for self-directed learning can be measured and does predict the degree to which a student can or will be a self-directed learner with a high degree of accuracy. Further implications will be discussed in the discussion section.

2. There was no difference in mean readiness for self-directed learning scores or mean self-efficacy scores between men and women. This supports the findings of all past studies done by Hoban and Sersland.

3. There was a modest relationship between age of the student and SDLRS (r (.31) = .31, p<.05), and between age of the student and the Self-Efficacy for Self-Directed Learning scores (r (67) = .32, p<.01). Older students tended to have both higher Self-Efficacy for Self-Directed Learning and SDLRS scores. Age was not a significant variable in the 1998 study by Hoban and Sersland. They did find in previous studies that there was a significant relationship between self-efficacy for mathe-

matics performance, mathematics performance, and SDLRS among middle school and high students. However, there was not a significant relationship between self-efficacy for mathematics performance and SDLRS among adult students.

4. There was a significant difference in SDLRS scores among the students from the three universities, $(F (2,65) = 5.13, p<.01)$.

5. There was a significant difference in Self-Efficacy for Self-Directed Learning scores among the students from the three universities, $(F (2,67) = 9.13, p<.001)$.

DISCUSSION

The most significance finding of this study is the affirmation of the hypothesis: that self-efficacy for self-directed learning can be assessed and the validation of the 1998 study by Hoban and Sersland. This finding has a number of potential implications for National University. National University is moving towards putting most if not all of its academic programs on-line. These programs will be delivered in the intensive one-month, one-course-at-a-time format that has been so successful with adult learners. It would appear that students in an on-line program would have to have a high degree of self-directedness. The self-efficacy instrument that is easily administered and easily scored could be administered to all entering adult students to determine their confidence level in becoming self-directed learners. Those who score high would have a higher potential for success in self-directed education and those who score lower could be given assistance in different ways to become self-directed learners or could be advised to take coursework in a more traditional delivery format such as the classroom. Students may be highly successful in a self-directed learning environment for certain content areas but not for others.

Grow (1991) concluded that self-directedness is situational. It may be valuable to develop self-efficacy for self-directed learning instruments for specific content areas, enabling students to determine their self-efficacy for self-directed learning in one area of endeavor but not in another. This could allow the student the opportunity to choose the delivery method for each content area that would be suited for their learning needs. This may also be of value in industrial training programs, allowing employees to determine how best they learn in a given situation and selecting the delivery method to get the most out of their training.

In the Himmelberg article it stated that on-line training would continue to become a larger share of the training and development market. This delivery system requires individuals to be self-disciplined which would lead one to believe that they would also have to have a high degree of self-efficacy for self-directed learning. The 10 item National University questionnaire could be used to predict employees' self-efficacy for self-directed learning and assist in determining what would be the most effective delivery method for training activities. Employers may find that the delivery system is highly related to the subject matter and the employees' variable confidence level in attaining success that Grow (1991) termed situational self-directed learning. Employers may also want to provide employees with resources that will help them become more self-directed learners. They may also find as the results in this current study suggest that age is a determinant in the self-efficacy for self-directed learning.

The finding that age is positively related to the Self-Efficacy for Self-Directed Learning scores caused the researchers to reflect on previous studies as to why this was significant in this sample. The purely statistical explanation is there was more variance in age in this sample than in previous samples. But reflecting on previous studies, it appears that self-efficacy may have a cycle that is related to a person's life experiences. In the middle school and high school populations, Hoban and Sersland (1996, 1997) found that self-efficacy for mathematics performance was positively related to SDLRS. In samples from the adult learner population from National University, Wall, Hoban and Sersland (1995) and Hoban and Sersland (1998) found that the self-efficacy scores were not related to the SDLRS scores, however.

Early in a person's life, self-efficacy appears to track with performance, most likely because of the absence of negative experiences. As a person has more experiences, the probability of having unsuccessful outcomes is more likely, so there would be a period of time where self-efficacy and most likely performance would be low. At some point in a person's life, opportunities are afforded that result in positive outcomes. Self-efficacy and performance increases with the more positive experiences a person has. The sample for this study is educators who have been successful teachers and in some cases are already successful administrators. The previous samples of adult learners were in the teacher education program. These people had very little or no experience in teaching. Age and life experiences may also have been played a role in the significant findings among the three universities.

The significant differences in SDLRS and Self-Efficacy for Self-Directed Learning scores among the three universities were expected. The demographic make-up of the students at each university, and the learning environment at each university are different. The students from Chapman University were the youngest thus having less professional experience and lower SDLRS and Self-Efficacy for Self-Directed Learning scores. The format at Point Loma University is a semester whereas at National and Chapman Universities it is an intensive one-course-at-a-time structure. Further research would be necessary to be able to make any definitive conclusions. Another variable of interest would be how students select a university to attend. It is possible that students pre-select themselves to a university that would require them to have a high degree of self-efficacy for self-directed learning.

This study makes a strong case that self-efficacy for self-directed learning can predict readiness for self-directed learning. With National University moving in the direction for most if not all of its programs on-line in the near future, it would be a valuable service to students to be able to assist them in assessing their self-directed learning and to provide resources for them to increase it. Measuring self-efficacy for self-directed learning is a very broad construct. Students, however, generally focus on a specific program or, more specifically, a course within a program. In addition Grow (1991) agrues that self-directedness is situational. What this suggests is that a more useful tool would be an instrument that could assist students not only in measuring self-efficacy for self-directed learning by subject matter but also by instructional delivery mode. For example, an instrument that would measure self-efficacy in using computers could help students determine if on-line computer instruction in a particular subject is appropriate for them.

Himmelberg stated that, as on-line education becomes a more integral part of higher education, how adult students become *successful* self-directed learners is what should be studied. A measure of success should be determined and the relevant data collected.

REFERENCES

Bandura, A. (1977). Towards a unifying theory of behavioral change. Psychological Review, 84, pp.191-215.

Bloyd, R., Hoban, G., & Wall, D. (1995). Self-efficacy and the adult learner: Implications for the teaching of writing. In H.B. Long (ed.), New dimensions in self-directed learning, (pp.197-217). Norman. Oklahoma: Public Managers Center, College of Education, University of Oklahoma.

Grow, G. (1991/1996). Teaching learners to be self-directed. Adult Education Quarterly, 41(3), pp.125-149.

Guglielmino, L. (1988). Learning Questionnaire. Boca Raton, Florida: Guglielmino and Associates.

Himmelberg, M. "Online Learning," The San Diego Union (reprinted from The Orange County Register), January 18, 1999, D-1.

Hoban, G., & Sersland, C. (1997). Self-efficacy, self-directed learning, and the adult learner: A look backward and a look forward. Paper presented at the First World Conference On Self-Directed Learning, Montreal, Quebec.

Hoban, G., & Sersland, C. (1997). Self-directed learning in mathematics-an impossibility at the middle school? A study of self-efficacy, readiness for self-directed learning and the middle school student: Implications for math performance. In H.B. Long, (ed.). Expanding horizons in self-directed learning (pp.223-243). Norman. OK: Public Mangers Center, College of Education, University of Oklahoma.

Hoban, G., & Sersland, C. (1998). Self-directed learning, Learned or Unlearned? (a study of self-efficacy, readiness for self-directed learning, and mathematics performance at the high school level with comparisons to the middle school and adult learner populations.) In H.B. Long, (ed.) Developing paradigms for self-directed learning (pp.107-124). Norman. OK: Public Mangers Center, College of Education. University of Oklahoma.

Hoban, G., & Sersland, C. (1999). Developing Learning Plans for Adult Learners – Can Self-Efficacy Predict A Readiness for Self-Directed Learning to Determine Effective Modes of Instruction? In H.B. Long & Associates (ed.). Contemporary ideas and practices in self-directed learning (pp.49-61). Norman. OK: Public Mangers Center, College of Education. University of Oklahoma.

Wall, D., Sersland, C., & Hoban, G. (1996). The adult learner: Self-efficacy, readiness for self-directed learning, and gender: Implications for mathematics performance. In H.B. Long (ed.). Current developments in self-directed learning (pp.107-126.). Norman, OK: Public Managers Center. College of Education. University of Oklahoma.

CHAPTER EIGHT

IF LIFELONG LEARNING IS IMPORTANT...
THE RELATIONSHIPS BETWEEN STUDENTS'
SELF–DIRECTED LEARNING READINESS, THEIR
PSYCHOLOGICAL TYPE, LEARNING STYLE, AND
CREATIVE AND LOGICAL THINKING ABILITY

Carolin Kreber, Patricia Cranton & Keina Allen

OVERVIEW

To better understand the nature of self-directed learning, it becomes important to see how self-directed learning readiness is related to other characteristics of learners. Conceptually, one would expect that self-directed learning readiness is connected to such abilities and traits as logical reasoning, creative thinking, and psychological type preferences. If we can understand these connections, we will be better able to foster self-directed learning among our students.

OBJECTIVES AND BACKGROUND

The purpose of this study was to explore the following three questions:

1. Does psychological type predict self-directed learning readiness?
2. Do logical and creative thinking ability predict self-directed learning readiness?
3. Does learning style predict logical and creative thinking ability?

Self-directed learning has been recognized as an important goal of education (Boud, 1988; Candy, 1991; Knapper & Cropley, 1991) at a time when rapid social, political, and technological changes require us to gain new skills and knowledge throughout our lives. There is a common perception that personal and professional success depend increasingly on continued learning and development. The key to active involvement in lifelong learning is seen in the acquisition of the skills and attitudes associated with the concept of self-directed learning.

The relationship between critical thinking and self-directed learning has been discussed by various scholars (Brookfield, 1984, 1985, 1993; Cranton, 1994; Garrison, 1992; Mezirow, 1985). Empirical research exploring this question, however, is scarce. Nevertheless, over the years many techniques and strategies for promoting critical thinking and self-directed learning skills have been proposed (Brookfield, 1987; Kirschenbaum & Perry, 1982; Smith, 1977). Research on self-directed learning and critical thinking, to date, has largely ignored individual differences among learners, and there is still only a small number of books and articles that make suggestions as to how instruction should be organized for different learners. This study explores whether students' psychological type preferences (Jung, 1971), preferred learning style, logical reasoning ability, and level of creativity are related to self-directed learning.

Herbeson (1994) and Kreber (1998) found a strong positive correlation between scores on the extraverted intuitive dimension of psychological type and scores on the Self-Directed Learning Readiness Scale. Jung (1971) describes intuitives as being basically future oriented, creative, independent, compelled to search for new opportunities, and drawn to novelty. The correlation between intuition and the SDLRS perhaps should not come as a surprise as the factor structure of the SDLRS, as reported by

Guglielmino, includes a future orientation, openness to learning opportunities, initiative and independence in learning, and creativity. Based on a sample of 142 undergraduates, Kreber (1998) found a small positive relationship between two logical reasoning abilities, the ability to interpret evidence (r =.32; p<.001) and the ability to evaluate arguments (r =33; p<.001), and SDLRS scores. Torrance and Mourad (1978) report a correlation between creativity and self-directed learning readiness. Again, one may expect this to be the case for the same reasons as outlined earlier. It appears that there is both empirical evidence and conceptual reasons to believe that psychological type, critical thinking, and creative thinking are related to how people score on the SDLRS.

The relationships between learning style (Kolb, 1984) and self-directed learning are less clear. In a correlational study with professional nurses Geehan (1998) found no relationships between scores on the Kolb Learning Style Learning Inventory and on Guglielmino's SDLRS. By definition, self-directed learning should encompass all learning styles. If learners choose what to learn, it seems plausible to assume that the learner is also free to decide how something will be learned. Considered from this perspective it does not make too much sense to assume that a preference for a particular style of learning would correlate with the degree to which an individual perceives him or herself as possessing the skills associated with self-directed learning. Rather than style of learning, we would perhaps expect a learner's self-efficacy, self-concept, or locus of control to make a difference here.

Kolb's (1984) concept of learning style becomes interesting in relation to self-directed learning readiness when we consider the cyclical learning process from which it has been derived. Kolb (1984) argues that a genuine learning experience involves four distinct phases of learning. Learning style is defined by the phase of the cycle a person prefers or excels in. Should it turn out that logical reasoning ability and creative reasoning ability both predict self-directed learning readiness, and logical reasoning ability and creative thinking ability are associated with different learning styles, then Kolb's learning cycle would have profound implications for promoting self-directed learning readiness.

SAMPLE AND INSTRUMENTATION

In the fall of 1998, 87 undergraduate students from a large research university (42 students from educational psychology and 43 students from philosophy) completed five instruments: three subtests of the Watson and Glaser Critical Thinking Appraisal (CAT), Guglielmino's (1977) Self-Directed Learning Readiness Scale (SDLRS), Kolb's (1976) Learning Style Inventory (LSI), the Torrance Test of Creative Thinking (TTCT), and a psychological type indicator (the PET Type Check) (Cranton and Knoop, 1995). Data were collected on three different occasions during regular class time for a total of 1.5 hours.

The SDLRS is a fifty-eight item self-response questionnaire designed to measure the degree to which an individual perceives himself or herself as having the willingness and capacity to engage in self-directed learning. It yields one final score but Guglielmino reports that there are eight factors underlying the scale. She labels the factors as follows: openness to learning opportunities, self-concept as an effective learner, initiative and independence in learning, informed acceptance of responsibility for one's own learning, love of learning, creativity, future orientation, and ability to use basic study and problem-solving skills.

The Critical Thinking Appraisal (CTA) measures logical analytical reasoning ability. Three of the five subtests were used in this study. The first one assesses "students' ability to "recognize assumptions or presuppositions in given statements or premises" (Watson & Glaser, 1980, p.2), the second, ability "to weigh evidence and decide if generalizations or conclusions based on the given data are warranted" (Watson & Glaser, 1980, p.2) and the third, the degree to which they can "distinguish between arguments that are strong and relevant and those that are weak and irrelevant for a particular question at issue" (Watson & Glaser, 1980, p.2).

Hence the three subtests of the CAT yields three scores per respondent, one for each logical reasoning ability tested.

The P.E.T. Type Check (Cranton & Knoop, 1995) has been designed on the basis of Carl Jung's (1971) theory of psychological types and measures people's preferences for introverted thinking, extraverted thinking, introverted feeling, extraverted feeling, introverted sensing, extraverted sensing, introverted intuition, and extraverted intuition. The questionnaire uses a Likert-type response format and consists of eighty items, ten for each of the eight type scales. The PET Type Check yields eight scores per respondent.

The Kolb Learning Style Inventory (LSI) measures an individual's preference for four modes of learning: concrete experience, reflective observation, abstract conceptualization, and active experimentation. More specifically, the scale looks at how an individual prefers to take hold of an experience (through concrete experience or through abstract conceptualization) and how the individual prefers to transform this experience into knowledge (through reflection or through experimentation). The scale yields four scores per respondent.

The figural version of the Torrance Test of Creative Thinking (TTCT) is a timed test consisting of three parts. Ten minutes are allocated to each. In each subtest, the respondent is required to complete a given picture (*the stimulus*) by adding lines to it. Respondents are instructed to complete the drawings in ways that they perceive as unique or unusual. The test yields one final raw score which can be broken down five factor scores: fluency, originality, elaboration, abstractness of titles, and resistance to premature closure.

Pearson R correlations were calculated among all variables. Step-wise multiple regression analyses were then conducted in which self-directed learning readiness served as the criterion variable.

FINDINGS

Results are based on a sample of 86 respondents. The study is ongoing and we expect to add further data to our file during the academic year 1999/2000. The results, to date, indicate a strong positive correlation between extroverted intuition and scores on the Self-Directed Learning Readiness Scale ($r = .62$; $p<.001$). A smaller negative relationship was found between introverted feeling and self-directed learning readiness ($r = -.28$; $p<.001$). A regression analysis with SDLRS as the criterion variable showed that extraverted intuition accounted for 35 percent of the total variance in SDLRS scores. Extraverted sensing entered the regression equation at the second step and accounted for an additional four percent of the variance. As beta is negative, we can infer that extraverted sensing and SDLRS scores are inversely related. Despite the negative correlation between introverted feeling and SDLRS, introverted feeling was not a significant predictor. As extraverted intuition entered the regression equation first and extraverted intuition and introverted feeling are related ($r = -.26$; $p<.01$) introverted feeling did not account for any additional variance. These data suggest that extraverted intuition appears to be a strong predictor of SDLRS scores. This finding supports the result of an earlier study (Kreber, 1998).

None of the other psychological type scales correlated with any of the other variables. These relationships became further substantiated when all undifferentiated cases [1] were removed from the data file (extraverted intuition and SDLRS: $r = .65$; $p<.001$; introverted feeling and SDLRS: $r = -.37$; $p<.001$).

No relationships were found between scores on any of the three logical thinking scales—identifying assumptions, evaluating arguments, interpreting evidence—and scores on the SDLRS; hence, these findings do not support the results of an earlier study (Kreber, 1998). The total raw score of the TTCT test also did not

---

[1] Jung considers a person undifferentiated when the person does not seem to have a clear dominant function or type preference.

correlate with SDLRS scores. As was to be expected, learning style was not found to be related to self-directed learning readiness.

Since extraverted intuition was the only variable that showed a high correlation with the total score of the SDLRS, we decided to factor analyse the SDLRS scores and to re-calculate Pearson R correlations using factor scores rather than one total SDLRS score.

A principal components factor analysis of SDLRS scores would not converge with 30 iterations; varimax rotation failed to converge in 24 iterations. A maximum likelihood solution yielded 17 factors with Eigenvalues greater than one. Quartimax rotation did not yield an interpretable factor structure. Varimax and oblique rotation methods would not converge. We then decided to calculate point bi-serial correlations between all 58 items and the total SDLRS score with the goal of excluding those items that showed the weakest correlations with the total score. This process led us to exclude 16 items (2, 4, 6, 7, 8, 11, 13, 15, 16, 20, 21, 33, 36, 51, 56, 58). Once these variables were removed, a principal component factor analysis with subsequent varimax rotation yielded 11 factors, six of which, with Eigenvalues ranging from 1.52 to 12.77, were considered interpretable.

The first factor was clearly associated with *a love of learning* and accounted for 30.4 percent of the total variance. The second factor accounted for an additional 7.5 percent of the variance and was associated with *self-management and problem-solving*. The third factor addressed *an individual's confidence in his or her independence as a learner*. This factor accounted for 5.3 percent of the variance. Factor four was associated with *enthusiasm for novelty*, factor five with *persistence or task-orientation*, and factor six seemed to address *responsibility for learning*. Factors four to six accounted for 3.6 to 3.9 percent of the variance. Table 8.1 gives the items which loaded on each factor. Factor scores were calculated using a regression method.

Calculations of Pearson R correlations of all variables including the six factor scores showed the following relationships (see Table 8.2): extraverted intuition correlated significantly with all six factors (with r ranging from .30 to .60), and most strongly

Table 8.1. Factor Loadings for the Six Interpretable Factors Emerging from Principal Component Analysis of SDLRS Scores (16 items excluded)

	Factor 1	Factor 2	Factor 3	Factor 4	Factor 5	Factor 6
Label	Love of learning	Self-management and Problem-solving	Confidence in one's independence as a learner	Enthusiasm for novelty	Persistence and Task-orientation	Responsibility for Learning
Items	V 1 (.72)	V 3 (.75)	V27 (.62)	V30 (.65)	V35 (.65)	V18 (.44)
	V 5 (.59)	V10 (.63)	V28 (.76)	V34 (.41)	V40 (.60)	V22 (.46)
	V17 (.63)	V12 (.60)	V38 (.50)	V37 (.63)	V42 (.34)	V24 (.63)
	V23 (.72)	V19 (.52)	V55 (.36)	V52 (.47)		V50 (.74)
	V31 (.52)	V39 (.48)				
	V32 (.61)	V41 (.53)				
	V45 (.69)	V44 (.56)				
	V47 (.80)	V57 (.58)				
	V49 (.58)					
	V53 (.76)					
Eigenvalue	12.77	3.14	2.22	1.62	1.58	1.42
Percentage of variance	30.4	7.5	5.3	3.9	3.8	3.6

104

Table 8.2. Pearson R Correlation Coefficients for the Six SDLRS Factors and All Other Variables

	ET	EF	ES	EN	IT	IF	IS	IN	REC	INT	EVAL	CE	RO	AC	AE	CREATE
F1	.08	-.03	-.25	.43**	.15	-.10	.23	.24	.05	.09	.11	.13	-.15	.01	-.18	.09
F2	.24	.06	-.07	.50**	-.13	-.31	-.13	-.04	.17	.31	.18	.01	-.12	.22	.10	.10
F3	.23	.05	.01	.51**	.11	-.08	.17	.25	.13	.35	.22	.08	-.18	.16	.01	.14
F4	.14	.08	-.10	.60**	.04	-.24	.16	.29*	-.01	.10	-.02	.12	-.18	-.01	-.01	.15
F5	.09	.02	-.06	.41**	-.15	-.34	-.11	-.03	.07	.18	.13	.05	-.31*	.17	.04	.11
F6	.03	-.01	-.05	.30*	.02	-.13	.08	.12	.01	.14	.01	.08	-.08	.01	.03	.10

* p < .01
**p < .001

ET to IN	=	extraverted thinking, feeling, sensing, intuition, introverted thinking. Etc.
REC	=	recognition of assumptions
INT	=	interpretation of evidence
Eval	=	evaluation of arguments
CE	=	concrete experience
RO	=	reflective observation
AC	=	abstract conceptualization
AE	=	active experimentation
CREATE	=	creativity as measured by TTCT

105

with factor four, *enthusiasm for novelty* (r =.60; p<.001). Introverted intuition also correlated positively with factor four but the
correlation was less strong (r =.29; p<.01). A small yet significant
negative correlation was found between introverted feeling and
factor two, *self-management and problem-solving* (r = −.31; p<.01)
and factor five, *persistence or task-orientation* (r = −.35; p<.001).

With respect to the scores on the CAT, a relatively small
positive correlation was found between the ability to interpret
evidence and factor two, *self-management and problem-solving*, as
well as the ability to interpret evidence and factor three, *confidence
in one's independence as a learner* (r =.31; p<.01 and r =.35;
p<.001 respectively).

A small negative correlation was found between one of the
learning style scales, reflective observation, and factor five,
persistence or task-orientation.

Multiple step-wise regression analyses, with each of the six
SDLRS factors successively serving as the criterion variable,
showed that extraverted intuition entered the regression equation
on the first step for all six factors (Table 8.3). As for factor one
(*love of learning*), extraverted intuition accounted for almost
sixteen percent of the variance (p<.001). Extraverted sensing
entered the regression equation at a second step and accounted for
an additional eleven percent of the variance (p<.001). As Beta is
negative, this suggests an inverse relationship between factor one
and extraverted sensing. Extraverted intuition accounted for the
first twenty-one percent of the variance for factor two (*self-
management and problem-solving*) (p<.001). One of the logical
thinking skills, interpretation of evidence, accounted for an
additional four percent (p<.001). As for factor three (*confidence in
one's independence as a learner*), extraverted intuition accounted
for twenty-two percent of the variance (p<.001), and interpreting
evidence again for an additional four percent (p<.001). A total of
forty-three percent of the variance of scores on factor four
(*enthusiasm for novelty*) was accounted for by extraverted intuition
(p<.001). Extraverted sensing accounted for a very small additional
amount of the variance (p<.001). As for factor five (*persistence or*

106

Table 8.3.   **Results of Step-Wise Multiple Regression Predicting SDLRS Factor Scores (N=89)**

	Step	Variable	Multiple R square	SE	Beta	p
F1 (Love of Learning)						
	1	EN	0.15	.08	.42	< .001
	2	ES	0.26	.10	-.33	< .001
F2 (Self-Management and Problem-Solving)						
	1	EN	0.21	.07	.42	< .001
	2	INT	0.26	.24	.21	< .01
F3 (Confidence in one's indepencence as a learner)						
	1	EN	0.22	.03	.44	< .001
	2	INT	0.26	.09	.20	< .05
F4 (Enthusiasm for Novelty)						
	1	EN	0.44	.018	.67	< .001
	2	ES	0.47	.023	-.16	< .05
F5 (Persistence or Task-Orientation)						
	1	EN	0.158	.028	.30	< .01
	2	RO	0.222	.018	-.28	< .01
	3	AC	0.26	.017	.24	< .01
	4	IF	0.31	.028	-.23	< .05
	5	ES	0.35	.033	-.20	< .05
F6 (Responsibility for Learning)						
	1	EN	0.05	.033	.23	< .05

task-orientation), extraverted intuition accounted for almost sixteen percent of the variance (p<.001). Perhaps surprisingly, an additional seven percent were accounted for by reflective observation. (p<.001) and another four percent by abstract conceptualization (p<.001), both variables representing learning style scales. As beta is negative for reflective observation, this suggests a negative correlation between persistence/task-analysis and reflective observation. Introverted feeling and extraverted sensing each accounted for an additional four percent of the total variance (p<.001). Extraverted intuition was the only variable entering the regression analysis for factor six (*responsibility for learning*), where it accounted for only .05 percent of the total variance (p<.05).

The total raw score of the TTCT did not correlate with any of the six factor scores nor with any of the other variables used in this study. We therefore decided to calculate Pearson R correlations using the TTCT factor scores of fluency, originality, abstractness of titles, elaboration, and resistance to premature closure.

Fluency refers to the number of ideas a person expresses through interpretable responses that use the stimulus in a meaningful manner. The essence of the idea may be expressed through the title, but the stimuli must be used.

Originality is inferred from the statistical infrequency and unusualness of the response. Focus is placed on the use of the stimulus rather than on the title. There are specific common responses listed which are eliminated from the scoring of this factor. There are also bonus points given for the appropriate use of combined stimuli.

Abstractness of Titles is based on the synthesis and organization that are required to produce good titles. At the highest level, there is the ability to capture the essence of the information involved, to know what is important. The scoring is an attempt to represent this quality of a person's thinking.

Elaboration is based on two assumptions: the minimum and primary response to the stimulus figure is a single response; the imagination and exposition of detail is a function of creative ability. Credit is given for each pertinent detail added to the original stimulus figure, its boundaries and/or its surrounding space. Examples are decoration, shading, elaboration of title, and each major meaningful variation of design.

Resistance to Premature Closure is based on the assumption that the creative person is able to keep open and delay closure long enough to make the mental leap that makes original ideas possible. Less creative persons tend to leap to conclusions prematurely without considering the available information.

Pearson r correlation coefficients for all variables indicated no relationships between the five creativity factors and any of the six SDLRS factor scores. There were also no relationships found between the creativity factors and any of the other variables (Table 8.4).

Table 8.4. **Pearson R Correlation Coefficients for the Five TTCT Factors and all Other Variables**

	C1	C2	C3	C4	C5
F1	.02	.03	.20	-.02	.03
F2	.01	.13	.07	.01	.06
F3	.11	.15	-.01	.02	.02
F4	.12	.17	.07	-.03	-.01
F5	.05	.13	.20	.01	.01
F6	.13	.14	-.08	-.07	-.09
ET	-.08	.03	-.14	.05	.05
EF	-.09	.03	-.08	-.07	.01
ES	-.01	.01	-.11	-.15	-.01
EN	.16	.15	.03	.03	-.16
IT	.02	.04	.10	.20	.05
IF	-.14	-.14	-.10	.03	-.01
IS	.16	.13	.06	.12	.03
IN	.04	-.01	.03	.08	-.08
REC	-.07	.02	.11	-.03	.11
INT	.02	.06	.01	.04	.19
EVAL	.03	.01	.10	.04	-.04
CE	.04	-.01	-.01	-.03	.12
RO	-.01	-.06	-.16	.14	-.01
AC	-.10	-.01	-.05	.11	.01
AE	.10	.16	-.12	.04	-.08
SDLRS	.12	.20	.12	-.01	.01

C1 = Fluency   C4 = Elaboration
C2 = Originality   C5 = Resistance to Premature Closure
C3 = Abstractness of Title

SUMMARY

Undergraduate students' scores on Guglielmino's Self-Directed Learning Readiness Scale seem to be associated with their preference for intuition. No relationship was found between logical reasoning and SDLRS scores or creative thinking and SDLRS scores. When factor scores were used, one logical thinking scale, interpreting evidence, accounted for a small amount of the variance of factor two (self-management and problem-solving) as well as of factor three (confidence in one's independence as a learner).

Contrary to what might have been expected, creativity, as measured by the TTCT, did not correlate with any of the SDLRS factor scores. No correlations were found between any of the four learning styles and any of three logical reasoning scales. Also, no correlations were found between any of the four learning style scales and any of the five creative thinking factor scores. Extraverted intuition accounted for most of the variance of all six SDLRS factor scores.

What are the implications that arise from these findings? We expected to find strong relationships between psychological type and self-directed learning readiness, between logical and creative thinking and self-directed learning readiness, between logical and creative thinking and psychological type, and between logical and creative thinking and learning style. Of these predictions, only the first one was supported. Extraverted intuition clearly predicts scores on the Self-Directed Learning Readiness Scale. While logical reasoning (interpreting evidence) accounted for some of the variance on two SDLRS factor scores, the relationship is much weaker than expected. How could one explain these results?

Clearly, a larger sample size would have been desirable in this study. It should be emphasized that the factor analysis, in particular, was exploratory in nature as it had not been our intent, initially, to use factor scores. It was only when no correlations were found with either creative thinking or logical reasoning and the total score of the SDLRS that we decided to explore whether such relationships might be revealed when individual factors are used. The observed trend would need to be replicated in studies with a much larger sample to enhance our confidence in the findings of this study. However, some interesting observations can be made.

The literature on SDL clearly suggests a relationship between critical and creative thinking and self-directedness in learning. It makes also intuitive sense to expect relationships between Kolb's learning style scales and logical and creative thinking. This study did not yield any empirical evidence that would support these assumptions. In interpreting these results it seems important to revisit the specific instruments used to collect the data. Three of the instruments used in this study (LSI, PET Type Check, SDLRS) relied on students' self-report; i.e., the scores reflect their personal perception of their abilities or preferences. Two instruments measured competence (CTA, TTCT) objectively. If students' perception of their capacity to engage in self-directed learning is distorted, for example, would we still expect to find a strong correlation between their scores on the Watson and Glaser Critical Thinking Appraisal and their scores on the SDLRS? Likewise, if students' responses to the PET Type Check were biased towards greater perceived social desirability, would we still expect a relationship between their scores on the Type Check and their scores on the CAT or TTCT? Also, when completing the LSI, respondents rank a series of statements describing their personal approaches to learning. While a person perceives him-or herself as being "a logical person," for example, the same person may not demonstrate much logic when completing the CAT; and someone describing him-or herself as "I'm a creative person" may not demonstrate much creativity when completing the TTCT.

Furthermore, while there is reason to assume that creative thinking, logical reasoning and self-directed learning are related, one may question whether it is indeed this relationship that is investigated when the SDLRS, the TTCT, and CAT are administered. The nature of the task of completing the TTCT, for example, is to express ideas in the form of pictures and to do so under time pressure. Is this the type of creativity that one expects to find in a self-directed learner?

Also, is it possible that self-directed learning may encompass more characteristics than addressed by the SDLRS? While the items on the SDLRS represent many important aspects of self-directed learning, an instrument that is based on an even broader conceptualization of SDL may be needed to identify the relationships between self-directed learning and creative and logical thinking.

One could argue that a perceived willingness and capacity to engage in SDL can be fostered by assisting learners in developing both their intuition and also, to some extent, their logical reasoning skills. However, as we show elsewhere (Cranton & Kreber, 1999), the items on the Self-Directed Learning Readiness Scale appeal to the intuitive types, and the high correlation between scores on the intuition scale and SDLRS scores, for this reason, is not surprising. Whether or not intuitives indeed have a greater "readiness" for self-directed learning, however, is a different question. The SDLRS may not measure readiness for self-directed learning in general but only those aspects of self-directed learning that naturally appeal to intuitive types.

The literature on self-directed learning suggests that there are good reasons to believe that important relationships exist between logical reasoning, creative thinking, psychological type, learning style, and self-directed learning. Understanding these relationships could greatly assist us in fostering self-directed learning. The results of this study, to date, did not support these hypotheses, however. As the results are counter-intuitive, we offer the following conclusion.

We suggest that there are at least three critical issues to be considered in empirical research on self-directed learning and its relationships to other variables: first, the nature of the task underlying the completion of the instruments used in the study; second, the nature of the assessment (whether the score represents a subjective self-report or *perception* of competence or an *objective assessment* of competence); third, the specific definition or construct underlying the particular variable the instrument is supposed to measure. It might be that different instruments are needed, or new instruments need to be developed, to investigate the complex relationships between critical thinking (logical reasoning and creative thinking ability) and self-directed learning competence.

REFERENCES

Boud, D. (Ed.). Developing student autonomy in learning, 2nd edition. London: Kogan Page.

Brookfield, S. (1984). Self-directed adult learning: a critical paradigm. Adult Education Quarterly, 35(2), pp.59-71.

Brookfield, S. (1985). Self-directed learning: A critical review of research. In S. Brookfield (Ed) Self-directed learning: From theory to practice. New Directions for Continuing Education, 25, pp.5-16. San Francisco, CA: Jossey-Bass.

Brookfield, S. (1987). Developing critical thinkers. San Francisco, CA: Jossey-Bass.

Brookfield, S. (1993). Self-directed learning, political clarity, and the critical practice of adult education. Adult Education Quarterly, 43(4), pp.227-242.

Candy, P.C. (1991). Self-direction for lifelong learning. San Francisco, CA: Jossey-Bass.

Cranton, P.A. (1994). Self-directed and transformative instructional development. Journal of Higher Education, 65(6), pp.726-744.

Cranton, P.A. & Knoop, R.(1995). P.E.T. Type Check. Victoria, BC: Psychological Type Press.

Cranton, P.A., & Kreber, (1999). The Self-Directed Learning Check: An Assessment of Self-Directed Learning Orientation Based on Jungian Psychological Type Theory. Paper presented at the 13th International Self-Directed Learning Symposium, Scottsdale, Arizona, February 26, 1999.

Garrison, D.R. (1992). Critical thinking and self-directed learning in adult education: An analysis of responsibility and control issues. Adult Education Quarterly, 42(3), pp.136-148.

Geehan, K. (1998). Psychological type and learning style among nurses. In Cranton, P. (ed.) Psychological Type in Action. Sneedville TN: Psychological Type Press.

Guglielmino, L.M. (1977). Development of the self-directed learning readiness scale, Unpublished doctoral dissertation. University of Georgia, Athens, Georgia.

Herbeson, E. (1992). Personality type and self-directed learning. The Canadian School Executive, 12, pp.8-15

Jung, C.G. (1971). Psychological types. Princeton, N.J.: Princeton University Press.

Kirschenbaum, D., & Perry, M. (1982). Improving academic competence in adults: A review of recent research. Journal of Counseling Psychology, 29(1), pp.76-94.

Knapper, C.K., & Cropley, A.J. (1991). Lifelong learning and higher education (second edition). London, UK: Kogan Page.

Kolb, D.A. (1984). Experiential learning. New Jersey: Prentice-Press.

Kreber, C. (1998). The Relationships between self-directed learning, critical thinking, and psychological type, and some implications for teaching in higher education. Studies in Higher Education, 21(3), pp.71-86.

Mezirow, J. (1985). A critical theory of self-directed learning. In S. Brookfield (Ed.), Self-directed learning: From theory to practice. New Directions for Adult and Continuing Education, 25. San Francisco: Jossey-Bass.

Smith, D. (1977). College classroom interactions and critical thinking. Journal of Educational Psychology, 69(2), pp.180-190.

Torrance, E.P., & Mourad, S.A. (1978). Some creativity and style of learning and thinking correlates of Guglielmino's Self-directed Learning Readiness Scale. Psychological Reports, 43, pp.1167-1171.

Watson, G., & Glaser, E.M. (1980). Critical Thinking Appraisal Manual. Orlando, Fl.: Harcourt Jovanovich.

CHAPTER NINE

PREREQUISITES TO SELF-DIRECTED LEARNING: MOTIVATION AS A PRECURSOR TO INITIATIVE IN YOUNG LEARNERS

Travis S. Plowman

STARBASE-Atlantis, Hampton Roads is a non-traditional education program designed for "at-risk" fifth graders conducted as a community outreach partnership between Fleet Training Center, Norfolk and Norfolk Public Schools, VA. As part of a continuing research effort to analyze program success, the Hampton Roads site participated in this study.

INTRODUCTION

The STARBASE-Atlantis Hampton Roads program brings military resources, Navy volunteers, teachers, professionals, and "at-risk" students together in a unique educational experience, a school without walls. The program focuses on math, science, computer literacy, technology, drug demand reduction, and goal setting activities. The program exposes "at-risk" students and their teachers to real-world applications of math and science through experiential learning, simulations, experiments in aviation, space-related fields, and tours of base activities. A summary case study of the first three years of operation reported significant performance by students and all group means (gender, ethnicity, regular ed./special ed.) (Lee-Pearce, Plowman, & Touchstone, 1998).

In a program as short as five days in which students attend one day per week for five weeks, long term cognitive gains are difficult to measure. Attempts to do so go beyond the program's goals and reasonable expectations of any program so short in duration. The underlying negative conditions that "at-risk" students bring into the learning environment are far more important issues to focus on in a short-term program than cognitive gains. Learning related issues that affect the conate areas can be stimulated in a very short period of time with dramatic long-term effects. STARBASE-Atlantis attempts to use the curriculum simply as a vehicle to address the more deeply rooted areas affecting learning in young "at-risk" students such as desire to learn, initiative, resourcefulness, and persistence.

PURPOSE OF THE STUDY

Lee-Pearce, Plowman, and Touchstone (1998) in a case study of this program found significant results in total population as compared to a control group, and within correlated pairs of gender, ethnic, and regular education/special education groups. Two pilot studies investigated whether there was anything about the STARBASE-Atlantis environment that influenced this measurable result (Plowman, 1999). Students appeared to become more self-aware of basic skills weaknesses and in the program's challenging environment wanted to improve their reading abilities. Conclusions of this study warrant further investigation to determine exactly how or why STARBASE-Atlantis was stimulating these kinds of results. Instrumentation, which was designed for adults, confounded the study as random selection of the population provided a sample group weak in reading skills (Plowman, 1999). The irony of the weakness of the previous study is the basic skill that provided a confounding element in the study became the self-identifier in the sample group. The study did identify weaknesses and obstacles in the basic skill areas, of which the learner was aware, that needed to be overcome.

This study was designed to analyze the environment at STAR-BASE-Atlantis, and students' self-perceptions of their learning interests. The Pilling-Cormick Self-Directed Learning Perception Scale (SDLPS) (1998) was used to analyze the learning environment, and the Learning Profile Questionnaire, with the same sample population, surveyed students' self-perceptions about learning. It combines both SDL instruments, previously used (Plowman, 1999) in separate pilot studies, with the same groups and utilizes a more robust Dunnett test to compare content gains against a control group.

RESEARCH QUESTIONS AND HYPOTHESES

The null hypotheses are as follows:

- There are no significant differences as measured in content material gains in the two experimental groups attending the program as compared to a single control group not attending.
- There are no significant indicators of a self-directed environment as measured by the SDLPS at the Virginia site.
- There are no significant cognate areas as determined by the LPQ.

REVIEW OF THE LITERATURE

Identifying children who are not performing has been a major thrust of educational research at the policy-making level for over ten years (NCES, 1995a). Public education's strength has been in preparing the masses for participation in society. Students finishing high school continue their education through adult vocational training programs, college and university training, or seek employment in the private sector. The picture is not good for all of our nation's students (NCES, 1996b; NCES, 1997b; NCES, 1998), however. Minority students are dropping out of high schools at high rates (NCES, 1996a; NCES, 1997a; Lee-Pearce et al, 1998).

Recognizing this problem, reform efforts, albeit inadequate, have been underway for the past 30 years (Gregory, 1993; NCES, 1996c; NCES, 1997c). Education of the masses evolved as a necessity driven by the industrial revolution to provide a responsive educated work force (Toffler, 1980). Vaill (1996) uses the image of permanent white-water as a metaphor for the only constant in today's information age is change. As society changes from the industrial age to the informational age increasingly large numbers of learners do not conform to the cookie cutter mass education model.

Confessore and Herrmann (1997) say that societies invest in formal education for reasons that include the intention to develop in individuals the capacity to continue to learn beyond those opportunities provided at the expense of society. The payoff could be in terms of less reliance on social welfare systems, low crime rate, healthier population, low unemployment rate, little or no drug abuse. On a more positive note, it would produce students who are capable of thinking critically, solving problems, collaborating with others, aspiring to be lifelong learners, and handling change (Lee-Pearce et al, 1998).

The students need to be approached from an instructional perspective that works for them individually and not necessarily as the "norm" would be perceived. Large studies utilizing populations representative of the nation have identified many statistically significant characteristics of learners at risk of failure in school (NCES, 1995a; NCES, 1996d). These characteristics form an increasing number of students identified "at-risk" (NCES, 1996a).

Simply identifying "at-risk" students and predicting their failure is depressingly defeatist without further interdiction. All of these learners bring and face obstacles into their learning environments that must be addressed before they can progress substantially as independent learners. "At-risk" students who already have a bad attitude towards school are not going to derive the most benefit from more academic programs. The result is a waste of time with learners already academically behind (Touchstone, personal communication, December 13, 1998). Prerequisites to learning must be addressed prescriptively to aid the learner in overcoming obstacles, and providing proven success to build the student's learning self-efficacy. Programs must be targeted to impact "at-risk" students early before hopelessness overwhelms a student's self-esteem.

Most students who drop out of school do not make the decision on a whim. An increasing number of dropouts demonstrate at least one family or one academic risk factor (NCES, 1996a). It clearly results from years of failing to navigate the current educational system. Students can be identified accurately as potential dropouts by the third grade (Barrington & Hendricks, 1989). Gaustad (1991) indicates that academic problems were clear early in the academic careers of students. Beekman (1987) and the Carnegie Council (1995) suggest that "dropping out" is the result of problems that had their antecedent in childhood. One national characteristic of "at-risk" students that transcends ethnic boundaries is socioeconomic in nature. Fuchs (1990) says the welfare system has undermined the existence of the family unit by not providing assistance to families with the father in the home. The father's absence or unemployment during the child's life may be reflected in the child's inability to cope in our present educational system.

Given the ability to identify children "at-risk" as dropout candidates as early as third grade, why are these students allowed to continue in the setting offering them little chance of success? If the system can identify these students, predict their failure, and attempt to educate them traditionally on a collision course to disaster, where is the logic? Fouad (1995) says that by the time students reach high school, counseling decisions already have been made regarding a student's math and science preparation, decisions that place "at-risk" students in difficulty. Forty-one percent of low-income students reported in the eighth grade that they did not expect to finish college. There was no substantial change in these expectations by family income or race-ethnicity by their senior year (NCES, 1997a). Lee-Pearce et. al. (1998) contend that these judg-

119

ments are being made as early as elementary school and usually are not remedied. Retention continues the same unsuccessful formula that caused the problem. Currently, there are few alternatives. Non-traditional programs seek to overcome these obstacles by providing linkage to the real world beyond the limited environment of the "at-risk" student.

STATEMENT OF THE PROBLEM

Concrete experiences that require use of children's senses provide a strong framework for abstract thinking later in life (Rillero, 1994). Unfortunately, not all children have a childhood filled with rich experiences. Nor do all children begin school with a wealth of knowledge in pre-reading, math, or science skills (Lee-Pearce et al, 1998). Children raised in poverty are especially "at-risk". "At-risk" children bring different cultural and linguistic paradigms into schools that are not accounted for within instructional approaches (Ladson-Billings, 1994; Orr, 1987/1997).

The most cost effective way to impact the "at-risk" population would be to provide programs as early as third grade to prevent the student from failing. Since this is not being done, relying upon data supplied from researchers about the most effective way to work with this population is the next best remedy (Lee-Pearce et al, 1998). The result would be to utilize that research in a prescriptive way to nurture an "at-risk" student to become a healthy learner.

Plowman (1999) conducted two initial pilot studies that indicated a special program was providing a stimulating learning environment and that it was stimulating the learner. This study further validates the use of the SDLPS and LPQ with young learners. It attempts to identify more specifically the qualities of the program that are stimulating the learner. This is important in identifying success with "at-risk" learners, replicating, and sustaining those results. When these questions are answered, then researchers will be able to apply a prescriptive technique to design effective programs elsewhere.

RESEARCH DESIGN

The research design utilized the SDLPS and the LPQ. Data collected on a student sample population in the spring of 1998 in a study to determine the effectiveness of the SDLPS and LPQ for use with an "at-risk" fifth grade population were examined. The program's content focused pretest/posttest was compared with scores of a control group using a Dunnett Test. The SDLPS was used to analyze the non-traditional classroom environment to ascertain its ability to support self-directed learning. The LPQ was given in pretest-posttest format to identify significant movement or events within the learning conate areas. Particular focus was whether such a short program could affect motivation in at-risk students.

The analysis of the SDLPS was completed by J. Pilling-Cormick, and for the LPQ by G. Confessore. Two classes were assigned to take the SDLPS that more closely represented a national average than the mono-ethnic representation attained randomly in the previous pilot (Plowman, 1999). The classes were chosen because of their gender balance, ethnic diversity, and ability (all students were working at grade level and reading at or above fifth-grade level). Use of the LPQ in a pre/post format further attempted to identify any movement by students in the conate areas of basic skills, motivation, desire to learn, resourcefulness, and initiative in general as well as self-reported in a specific learning project.

The intent of this study was to assign students from the same urban public school district that had attended STARBASE-Atlantis since May 1995. A class of 21 students was selected to take the SDLPS on their last day attending the program. This class was typical of the classes attending the Norfolk program. In October, a second class of 23 students from a different elementary was selected to take the LPQ as a pretest and five weeks later to take the LPQ as a posttest. Analysis was based on a movement in any of the self-directed cognitive areas.

The STARBASE-Atlantis environment was observed by taking the SDLPS on the last day of program attendance. The LPQ class was observed by pre-LPQ, followed by attending STARBASE-ATLANTIS for one day per week for five consecutive weeks. At the conclusion of the session, a post-LPQ comparison was made. Attending the STARBASE-Atlantis program acted as the treatment condition.

Sample, Population, or Subjects
The total population consisted of 32 Mid-Atlantic region urban public school fifth-grade students attending STARBASE-ATLANTIS in the spring term of 1998. Schools were assigned by the public school district from schools consisting of at least 50% minority population and 65% or greater on free or reduced lunch subsidies. The two classes were from an integrated school where students were bused from several locations within the school district, thereby achieving a diverse population. Multicultural schools represent 5/12ths of the schools attending STARBASE-Atlantis each year.

One class of 20 students formed Experimental Group 1 (E1), the second class of 24 students formed Experimental Group 2 (E2), and a class of 26 students not attending the program formed the Control Group (C). Thirteen students in E1 and 20 students in E2 took both the STARBASE-Atlantis Pretest and Posttest (validity and reliability analysis in Lee-Pearce et. al. 1998). Twenty-one students in the C Group took both the pretest and posttest. A modified percentage gain was used to amplify descriptive statistics (CNET, 1996). A Dunnett comparison was utilized to compare the two experimental groups of different sizes to a single control group (see Table 9.1). Of the 13 students in E1 and the 20 students in E2 taking both pre and post LPQ, there were 29 useable pairs of surveys. Of the 17 students in E1 taking the SDLPS, there were 17 useable surveys and of the 22 students in E2 taking the SDLPS, there were 20 useable surveys. There were four students in E1 and two students in E2 that completed the SDLPS, but did not attend all five days of the program. Classes attended STARBASE-Atlantis as a regular classroom group with the regular classroom teacher for the treatment phase of the design. The resulting cell design left classes intact.

Table 9.1.   STARBASE-Atlantis Descriptive Statistics

Group	N	Pre Raw	Post Raw	Mean Gain	Modified Gain %	Gender	Ethnicity
E1	13	7.73	13.82	6.09	50%	8 F/5 M	5 W/8 B
E2	20	8.71	16.26	7.77	67%	10 F/10 M	5 W/15 B
C	21	8.79	7.70	−1.10	−10%	10 F/11 M	4 W/17 B

Instrumentation and Materials

The SDLPS was utilized to analyze the environment created at STARBASE-Atlantis. Prior to Plowman (1999), this instrument had been validated and only used with adults in an adult education or university setting. Pilling-Cormick (1998) reported the reliability of the SDLPS with an adult population provided an overall Cronbach-alpha coefficient of .93. I report that the readability grade level of the SDLPS is 5.7 on the Flesch-Kincaid Grade Level Scale. The LPQ was utilized to assess self-awareness of abilities and movement in any of the self-directed learning cognate areas. The LPQ has been used with elementary students previously, but not extensively with "at-risk" students. The LPQ's readability by analysis, using the Flesch-Kincaid Grade Level Scale, is 7.9. The LPQ was read aloud to students to account for readability difficulties. The STARBASE-Atlantis Pretest/Posttest comprises a 20 question multiple choice test that tests cognitive gains made by students involving application, analysis, and synthesis. Readability of the instrument is .5 grade Flesch-Kincaid Grade Level Scale. Validity and reliability were assessed using a Kuder-Richardson split-half test (Lee-Pearce et. al., 1998).

DATA ANALYSIS

According to data reported in Table 9.2, both Group E1 and E2 performed at significant levels on the Dunnett comparison of content material gains during the program.

Table 9.2.   **Dunnett Comparison of Program Gains**

Dunnett t (2-sided) Dependent Variable			Mean Difference	Std. Error
Post	E1	C	6.52*	.866
	E2	C	9.07*	.748
Pre	E1	C	-0.87	.978
	E2	C	0.18	.845

Based on observed means.
*The mean difference is significant at the < .05 level.

The SDLPS E1 group (N=17) revealed significant characteristics toward self-directed learning in reaction to the STARBASE-Atlantis environment. The SDLPS E1 Group Score (N=17) was 336 with a standard deviation of 38. The range was 149 with the maximum score being 389 and the minimum being 239. These results are at the high end of an environment rated as moderate. The SDLPS E2 Group Score (N=20) was 310 with a standard deviation of 22. The range was 71 with a maximum score being 343 and the minimum being 272. The group scores of E1 and E2 would indicate a moderate rated environment supportive of self-directed learning. Table 9.3 reports related information.

Table 9.3.   **SDLPS Learning Environment Factors**

SDLPS	Group Score Evaluation	N	N Useable Forms	Group Score (Mean)	Std. Dev.	Range	Max. Score	Min. Score
E1	Moderate	17	17	336	38	149	389	239
E2	Moderate	22	20	310	22	71	343	272

The LPQ E1 group and LPQ E2 group (N=29) demonstrated no significant differences between pre and post questionnaires in any general conate areas. Both groups demonstrated a significant difference in motivation t scores in describing the specific learning project the student chose to self-report. LPQ E1 SMOT t-scored 12.138 with a standard deviation of 3.492. The LPQ E2 SMOT t-scored 14.966 with a standard deviation of 4.187. Most students taking the post-LPQ chose to describe an STARBASE-Atlantis activity as their learning project (84.5%). Table 9.4 reports related information.

Table 9.4.		LPQ Specific Motivation Scores	
LPQ	N	SMOT t score	Std. Deviation
E1	10	12.138*	3.492
E2	19	14.966*	4.187

*Significant at <.05 level (.003 actual)

DISCUSSION

Significant progress was made in analyzing usefulness of the SDLPS in the young learner environment. One group (SDLPS E1) could be evaluated as a high self-directed learning environment extremely helpful to self-directed learning areas. Both groups under conservative analysis were rated as moderate. Moderate SDLPS Group Scores indicate that some helpful areas identified in the SDL literature are present. STARBASE-Atlantis is not designed to be a self-directed program, but allows students to discover more than one right answer. Stressing a student-directed hands-on approach has roots in SDL literature.

The LPQ yielded inconclusive results. While not significant in any conate areas, some results encourage additional study. In spite of limitations and reliability questions posed by the readability issue, students had significant t-scores for the specific motivation factor describing the specific project they self-reported. That specific project reported on the post-LPQ was a STARBASE-Atlantis project. It could be expected that a large percentage of students would describe a program project that was near to the time proximity that the LPQ was given. On the other hand, it would not be predictable that the program projects described by students would produce significant motivational scores, unless there was something inherently motivational in those projects. STARBASE-Atlantis appears to have had a positive influence on students' learning projects and provided them some degree of freedom to choose their project. The program had a significant impact on motivation and initiative of students. It is unknown what long term affects this short-term motivation will have.

The STARBASE-Atlantis projects typically described by students as their specific learning project were: rocket construction, rocket launch, flying a full-motion Navy flight simulator, and Eggbert (a teamwork). Students become excited doing these projects. Positive external stimulation in a learning environment can stimulate an interest in learning, which provides an external motivation to learn. This external motivation provides a stimulating opportunity for learning success that further intensifies an interest in learning. The renewed desire to learn in the "at-risk" student contributes to growth in self-efficacy that shows up in specific internal initiative to complete the project. When outside resources are provided in a stimulating learning environment, the stage is set for the learner to persist in the learning project to successful completion. Translating that process into real tangible "critical" learning experiences that the student can see, touch, and participate, provides a learning launch pad that puts an "at-risk" learner moving in the right direction. Mazlow called these critical events as "peak experiences."

Plowman (1999) raised the question as to whether students at a much younger age learn more effectively using andragogical approaches than pedagogical techniques. Lee-Pearce et. al. (1998), Plowman (1999), and now this study all reported consistently significant cognitive gains using progressively more robust statistical analysis. The Dunnett comparison would indicate that "at-risk" students are performing at significant levels using andragogical techniques. Teacher education programs locked into the tradition of mass education of "at-risk" students, using techniques designed to fail, should look for a successful process.

This study would indicate a need to revise the LPQ to adjust its readability to the fifth-grade level. A pilot of the modified instrument would be needed to validate its reliability before continued use. Its application to the specific learning projects of young learners makes it a future tool of choice to analyze young learners responsiveness to the conate areas as they describe their learning projects. That work is currently in-progress.

REFERENCE

Bandura, A. (1977). Social learning theory. Englewood Cliffs, NJ: Prentice-Hall.

Bandura, A. (1986). Social foundations of thought and action: A social cognitive theory. Englewood Cliffs, NJ: Prentice Hall.

Bandura, A. (1997). Self-efficacy: The exercise of control. New York: W.H. Freeman & Co.

Barrington, B.L., & Hendricks, B. (1989). Differentiating characteristics of high school graduates, dropouts, and non-graduates. The Journal of Educational Research, 82(6), pp.309-319.

Beekman, N. (1987). The dropout's perspective on leaving school. Ann Arbor, MI: Clearinghouse on Counseling and Personnel Services. (ERIC Document Reproduction Services No. ED 291 015.)

Bolman, L.G., & Deal, T.E. (1991). Reframing organizations. San Francisco, CA: Jossey-Bass.

Boyer, E.L. (1983). High school: A report on secondary education in America. New York: Harper & Row.

Brockett, R.G., & Hiemstra, R. (1991). Self-direction in adult learning: Perspectives on theory, research, and practice. New York: Routledge.

Bybee, R., & Landes, N. (1990). Science for life and living. The American Biology Teacher, 52(2), pp.92-98.

Carnegie Councils on Adolescent Development. (1995). Great Transitions: Preparing Adolescents for the New Century. New York: The Carnegie Corporation of New York.

Chief of Naval Education and Training (CNET). (1996). STARBASE-Atlantis operations manual. Unpublished manuscript.

Cicourel, A.V., & Kitsuse, S.I. (1963). The educational decision-makers. Indianapolis, IN: Bobbs-Merrill.

Confessore, G., & Herrmann, R. (1997). Developing self-efficacy among baccalaureate students: Pygmalion revisited. In H.B. Long & Associates, Expanding horizons in self-directed learning. Norman, OK: Oklahoma Research Center for Continuing Professional & Higher Education, University of Oklahoma.

Confessore, S.J., & Confessore, G.J. (1994). Learner profiles: A cross-sectional study of selected factors associated with self-directed learning. In H.B. Long & Associates, New ideas about self-directed learning. Norman, OK: Oklahoma Research Center for Continuing Professional & Higher Education, University of Oklahoma.

Cunningham, W.G., & Gresso, D.W. (1993). Cultural leadership: The culture of excellence in education. Boston: Allyn & Bacon.

Ekstrom, R., & Lee, V. (1988). Starting on the right track. In ETS policy notes: News from the ETS Policy Information Center, V.1, N. 1-3. Princeton, NJ: Research Publications, ETS. ERIC Document Reproduction Service No. ED 338632.

Fouad, N.A. (1995). Career linking: An intervention to promote math and science career awareness. Journal of Counseling and Development, 73, pp.527-534.

Fuchs, L. (1990). The American kaleidoscope: Race, ethnicity, and the civic culture. Hanover, NH: University Press of New England.

Gaustad, J. (1991). Identifying potential dropouts. Eugene, OR: Clearinghouse on Educational Management. (ERIC Document Reproduction Service No. ED 339 092).

Gregory, R. (1993). Making high schools work. New York: Teachers' College Press.

Kimball, W.H., Swap, S.M., LaRosa, P.A., & Howick, T.S. (1995). Improving student learning. In R.T. Osguthorpe, R.C. Harris, M.F. Harris, & S. Black (Eds.), Partner schools: Centers for educational renewal. San Francisco: Jossey-Bass.

Ladson-Billings, G. (1994). The dreamkeepers: Successful teachers of African American children. San Francisco: Jossey-Bass.

Lee-Pearce, M., Plowman, T.S., & Touchstone, D.A. (1998). STARBASE-ATLANTIS a school without walls: A comparative study of an innovative science program for "at-risk" urban elementary students. Journal of Education for Students Placed At Risk, 3(3), pp.223-235.

Orr, E.W. (1987/1997). Twice as less: Black English and the performance of Black students in mathematics and science. New York: W.W. Norton.

Pilling-Cormick, J. (1998). Self-directed learning perception scale (SDLPS): Guide. Burlington, Canada: Professional Learning & Training.

Plowman, T.S. (1999). STARBASE-Atlantis: Examination of Movement Toward Self-Directed Learning in a Non-Traditional Fifth Grade Science Program. In H.B. Long (Ed.), Contemporary ideas and practices in self-directed learning. Norman, OK: H.B. Long & Associates.

Racosky, R. (1996). Dreams + Action = Reality: A step-by-step guide to lifelong success for youth. Boulder, CO: Action Graphics Publishing.

Rillero, P. (1994). Doing science with your children. Columbus, OH: ERIC Clearinghouse for Science, Mathematics, and Environmental Education. (ERIC Document Reproduction Service No. ED 372 952).

Rosenbaum, M. (1990). Learned resourcefulness: On coping skills, self-control, and adaptive behavior. New York: Springer.

Sadker, M., & Sadker, D. (1994). Failing at fairness: How our schools cheat girls. New York: Touchstone.

Shon, D.A. (1983). The reflective practitioner: How professionals think in action. New York: Basic Books.

Sykes, C.J. (1995). Dumbing down our kids: Why American children feel good about themselves but can't read, write, or add. New York: St. Martin's Griffin.

Toffler, A. (1980). The third wave. New York: William Morrow & Co.

U.S. Department of Education. National Center for Education Statistics. (1995). "At-risk" eighth-graders four years later. NCES 95-736. Washington, D.C.: U.S. Government Printing Office.

U.S. Department of Education. National Center for Education Statistics. (1996a). A comparison of high school dropout rates in 1982 and 1992. NCES 96-893. Washington, D.C.: U.S. Government Printing Office.

U.S. Department of Education. National Center for Education Statistics. (1996b). The condition of education 1996. NCES 96-304. Washington, D.C.: U.S. Government Printing Office.

U.S. Department of Education. National Center for Education Statistics. (1996c). Students staying in school, studying more. Washington, D.C.: U.S. Government Printing Office.

U.S. Department of Education. National Center for Education Statistics. (1996d). Urban schools: The challenge of location and poverty. NCES 96-184. Washington, D.C.: U.S. Government Printing Office.

U.S. Department of Education. National Center for Education Statistics. (1997a). <u>Access to post-secondary education for the 1992 high school graduates</u>. NCES 98-105. Washington, D.C.: U.S. Government Printing Office.

U.S. Department of Education. National Center for Education Statistics. (1997b). <u>The condition of education 1997</u>. NCES 97-388. Washington, D.C.: U.S. Government Printing Office.

U.S. Department of Education. National Center for Education Statistics. (1997c). <u>High school course taking in the core subject areas</u>. NCES 97-925. Washington, D.C.: U.S. Government Printing Office.

U.S. Department of Education. National Center for Education Statistics. (1998). <u>The condition of education 1998</u>. NCES 98-013. Washington, D.C.: U.S. Government Printing Office.

Vaill, P.B. (1996). <u>Learning as a way of being: Strategies of survival in a world of permanent white-water</u>. San Francisco, CA: Jossey-Bass.

Zimmerman, B. (1995/1997). Self-efficacy and educational development. In A. Bandura (Ed.), <u>Self-efficacy in changing societies</u>. Cambridge, UK: Cambridge University Press.

CHAPTER TEN

BECOMING AN EXPERT UNIVERSITY TEACHER:
A SELF–DIRECTED PROCESS

Carolin Kreber

Exceptional competence in teaching can be found on all levels of
schooling including college and university education. Most of us
would not have trouble listing at least some individuals whose
conduct as university teachers suggested *exceptional* competence
to us. While the criteria we use to discriminate between these
unique individuals and other teachers we have known may differ
for each of us, we still base our individual judgements on a set of
specific features upon which we decide what constitutes reasonable
teaching and what constitutes *exceptionally* competent teaching. In
all likelihood the persons identified as *exceptionally* competent
will have in common that they are not new to the teaching profession but have accumulated considerable experience as evidenced
by many years on the job. However, if length of service as a
teacher was the decisive factor in acquiring exceptional competence in teaching, why would so many of the experienced teachers
we have known fail to make their way on our initial list?

One might argue that although length of service does not appear to be the critical variable in the development of exceptional
competence, there must be an additional dimension to the experience of exceptionally competent teachers which leads to their developing high levels of work-related skill and knowledge. One may
speculate, therefore, that it is not the length of experience, or the

number of years on the job, that distinguishes the exceptionally competent teacher from other teachers, but the quality of their experience.

In this conceptual paper I develop the argument that acquiring exceptional competence in teaching, and any other profession, is by definition a self-directed learning process which can be facilitated through specific professional development interventions. Using personal construct psychology as the theoretical framework (Candy, 1991; Kelly, 1955, Neymeier & Neymeier, 1995) I draw on both the literature on the development and nature of expertise (Bereiter & Scardamalia, 1993) as well as a recently developed model that explains the acquisition of teaching scholarship (Kreber, in press; Kreber & Cranton, 1996, submitted manuscript) in order to demonstrate how acquiring expertise in teaching is essentially a self-directed learning process. The paper concludes with practical suggestions as to how this self-directed learning process can be facilitated.

FRAMEWORK

Coining the metaphor "man-as-scientist," Kelly (1955) proposed that a person, just like a scientist, develops hypotheses or personal constructs by which to predict the outcome of events. In case future experience teaches that these constructs, or anticipatory schemes, were wrong, the constructs are revised to better predict next time. As a result of experience, a person continuously revises his or her construct system in the general direction of increased predictive efficiency. A person develops construct systems for particular domains of experience. A faculty member, for example, holds a construct system of what it means to be a teacher in a university setting. In this paper I will argue that as faculty acquire expertise in teaching, they revise their construct system by developing increasingly sophisticated and effective strategies to solve the problems constitutive of their teaching. I will discuss why this is essentially a self-directed process.

132

HOW EXPERTISE IS ACQUIRED

Bereiter and Scardamalia (1993) and Tennant and Pogson (1995) criticize the literature on expertise as primarily highlighting differences between novices and experts (Chi, Glaser, & Farr, 1988; Ericsson & Smith, 1991) or describing the stages of development from novice to expert (Benner, 1984; Dreyfus & Dreyfus, 1986), without addressing the question as to why some people learn from experience and become experts, and others remain experienced non-experts. They argue that experience and time do not by themselves bring about expertise, but it is how individuals learn from experience that distinguishes the experienced expert from the experienced non-expert.

Distinguishing Efficiency from Expertise

Following Bereiter and Scardamalia (1993), I argue that the decisive factor underlying the acquisition of expertise in teaching, or exceptional competence in teaching, is not the number of years spent teaching, but the continued effort and motivation expert teachers exert in going above and beyond what is needed to achieve efficiency in teaching. Efficiency, the result of automatization and pattern learning which both come about through experience and repetition, is a state many teachers attain after years on the job. Efficient teachers are "good" teachers in a sense that they have established for themselves a workable set of routines and algorithms for solving teaching-related problems. The moment a problem is encountered, the efficient teacher reverts to an already-known problem-solving procedure to deal with the situation. Expert teachers, however, go above and beyond efficiency as they reinvest the mental resources and energies set free by the process of automatization and pattern learning into problems that are constitutive of their particular teaching context. This reinvestment of mental resources into the specific tasks associated with teaching, I propose, leads them to reframe tasks at increasingly higher levels of complexity resulting in more in-depth analyses of tasks and a more sophisticated structure of knowing about teaching. The non-expert teacher, by confining him or herself to already established algorithms of problem-solving is bound to interpret the problem continuously in the same way and thereby, while being efficient, is deprived of the opportunity of developing more complex conceptual structures of construing. What distinguishes the expert from the non-expert seems to be the underlying effort and motivation of the expert to advance his or her learning about teaching by engaging in progressive problem-solving.

<u>Progressive Problem–Solving</u>
Progressive problem-solving is the process by which the problem-solver steadily advances previous problem interpretations and corresponding problem-solving strategies by taking more and more variables into account when analyzing the problem situation. In other words, the expert teacher, while using previous experience and knowledge when solving problem situations, is inclined to look at the problem in increasingly complex ways. One may argue that the individual engaging in progressive problem-solving goes above and beyond what is expected if the efficient application of routines is considered sufficient . The question that should interest us then is what are the motivational factors that lead an individual to engage in such a continuous learning process or, as Garrison (1997) recently stated with respect to people assuming responsibility for their learning, "the theoretical challenge is to define the variables that influence the decisional process leading to a goal commitment" (p.27).

<u>Motivation</u>
Motivation is typically understood as a combination of perceived expectancy and valence that lead an individual to exert effort towards a particular goal (Vroom, 1964). Expectancy refers to the individual's beliefs that desired goals can be reached. The individual's competence and the contingencies of the situation influence this perception and determine the degree of control the person anticipates during the experience (Garrison, 1997). Valence refers to how much value the individual attributes to the task. According to

this theory a person will exert great effort to reach certain goals if the person expects to be successful with the endeavor (expectancy) and the person perceives the effort to satisfy a particular need or preference (valence). How does this model explain the acquisition of expertise in teaching?

While exceptions do exist, at larger research universities in particular the expectation for faculty is to demonstrate excellence in tasks associated with research; the expectations for teaching-related tasks are typically much lower. As long as a faculty member's teaching does not suggest overt problems, as evidenced for example by recurring poor student ratings of instruction, poor peer review, complaints from students, or grades of student learning that are consistently below average, the performance usually meets the expectation. What we observe at many campuses is that demonstrating excellence in research, in the forms of bringing in extramural funding and research awards, is becoming increasingly important for tenure and promotion, while demonstrating excellence in teaching usually goes beyond what is expected. As a result, a faculty member's excellence in teaching often remains unrewarded by the institution whereas rewards for excellence in research increase at a time when universities depend more and more on faculty bringing in external funding.

Extrinsic Versus Intrinsic Motivation

When motivation is influenced by external conditions such as rewards offered by an institution, we speak of extrinsic motivation. When these rewards, or the sense of satisfaction a person experiences as a result of the engagement with the task, come from within the person we speak of intrinsic motivation. While in some cases extrinsic motivation may complement or even enhance intrinsic motivation, according to Garrison (1997), it is the intrinsic motivation that leads to responsible, worthwhile, and continuous self-directed learning. One could speculate that most faculty holding positions at research institutions, due to their graduate experience and decision to join the professoriate, are intrinsicall vated to be actively involved in research. We may suspe these faculty would continue pursuing their research interests, though in some cases perhaps at a lower rate of productivity, if external rewards for publications were not in place. We may also speculate that due to their graduate experience most faculty have a genuine interest in working with students, and value the sense of fulfillment and gratification they gain through interacting with learners; however, their intrinsic motivation to learn more about teaching, and hence to enhance their teaching competence, might be curtailed by their having little control over the professional development initiatives offered at their campus. Moreover, faculty's extrinsic motivation to commit towards excellence in teaching is curtailed by the institutional demands and external rewards for increasingly greater productivity in research. External rewards (or punishments) for growth in teaching often do not go beyond awarding (or denying) tenure for "reasonable" teaching performance.

Garrison (1997) argues that "learners are intrinsically motivated to assume responsibility for constructing meaning and understanding when they have some control over the learning experience" (p.29). I suggest, therefore, that faculty learning about teaching are adult learners whose effort to engage in progressive problem-solving on teaching-related tasks is influenced by their level of intrinsic motivation. This intrinsic motivation is the result of the degree to which they value the satisfaction gained from successful teaching (valence), the degree to which they believe that their efforts to learn about teaching will be successful (expectancy), the latter variable being moderated by the degree of control they anticipate to exert while pursuing their goal of enhancing their teaching competence. I would argue that the continued effort and motivation that give rise to the acquisition of expertise in teaching are crucial elements of self-directed learning and self-regulated learning (Garrison, 1997; Zimmerman, 1989).

Whether or not individuals are motivated to exert effort is a matter of personal choice. Furthermore, it seems when faculty develop expertise they do so *not* primarily as a result of involvement in a formal or informal *other*-directed learning environment; instead, it seems more likely that they are involved in a process of identifying their own learning needs, choosing solution strategies, and evaluating the effectiveness of their learning. This may or may not involve participation in formal professional development activities such as workshops and seminars, peer consultation programs, or mentoring programs. The learning takes place because the individual has made the choice to attend to a particular teaching problem that he or she identified as significant, to resist the temptation to revert to familiar solution strategies, and to invest mental effort in reanalyzing and solving this problem at increasingly deeper levels of sophistication.

Professional development for teachers, in order to be effective, that is, lead to changes in thinking and doing, needs to be a self-directed process where individuals are in charge of identifying their learning needs, choosing strategies, and evaluating their learning. This is in line with Knowles' (1975) original definition of self-directed learning as "a process in which individuals take the initiative with or without the help of others in diagnosing their learning needs, formulating goals, identifying human and material resources, and evaluating learning outcomes (p.18) and Candy's (1991) notion of self-management in learning which he defines as "the manifestation of a certain independence of mind and purpose in learning situations" (p.411).

The acquisition of expertise in teaching involves three factors. First, faculty assume responsibility for their own learning. This is enhanced by faculty having control over the learning process which determines whether or not they expect the learning endeavor to be successful. Second, faculty experience a sense of gratification and job satisfaction as a result of success in teaching. Third, faculty go beyond the efficient application of routines by reframing the tasks constitutive of their teaching context at increasingly higher levels of complexity. In the next section of this paper I illustrate how the process of progressive problem-solving on teaching-related tasks can be fostered.

BECOMING AN EXPERT TEACHER: A MODEL

I argue elsewhere that Mezirow 's (1991) theory of perspective transformation has the potential to explain how teachers develop scholarship in teaching (Kreber, in press; Kreber, 1998; Kreber & Cranton, 1996, 1997, submitted manuscript). In line with transformative learning theory and constructivist psychology (Kelly, 1955; Neymeier & Neymeier, 1995) I suggest that how teachers conceptualize the various tasks or problems associated with teaching is the determining factor for their actions. Conceptualizations may change as a result of critical reflection. Mezirow proposes that reflection can take place on three levels. Content reflection is geared to one's present explanation or conceptualization of the problem situation. Process reflection is concerned with how a certain conceptualization of the problem, and resulting problem-solving strategy, has come about. Premise reflection refers to why it is important to conceptualize a particular problem (Kreber, 1998; Kreber, in press). The three kinds of reflection represent three invariant levels of cognitive processing.

We propose that competence in teaching is the result of teachers constructing knowledge in three distinct yet overlapping domains of knowledge. The first knowledge domain, *instructional knowledge*, is concerned with the strategies teachers need for planning and delivering instruction. The second knowledge domain, *pedagogical knowledge*, refers to the knowledge teachers need in order to assist students in solving the learning tasks associated with understanding a particular concept. The third domain, *curricular knowledge*, pertains to the rationale and purpose underlying the educational experiences that teachers decide to provide for their learners. Knowledge in all three domains is needed for effective teaching to take place. Pedagogical knowledge provides a foundation for instructional knowledge, and instructional and pedagogical knowledge would have less purpose and meaning without curricular knowledge.

Knowledge about teaching is constructed as teachers engage in content, process, and premise reflection in each of the three domains. As faculty construct this knowledge, the reflect on both their personal teaching experiences as well as the research-based knowledge of teaching. Thus, there are nine distinct ways of reflection: Content, process, and premise reflection on experienced-based and research-based instructional, pedagogical, and curricular knowledge. Table 10.1 shows the questions faculty may ask when engaging in each type of reflection.

Table 10.1.   Questions that Trigger Content, Process, and Premise Reflection in Each Knowledge Domain

<u>Instructional Knowledge</u>

Content Reflection	*What should I do in course design, selecting materials, and methods?*
Process Reflection	*How did I do? Were my methods, materials, and course design effective?*
Premise Reflection	*Why does it matter what methods, materials, or course design I use?*

<u>Pedagogical Knowledge</u>

Content Reflection	*What do I know about how students learn, what should I do to best facilitate learning?*
Process Reflection	*How did I do? Am I successful in facilitating student learning?*
Premise Reflection	*Why does it matter if I consider how students learn?*

<u>Curricular Knowledge</u>

Content Reflection	*What do I know about the goals and rationale for my courses/program?*
Process Reflection	*How did I/we arrive at the goals and rationale for courses/programs?*
Premise Reflection	*Why do our goals and rationale matter?*

I suggest that the process of professional development in teaching, as suggested by this model, is self-directed by definition. The person learning about teaching decides on his or her own, or with the help of others, what problems to address, on what level the problem will be addressed (content, process, or premise), on the strategies employed to solve the problem, and on whether desired outcomes were attained. Throughout the process the learner has as much control over the learning process as desired. This perception or anticipation of control, we saw earlier, is a crucial factor in the degree of motivation the person experiences in becoming involved in the learning process.

The resulting knowledge is personally constructed (Kelly, 1955) as faculty actively engage with the problems constitutive of their particular teaching context. This knowledge, on a structural level, can be conceived of as an interrelated system of personally constructed hypotheses or anticipatory schemes (Kelly, 1955) by which teachers predict the outcome of their problem-solving procedures. In case the prediction was wrong, the personal construct is revised to better predict next time. As individual constructs change (or sets of hypotheses change), the entire construct system (or perspective on teaching) gradually moves towards further sophistication and complexity, characterized by greater integration, greater discrimination, and greater permeability of the construct system. Jack Mezirow (1991) describes this process as perspective transformation. I suggest that it is this transformative process that is underlying the expert's acquisition of increasingly sophisticated knowledge structures through progressive problem-solving (Bereiter and Scardamalia, 1993). The process underlying perspective transformation is essentially self-directed, relying on self-regulatory skills.

IMPLICATIONS FOR PROFESSIONAL DEVELOPMENT

The two factors influencing motivation are the value a person attributes to the goal and the belief that the endeavour will be successful (Vroom, 1964). With respect to learning about teaching we saw that the latter factor in particular is moderated by the degree to which the person perceives him or herself as being in control of the learning experience. As a result of having worked as a university teacher, and worked with faculty in my roles as instructional developer over several years, I believe that most faculty gain personal satisfaction and meaning from their interactions with students and as such have some intrinsic motivation to become good teachers. However, this intrinsic motivation is curtailed by two factors. First, the steady increase of external rewards for greater productivity in research and the relative scarcity of rewards for excellence in teaching impedes extrinsic motivation. Second, their perceived lack of control over the learning endeavor, as is the case when the faculty development program is organized without consultation with faculty regarding their needs and goals, and hence their diminished expectation that the endeavor will result in successful learning and better teaching impedes intrinsic motivation.

Many faculty are sceptical towards instructional development initiatives that they perceive as not addressing their real needs and as not being grounded in research or scholarship. If the goal is to enhance faculty's confidence in instructional development it seems that they need to be involved in the planning, practising, and evaluating of their own instructional development initiatives (Cranton, 1994). We should be cautious, however, not to lose sight of the fact that providing learners with greater control over their learning can also be met with suspicion and initially lead to a lack of perceived credibility of the professional developer trying to foster faculty's self-directed learning about teaching. Learner control should be introduced gradually considering the individual faculty member's present stage of self-directedness (Grow, 1991).

CONCLUSION

On the basis of this analysis of the process of constructing knowledge about teaching I argue that professional development programs for faculty need to provide support for self-directed learning. Professional development programs on teaching should assist faculty in their efforts and motivation to engage in progressive problem-solving by reflecting on the content, process, and premises underlying the tasks that are constitutive of their teaching context.

REFERENCES

Benner, P. (1984). From novice to expert. Excellence and power in clinical nursing practice. Menlo Park, CA: Adison-Wesley Publishing Company.

Bereiter, C., & Scardamalia, M. (1993). Surpassing ourselves. Chicago and La Salle: Open Court.

Berliner, D. (1986). In pursuit of the expert pedagogue. Educational Researcher, 15(7), pp.5-13.

Candy, P. (1991). Self-direction for lifelong learning. San Francisco: Jossey-Bass.

Cranton, P.A. (1994). Self-directed and transformative instructional development. Journal of Higher Education, 65, pp.726-744.

Ericsson ,K.A., & Smith, J. (eds.) (1991). Toward a general theory of expertise. Cambridge, NY: Cambridge University Press.

Garrison, D.R. (1997). Self-directed learning: toward a comprehensive model. <u>Adult Education Quarterly, 48</u>(1), pp.18-34.

Glaser, R.,& Chi, M.T. (1988). Overview. In M. Chi, R. Glaser, & M. Farr (eds.), The nature of expertise (pp.xv-xxxvi). New Jersey: Erlbaum.

Grow, G.O. (1991). Teaching learners to be self-directed. <u>Adult Education Quarterly, 41</u>(3), pp.125-149.

Kelly, G.A. (1955). <u>The Psychology of Personal Constructs, 1</u>. New York, NY: Norton & Company.

Kreber, C. (in press). A course-based approach to the scholarship of teaching. <u>Teaching in Higher Education, 4</u>(3), pp.309-325.

Kreber, C. (1998). Perfektion durch Reflektion: Das Lehrportfolio zur Beurteilung und Professionalisierung der Hochschullehre" (Engl: Perfection through reflection: the teaching portfolio to evaluate and professionalize university teaching). In <u>Handbuch Hochschullehre: Handreichungen zur Hochschuldidaktik</u> (section 18, pp.1-24). Bonn, Germany: Raabe Verlag.

Kreber, C., & Cranton, P.A. (1996). The scholarship of teaching. Proceedings of the 26th conference of the Canadian Society for the Study of Higher Education (CSSHE), Brock University, St. Catharines, ON, May 1996.

Kreber, C., & Cranton, P.A. (submitted manuscript). Exploring the scholarship of teaching. <u>Journal of Higher Education, 71</u>.

Mezirow, J. (1991). Transformative dimensions of adult learning. San Francisco: Jossey-Bass.

Neimeyer, R.A., & Neimeyer, G.J. (Eds.). (1995). <u>Advances in Personal Construct Psychology, 3</u>. Greenwich, Connecticut: JAI Press.

Tennant, M., & Pogson, P. (1995). Learning and change in the adult years. San Francisco: Jossey-Bass.

Vroom, V. (1964). Work and motivation. New York: John Wiley.

Zimmerman, B.J. (1989). A social cognitive view of self-regulated academic learning. <u>Journal of Educational Psychology, 81</u>, pp.329-339.

CHAPTER ELEVEN

CONTRACT LEARNING IN ORGANIZATIONAL LEARNING & MANAGEMENT DEVELOPMENT

Michael A. Beitler

Contract learning was advocated throughout the 1970s and 1980s by Knowles (1975, 1986). Knowles, who taught graduate students at Boston University and North Carolina State University, found lecturing to *older* students ineffective because of their unique backgrounds and needs. Knowles decided to write a learning contract with each of his students. The contract was an agreement between teacher and student; it detailed what would be learned, and how it would be learned (Knowles, 1986). Knowles' conception of the learning contract has been implemented in numerous graduate schools; including Norwich University and The Union Institute. Many graduate students have reported great success with contract learning (Beitler, 1998).

Throughout the 1990s, I have advocated the use of contract learning with mid-career professionals (Beitler, 1999a, 1999b). While I have been a vocal advocate of contract learning, I have always kept Knowles' ominous warning in mind. Knowles (1986) warned, "some people get so enamored of one technique that they use it in every situation, whether it is appropriate or not" (p.3). To heed his admonition, I have attempted to determine when contract learning is appropriate (or not appropriate) in management development.

SELF–DIRECTED LEARNING (SDL)

Over the past twenty years, a substantial amount of research has revealed the power of self-directed learning (SDL)—where adult learners are empowered by the opportunity of studying what is important to them. The trick is to harness this empowered learning for the benefit of the entire organization.

Tough (1979) believed self-directed learning (SDL) was powerful because the learners themselves made decisions about what to learn, how to learn it, and at what pace the learning should proceed. While these self-directed learners sought information and advice from others, the responsibility for and control over the learning remained theirs.

Knowles (1975, 1980) focused on the importance of establishing a climate supporting SDL. Spear and Mocker (1983) claimed the environment has a significant influence on the type of SDL projects undertaken. Confessore and Kops (1998) believe "the organization's goals, values, and work environment affect the degree to which SDL will take place within the organization" (p.371).

SDL IN THE WORKPLACE

Nobody denies that self-directed learning takes place in organizations. Long and Morris (1995) found more than fifty articles and papers published between 1983 and 1993 concerning SDL in business and industry.

Foucher's (1995) interviews with HR practitioners revealed four organizational variables that promote SDL in the workplace:

1. the presence of a participative management style;
2. a supportive environment in which employees enjoy
3. support for experimentation and tolerance for error; and
4. support for unplanned, non-sequential learning activities.

Foucher's (1995) work corroborates Baskett's (1993) findings in his study of workplace learning. Baskett found the following factors important in enhancing organizational learning:

1. employees can contribute to the organization's goals and values,
2. an environment of trust and mutual respect,
3. support for risk taking and innovation, and
4. collaboration among organization members.

ORGANIZATIONAL LEARNING TO LEARNING ORGANIZATIONS

The literature on organizational learning speaks of individuals learning new KSAs (knowledge, skills, and attitudes) for the benefit of the organization. It is important to analyze the learning needs of both the individual and the organization. The new individual KSAs must be available for the benefit of the organization. Confessore and Kops (1998) stated, "the learning organization must account for the learning needs of both the individual and the organization" (p.371).

Confessore and Kops (1998) believe, "all the perspectives used to describe organizational learning include some dimension of transforming individual knowledge into collective knowledge—that is, knowledge determined, shared, interpreted, and used collectively throughout the organization" (p.366). Dixon (1994) defined organizational learning as a process by which information, determined by the organization as meaningful, is communicated by and throughout the organization.

In the 1990s, many authors abandoned the term "organizational learning" for the idea of a "learning organization." Writers, including Senge (1990), emphasized the importance of a systemic approach to learning in the organization.

Watkins and Marsick (1993) defined six imperatives for a learning organization:

1. creating continuous learning opportunities,
2. promoting inquiry and dialogue,
3. encouraging collaboration and team learning,

4. establishing systems to capture and share learning,

5. empowering people to have a collective vision, and

6. connecting the organization to the environment.

SDL & LEARNING ORGANIZATIONS

The environment for successful SDL and the environment for a flourishing learning organization share the same characteristics. Confessore and Kops (1998) found five characteristics reflected in both bodies of literature:

1. tolerance for errors, support for experimentation and risk taking, and an emphasis on creativity and innovation;

2. the use of a participative leadership style and delegation of responsibility to organizational members;

3. support for learning initiatives that are linked to the organization's goals and values;

4. encouragement of open communication and of information systems that provide for collaboration and teamwork, and the use of both internal and external learning resources; and,

5. provision of opportunities and situations for individual learning.

MANAGEMENT DEVELOPMENT

The creation of a learning organization environment, which encourages self-direct and self-initiated learning, clearly enhances our efforts at management development.

An essential aspect of management development in any organization is the acquisition and use of self-directed learning skills. Kops (1993, 1997) interviewed mid-level managers and found five conditions that affected their ability to learn:

1. supportive and challenging organizational settings, characterized by open communication, active experimentation, and tolerance of mistakes;

2. clear expectations and outcomes that allow for the alignment of SDL efforts with the goals of the organization;

3. discretionary time for learning and maintenance of resources that support learning;

4. opportunities for making internal and external contacts, and for building networks with colleagues and associates; and,

5. development of employees' ability to engage in SDL.

McCall, Lombardo, and Morrison (1989) found independent learning to be a key aspect in executive development. Vaill (1996) stated that leaders must model self-directed learning behavior, and require it of others.

MY FINDINGS

In previous publications (1997, 1998, 1999b), I shared my findings from interviews with mid-career executives and professionals. Understandably, they showed little interest in debating the merits of teacher-directed versus self-directed learning. The mid-career learners I interviewed were very pragmatic. Their criterion for evaluating a learning scenario was based on one question: "Did I learn anything?"

The adult learners in my research expressed satisfaction with both teacher-directed and self-directed learning—seemingly diametrically opposed methodologies. Only after a second round of interviews did I begin to understand what they were telling me. In my second interviews, I asked questions about course content and the related teaching/learning methodology (teacher-directed versus self-directed learning). The appropriateness of teacher-directed or self-directed learning became obvious when related to course content. I then developed the following Continuum of Business Education (Table 11.1):

Table 11.1.   The Continuum of Business Education

Teacher-Directed (Training)		Learner-Directed (Development)
Technical Skills	People Skills	Conceptual Skills
Courses	Courses	Courses
accounting	group dynamics	strategy
finance	organizational behavior	ethics

Source: Beitler, M.A. (1999b).

147

TEACHING/LEARNING METHODOLOGIES

In American business schools, and in corporate HRD departments, we talk about the importance of executives and managers acquiring three types of skills: technical skills, people skills, and conceptual skills. All three types of skills are necessary for success as an executive or manager.

Technical skills, including accounting and finance, involve acquisition of a "block of knowledge." This well-defined "block" includes the principles and fundamentals that provide a basic understanding of these fields. The non-accountant/non-financial professional is blissfully unaware of what they don't know. In these areas teacher-direction is a necessity. Classroom training is appropriate because all the participants need the same minimal block of knowledge.

People skills (such as group dynamics) and conceptual skills (such as corporate strategy) do not involve clearly defined disciplines. In fact, people skills and conceptual skills are interdisciplinary in nature. In these areas, professionals have a better sense of what they don't know. Individuals know if they are weak in communication skills, team-building skills, task prioritizing, strategic planning, or stakeholder management skills. If they haven't figured it out on their own, they should have been made aware of it through their organization's evaluation system (whether 360 degree or supervisor).

Learner-direction or learner-participation is very powerful in the acquisition of people skills and conceptual skills. In these two areas, no two managers have the same needs. A customized, or individualized, plan is appropriate.

Teacher-directed learning appears to be appropriate in acquiring the technical skills of accounting or finance; whereas, learner-directed learning (SDL) is appropriate in the acquisition of people skills and conceptual skills.

HARNESSING INDIVIDUAL LEARNING IN THE ORGANIZATION

While I can argue for the use of both teacher-directed learning and self-directed learning in the organization, it is more important to discuss how to harness individual learning for the benefit of the entire organization.

That brings us back to considering contract learning. A contract between the supervisor, the individual manager/learner, and an HRD representative can incorporate teacher-directed and self-directed learning, as appropriate.

These contracts not only provide guidance for the individual manager; they provide a way to capture, document, and share knowledge throughout the organization. These contracts can provide the foundation for a learning organization in which individuals engage in self-directed study and participate in discussions with fellow managers. These group discussions enhance the critical thinking skills of the individual, and add to the knowledge base of the organization.

Contract learning is an invaluable tool in organizational learning and management development. Contract learning, along with group discussions, offers exciting possibilities for developing the organization and the individual manager.

REFERENCES

Baskett, M. (1993). Workplace factors that enhance self-directed learning. (Text No. 93-01-002).Montreal, Canada: Group for Interdisciplinary Research on Autonomy and Training, University of Quebec at Montreal.

Beitler, M.A. (1997). Midlife adults in self-directed learning: A heuristic study in progress. In H.B. Long & Associates (Eds.), Expanding horizons in self-directed learning. Norman, OK: College of Education, University of Oklahoma.

Beitler, M.A. (1998). Mid-career adults in self-directed graduate programs. In H.B. Long & Associates (Eds.), Developing paradigms in self-directed learning. Norman, OK: College of Education, University of Oklahoma. (ERIC Document # 415-361)

Beitler, M.A. (1999a). Learning and development agreements with mid-career professionals. Performance in Practice, Fall 1999. American Society for Training and Development.

Beitler, M.A. (1999b). Contract learning: Appropriate for mid-career business students? In H.B. Long & Associates (Eds.), New dimensions in self-directed learning. Norman, OK: College of Education, University of Oklahoma.

Confessore, S.J., & Kops, W.J. (1998). Self-directed learning and the learning organization: Examining the connection between the individual and the learning environment. Human Resource Development Quarterly, 9(4), pp.365-375.

Dixon, N.M. (1994). Organizational learning: A review of the literature with implications for HRD professionals. Human Resource Development Quarterly, 3(1), pp.29-49.

Foucher, R. (1995). Enhancing self-directed learning in the workplace: A model and a research agenda (Text No. 95-01-005). Montreal: Group for Interdisciplinary Research on Autonomy and Training, University of Quebec at Montreal.

Knowles, M. (1975). Self-directed learning: A guide for learners and teachers. Chicago: Follett.

Knowles, M. (1980). The modern practice of adult education (Rev. Ed.). Chicago: Follett.

Knowles, M. (1986). Using contract learning. San Francisco: Jossey-Bass.

Kops, W.J. (1993). Self-planned learning efforts of managers in an organizational context. In H.B. Long & Associates (Eds.), Emerging perspectives in self-directed learning (pp.247-261). Norman, OK: College of Education, University of Oklahoma.

Kops, W.J. (1997). Managers as self-directed learners: Findings from public and private sector organizations. In H.B. Long & Associates (Eds.), Expanding horizons in self-directed learning (pp.71-86). Norman, OK: College of Education, University of Oklahoma.

Long, H.B., & Morris, S.(1995). Self-directed learning in business and industry: A review of the literature 1983-1993. In H.B. Long & Associates (Eds.), New dimensions in self-directed learning. Norman, OK: College of Education, University of Oklahoma.

McCall, M., Lombardo, M., & Morrison, A. (1989). Lessons of experience: How successful executives develop on the job. San Francisco: New Lexington Press.

Senge, P.M. (1990). The fifth discipline: The art and practice of the learning organization. New York: Doubleday.

Spear, G.E., & Mocker, D.W. (1983). The organizing circumstance: Environmental determinants in self-directed learning. Adult Education Quarterly, 35, pp.119-130.

Tough, A. (1979). The adult's learning projects (2nd ed.). Toronto: Ontario Institute for Studies in Education.

Vaill, P. (1996). Learning as a way of being. San Francisco: Jossey-Bass.

Watkins, K. & Marsick, V. (1993). Sculpting the learning organization: Lessons in the art and science of systematic change. San Francisco: Jossey-Bass.

CHAPTER TWELVE

A CORRELATION BETWEEN INSTRUCTOR RATINGS AND NURSING STUDENT SELF–DIRECTED LEARNING READINESS SCORES

Karen L. Barnes & Scott S. Morris

Current changes in the healthcare system, both social and techno-logical, posit problems for those concerned with delivery of healthcare, and educators who prepare practitioners. Registered nurses are being challenged to assume roles with greater auton-omy, responsibility, and scope of practice. To meet those chal-lenges, the professional nurse is expected to be committed to life-long learning. Consequently, there has been much attention in the nursing literature about ways to promote lifelong learning, specifi-cally self-directed learning. The ability to become a self-directed learner during nursing school and nursing practice is an expecta-tion of students in baccalaureate nursing programs in the United States and other countries (Barnes, 1999). The American Nurses Association has supported self-directed learning approaches in nursing program curriculum for decades (Bell & Bell, 1983). Im-plementation of these self-directed learning approaches, however, remains somewhat problematic for faculty and students (Long & Barnes, 1995).

Prior to implementing self-directed learning strategies to pro-mote self-direction in learners, it is beneficial for the nursing edu-cator to assess student readiness to engage in these approaches (Turunen, Taskinen, Voutilaninen, Tossavainen, & Sinkkonen, 1997). The most popular assessment method has been the use of

Guglielmino's (1977/1978) Self-Directed Learning Readiness Scale. Nursing faculty frequently evaluate students in their self-directed learning behaviors during the process of nursing education, particularly in the clinical setting. Identification of students exhibiting the ability to be self-directed in their learning would logically lead the nurse educator to find ways to promote and enhance this ability. How well nurse educators do this has not been a focus in the literature. Hence, the purpose of this study is to address two questions:

1. Are clinical nursing faculty perceptions of self-direction in learning an accurate predictor of students' self-reports of self-directed learning readiness?
2. Are faculty ratings of student self-direction in learning influenced by their perceptions of how well they know the student?

RELATED LITERATURE

There is a paucity of reported research regarding teacher ratings of self-direction in the learner. Long and Agyekum (1983, 1984) have published the most extensive studies on this topic. Their studies included multitrait–multimethod procedures to determine the validity of the SDLRS. Variables other than SDLRS and faculty ratings were examined: dogmatism, race, age, sex, and achievement level. The first study included 136 college students enrolled in two southern universities (63 black, 70 white, and 3 international students), and the second study included 92 students of similar racial mix. Results in the first study (Long & Agyekum, 1983) revealed no significant correlation (r =.03, p >.05) between student SDLRS and faculty ratings. The second study's (Long & Agyekum, 1984) results, however, revealed a correlation approaching significance (r =.20, p =.056). Further analysis indicated differences for instructor ratings, student race composition, and age. "In both studies black subjects were rated lower than white subjects and older subjects were rated higher than younger ones" (Long & Agyekum, 1984, p.714).

One study was identified in the nursing literature relating to faculty ratings. Crook (1985) asked nursing faculty and students to identify the three most effective self-directed learners in a) his/her group at the end of the first year in the program, and b) in his/her entire class at the end of the second year of the program. First and second year students completed Guglielmino's SDLRS (mean score = 222.3). Crook reports no significant correlation between faculty nominations and the SDLRS scores and comments that there is not necessarily "any assurance that peers or faculty within and among themselves have shared meanings of what a self-directed learner is" (p.278).

Jones (1989), while observing 26 adult basic education students, did find significant correlation between the students' self-directed learning readiness behavior and their SDLRS Score (r =.48, p =.018). Her findings suggesting a relationship between faculty ratings of students and the students' SDLRS score are in contrast to those studies previously mentioned.

HYPOTHESES

Based on the literature review, the evidence to support directional hypotheses is not conclusive. Therefore, four non-directional hypotheses, stated below in the null form, were tested using the alpha level of .05 for rejection.

Hypotheses

1. There is no significant relationship between student self-directed learning readiness and their faculty's rating on self-direction in learning.
2. There is no significant relationship between the faculty's rating on self-direction in learning and faculty's rating on how well they know their students.
3. There are no significant differences between faculty's educational level, employment status, and sex on their faculty's rating on self-direction in learning.
4. There are no significant differences between faculty's educational level, employment status, and sex on their faculty's rating on how well they know their students.

ASSUMPTIONS AND LIMITATIONS

Important assumptions upon which this research was based and which may affect the interpretation of the results are:

1. Students and faculty respond honestly and to the best of their ability when completing the instrument.
2. The SDLRS – A questionnaire is a valid, reliable, and objective instrument for the measurement of self-directed learning readiness of nursing students.
3. The faculty reporting questionnaire is a valid, reliable, and objective instrument for the measurement of a faculty member's perception of a) how well the instructor knows her/his student, and b) a student's level of self-directed learning readiness.

Generalization and interpretation of the findings may be hindered by the following limitations:

1. The SDLRS-A instrument was completed in environments beyond the control of the researcher, thus the response behavior of the subjects may have been affected by unknown ways.
2. The sample sizes of 90 students and 12 faculty members is small.
3. Generalization of the findings beyond the nursing academic setting should be made with caution.

METHODOLOGY

This study's research design is a one time, static group. Correlation methods were used to determine if the variables of primary interest (student SDLRS, faculty's ratings, and faculty perceptions of how well they knew the student). This study uses a convenience sample and cross-sectional design. The sample for the study consisted of two groups: nurse educators and nursing students from an accredited baccalaureate nursing program. The institutional setting is in a public comprehensive regional university in a south central state.

Date Collection

Junior and senior nursing students were asked to volunteer at the end of a class period. Upon agreement to participate, they were requested to sign a consent form and complete the packet materials

(SDLRS-A and biographical data sheet) outside of class during a quiet time. Student participants were given three weeks to complete the packet. Faculty were given the self-directed rating instrument and were asked to complete it within a two week period. The data collection occurred at the end of the spring semester.

<u>Instrumentation</u>
Two instruments were used: Guglielmino's Self-Directed Learning Readiness Scale (SDLRS-A) and Long and Agyekum's faculty rating of self-direction in learning instrument.

Self-Directed Learning Readiness Scale
Guglielmino's Self-Directed Learning Readiness Scale [SDLRS-A] is a Likert-formatted, 58 item, self-reporting questionnaire developed to evaluate one's readiness for self-directed learning (Guglielmino, 1977/1978). It originated as a 41-item questionnaire and has undergone several iterations of revision to its present 58-item format. A factor analysis of the original 41 item version of the instrument identified eight attributes describing the self directed learner: 1) Openness to Learning Opportunities, 2) self-concept as an Effective Learner, 3) Initiative/Independence in Learning, 4) Informed Acceptance of Responsibility for One's Own Learning, 5) Love of Learning, 6) Creativity, 7) Future Orientation, and 8) Problem Solving Skills. Straka and others (SDL International Symposium discussions) have challenged these original factor analysis conclusions.

The questionnaire has been widely examined for both its reliability and validity in measuring one's readiness for self directed learning. An abundance of supportive documentation acknowledges its value (Morris, 1997). Guglielmino (1977/1978) reported a population SDLRS score mean of 214.44 ($\underline{SD}$ = 25.59).

Faculty Rating Instrument
The instrument used in this study for faculty rating of student self-direction in learning is a modification of the instrument developed by Long and Agyekum (1983, 1984). Their instrument is based on

the following six statements Guglielmino (1977/1978) used to define a self-directed learner:

1. One who exhibits initiative, independence and persistence in learning.
2. One who accepts responsibility for his/her own learning and view problems as challenges, not obstacles.
3. One who is capable of self-direction and who has a high-degree of curiosity.
4. One who has a strong desire to learn or change and is self-confident.
5. One who is able to use basic study skills, organize his/her time, set an appropriate pace for learning, and to develop a plan for completing work.
6. One who enjoys learning, and has a tendency to be goal oriented. (Long & Agyekum, 1984, p.711).

Long and Agyekum (1984) revised their original six-item faculty rating instrument to include 15 discrete items to allow the faculty member more discrimination in evaluation. Items were recreated for this study using the model of the revised instrument (Long & Agyekum, 1984). The rationales for choosing this revised instrument was to assure that faculty share a common description of self-directed learner. For this study, faculty members were asked to circle the number (1-5) that is most consistent with their position on the descriptive item concerning their student in the clinical setting, and an additional question concerning the perception of how well the faculty member knows the student. An example of the instrument is as follows:

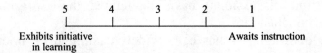

The 15 items were written in polar terms and three items (2, 10, 14) were reversed by alternating the positive concepts from right to left. The polar terms used for each item were:

1. Exhibits initiative in learning/Awaits instruction
2. Exhibits dependence in learning/Is independent
3. Exhibits persistence in learning/Effort is not sustained
4. Accepts responsibility for own learning/Expects others to be responsible

5. Views problems as challenges/Views problems as obstacles
6. Exhibits self-direction in learning/Depends on instructor-provided structure
7. Exhibits a high degree of curiosity/Exhibits a low degree of curiosity
8. Exhibits strong desire to learn or change/Desire to learn or change not evident
9. Exhibits self-confidence in learning situations/Lacks self-confidence
10. Lacks ability to use basic study skills/Exhibits ability to use basic study skills
11. Organizes time efficiently/Lacks ability to organize time
12. Sets an appropriate pace for learning/Depends on instructor to set pace for learning
13. Develops plan for work completion/Depends on instructor to develop plan
14. Apathetic towards learning/Exhibits joy in learning
15. Is goal oriented/Lacks goal orientation

The sixteenth item was constructed to determine the faculty's perception of how well they know the student:

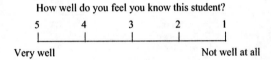

How well do you feel you know this student?

5   4   3   2   1

Very well   Not well at all

FINDINGS

Descriptive Findings

Of the 90 student nurses participating in the study, 79 were female. The mean age of the students was 29.1 years (SD = 8.34), their mean grade point average was 3.22 based on a four point system (SD = .36), and their mean SDLRS score was 234.77 (SD = 21.56) (Refer to Table 12.1). Of the 12 instructors participating in the study, ten were female, three were adjuncts, and one had attained a doctorate. Student and faculty demographic data are presented in Tables 12.2 and 12.3.

No significant relationship (r =.09, p =.397; refer to Table 12.4) was found between the instructors' rating of student self-directness and the students' self reporting of their readiness for self-direction. Therefore, the first hypothesis was not rejected. For each faculty member, there was no significant relationship between her/his faculty rating and the students' mean SDLRS score.

Table 12.1. Student Age, GPA, and SDLRS Data – Faculty Rating and "How Well They Know the Student" Scores

Variable	Mean	SD	Min.	Max.
Student Age [Years]	29.07	8.34	20	55
Student GPA	3.22	.36	2.50	3.98
SDLRS Score	234.68	21.56	166	275
Faculty Rating Score	61.72	9.15	35	75
Faculty "How Well They Know the Student" Score	3.89	.77	2.0	5.0

Table 12.2. Student Demographic Data (N = 90)

Variable		Percent %	Number
Sex	Female	88	79
	Male	13	11
Education Level	Senior	47	42
	Junior	53	48
Marital Status	Married	43	39
	Single, not Divorced	47	42
	Divorced	10	9
Ethnicity	Caucasian	91	82
	Other	9	8

Table 12.3. Faculty Demographic Data (N = 12)

Variable		Percent %	Number
Sex	Female	83	10
	Male	17	2
Education Level	Bachelor	17	2
	Master	75	9
	Terminal Degree	8	1
Employment Status	Tenured	33	4
	Non-Tenured	42	5
	Adjunct	25	3
Ethnicity	Caucasian	100	12

Support was found for the rejection of the second hypothesis. A strong relationship (r =.469, p <.005) was found between the mean faculty rating of student self-directedness and how well they reported knowing the student.

Table 12.4. **Correlation Data: Student to Faculty Relationships (Pearson's r value)**

	Age	Student GPA	Student SDLRS	Faculty Rating
Age				
Student GPA	.112			
Student SDLRS	.187*	.167		
Faculty Rating	−.172*	.249**	.090	
Faculty "*Well*"	-.090	−.044	.086	.469***

*= p <.10; ** = p <05; *** = p <.005

Table 12.4 indicates three additional relationships worthy of mention. A positive yet weak relationship (r =.187 p <10) is present between a student's age and her/his SDLRS score, indicating that one's propensity for self-directedness increases with age. Faculty, however, perceive (r = −.172, p <.10) that the older a student, the less likely she/he to be self-directed.

A stronger relationship (r =.249, p <.05) is indicated between a student's grade point average and the level with which an instructor rates her/his self-directedness. Students with high grade point averages tended to be perceived as being more self-directed in their learning readiness.

Table 12.5 identifies the significant relationships found related to the faculty "*Well*" score, faculty rating of student self-directedness, and student SDLRS scores when grouped by student and faculty characteristics. There is no evidence to reject the third hypothesis for no significance was found between faculty ratings of student self-directedness based on the sex, education level, or employment status of the instructor.

There is evidence to reject the fourth hypothesis. The faculty perception of how well they knew a student was related to their tenure status (t =2.400, p <.05) and their full time employment status (t =4.055, p <.005). Tenured instructors reported knowing the students better than did the non-tenured instructors, as did the full time employees versus those that were adjunct instructors.

Table 12.5.   **Relationship Significance Matrix: Grouped by Student and Faculty Attributes**

Group		Faculty "Well" Score	Faculty Rating	Student SDLRS
Students	Sex	None	None	None
	Junior/Senior	t =4.055, p <.005	None	None
	Marital Status	None	None	None
	Ethnicity	None	t =2.114, p <.10	None
Faculty	Sex	None**	None*	t =1.917, p <.10
	Education Level	None**	None*	None
	Full/Part Time	t =4.055, p <.005**	None*	None
	Tenure	t =2.400, p <.05**	None*	None

* Third Hypothesis parameters
** Fourth Hypothesis parameters

Table 12.5 indicates three additional relationships worthy of note. Faculty members reported that they knew the senior nursing students better than they did the juniors (t = 4.055, p < .005). Faculty ratings on student self-directedness were higher for the eight minority students (t =2.114, p <.10). Although this sample size is small, the finding does merit further investigation. Students with higher SDLRS scores tended to select the male instructor to be their advisor (t =1.917, p <.10).

Two additional analyses were performed concerning the faculty rating instrument: the Chronbach-alpha descriptive statistic and an Item-to-Item correlation. The Chronbach-alpha reliability coefficient was found to be .77. An Item-to-Item analysis of the contents of the faculty rating instrument indicated that 79 percent of the item-to-item pairs were significant at the five percent level and that five percent were significant at the ten percent level. Twenty percent of the item pairs failed the significance test. Refer to Table 12.6 for the item pairs lacking significance.

Table 12.6.	Faculty Rating Item-to-Item Analysis: Questions Lacking Significant Correlation (p <.05)		

Question	To	Question(s)
1		10, 14, 15*
2		7, 8, 10, 11, 14, 15
3		14
6		10*, 14, 15*
7		9, 11*, 13*, 15
8		9
9		14, 15

* = p < .10

DISCUSSION AND CONCLUSIONS

Results for the first hypothesis indicated no positive relationship between student SDLR and faculty ratings. These results support findings reported by others (Crook, 1985, Long & Agyekum, 1983, 1984). These findings raise two concerns:

1. Is the program's expectation of self-direction as a professional behavior confounding faculty ratings?
2. Is the narrow range of the faculty rating instrument too limiting for appropriate data analysis?

Instructor ratings were typically self-limiting to the upper half of the scale. Perhaps the scale needs to be expanded to allow for a greater range of response.

The second hypothesis testing revealed evidence that the better the faculty know the student, the higher the rating of student self-direction in learning. This finding raises the possibility of other intervening factors such as issues of personality that may include characteristics such as student friendliness, extroversion, introversion, submissiveness, or openness.

Educational level, employment status, and sex of the faculty members have no bearing on how they rate student self-direction in learning. This suggests that advanced educational preparation of the faculty, full-time status, tenure status, or sex do not enhance the ability of a faculty to judge self-direction in a nursing student. Tenure and full-time status, however, are positively associated with perceptions of how well they know the student. This finding could be explained by the observation that full-time tenured faculty have the greatest opportunity to become acquainted with students from the time of application and observe the students in a variety of situations (clinical, classroom, and/or student/campus activities).

IMPLICATIONS

This research suggests that nursing faculty inaccurately assess their students' propensity for self-direction in learning. A question then arises relevant to such assessment translated into the workplace. Are today's strategies for work assessment, including the 180 degree and 360 degree models effectively measuring worker learning behaviors?

RECOMMENDATIONS

Several recommendations for future research are generated by this study. Recommendations are as follows:

1. Expansion of the faculty rating instrument item scale to 9 points (1-9).
2. Eliminate faculty rating instrument reverse items.
3. Develop a method to quantify and monitor student/faculty interaction and/or supervision.
4. Administer the SDLRS–A to faculty to determine if "likes attract".
5. Vary the disciplines of the sample.
6. Use a sample with longer and more consistent observation/interaction opportunities.

REFERENCES

Barnes, K.L. (1999). Curiosity and self-directed learning readiness among a sample of baccalaureate nursing students. In H.B. Long & Associates (Eds.), <u>Contemporary ideas and practices in self-directed learning</u> (pp.31-47). Norman, Oklahoma: Public Managers Center, University of Oklahoma.

Crook, J. (1985). A validation study of a Self-Directed Learning Readiness Scale. <u>Journal of Nursing Education, 24</u>(7), pp.274-279.

Guglielmino, L.M. (1977/1978). Development of the Self-Directed Learning Readiness Scale, <u>Doctoral Dissertation</u>, Athens, Georgia: University of Georgia.

Jones, C.J. (1989). A study of the relationship of Self-Directed Learning Readiness to observable behavioral characteristics in an adult basic education program, <u>Doctoral Dissertation</u>, Athens, Georgia: University of Georgia.

Long, H.B., & Agyekum, S.K. (1983). Guglielmino's Self-Directed Learning Readiness Scale: A validation study. <u>Higher Education, 12</u>, pp.77-87.

Long, H.B., & Agyekum, S.K. (1984). Teacher ratings in the validation of Guglielmino's Self-Directed Learning Readiness Scale. <u>Higher Education, 13</u>, pp.709-715.

Long, H.B. & Barnes, K.L. (1995). Self-directed learning in nursing education: Analysis of the literature: 1983-1993. In H.B. Long & Associates (Eds.), <u>New dimensions in self-directed learning</u> (pp.217-242). Norman, Oklahoma: Public Managers Center, University of Oklahoma.

Morris, S.S. (1997). Item analysis of Guglielmino's Self-Directed Learning Readiness Scale: Revisiting the issue of internal consistency. In H.B. Long & Associates (Eds.), <u>Expanding horizons in self-directed learning</u> (pp.195-207). Norman, Oklahoma: Public Managers Center, University of Oklahoma.

Turunen, H., Taskinen, H., Voutilaninen, U., Tossavainen, K., & Sinkkonen, S. (1997). Nursing and social work students' initial orientation towards their studies. <u>Nurse Education Today, 17</u>, pp.67-71.

CHAPTER THIRTEEN

PERSONALITY AND COGNITIVE STYLE CHARACTERISTICS OF ADULT SELF-DIRECTED LEARNERS

Charles R. Nuckles

Brookfield (1993) asks, "If adult educators tell us that adults are naturally self-directed learners...then why bother making provision for their education? Won't they self-directedly take their own initiatives in learning anyway?" (p.240). Adult educators have not been able to answer Brookfield's question with confidence. Despite recurrent claims for the importance of personality factors for self-directed learning (Brookfield, 1986; Candy, 1991; Long, 1996; Oddi, 1987), "the literature does not provide a systematic study of the self-directed learner's personality apart from the ability to engage in a self-instructional process" (Oddi, 1987, p.27). As Merriam and Caffarella (1991) have put it, "to understand self-directedness in learning as a personal attribute, more in-depth study is required" (p.218).

Those attempts that have been made to broadly measure learners' propensity, or readiness, for self-direction (Guglielmino, 1977; Oddi, 1986) are based on an undifferentiated blend of attitudes, personality and cognitive factors, and typical learner behaviors. Studies that have attempted to explore the relationship of learner psychological orientation and self-direction (Bitterman, 1988; Johnson, Sample, & Jones, 1988; Kitson, Lekan, & Guglielmino, 1995; Tzuk 1985) have produced few insights. Self-directed learning, as measured by the Self-Directed Learning Readiness Scale (SDLRS) may be related to task assertiveness and self-confidence (Kitson, Lekan, and Guglielmino, 1995), a preference for an Intuitive style of information processing (Johnson, Sample, & Jones, 1988), and a field independent cognitive style (Bitterman, 1988). Tzuk (1985) reported a low correlation ($r = .24$) between high Group Embedded Figures Test (GEFT) scores and high SDLRS scores for a sample of graduate students. These previous research findings suggest that:

1. A positive relationship exists between the cognitive style of field-dependence/field-independence and self-directed learning process with higher field-independence scores associated with higher self-directed learning scores.

2. A positive relationship exists between the Myers-Briggs Type Indicator (MBTI) preference scale sensing (S)/intuition (N) and self-directed learning process with higher N scores associated with higher self-directed learning scores.

While such findings suggest a relationship between psychological factors and self-directed learning, a comprehensive examination of psychological orientation among a group of adult self-directed learners has yet to be conducted. Reliance on the SDLRS as the principal analog for self-direction may be one source for the lack of clear research direction. The most frequently used instruments have been the SDLRS, the Oddi Continuing Learning Inventory (OCLI) (Oddi, 1986), the Group Embedded Figures Test (GEFT) and the Myers-Briggs Type Indicator (MBTI). One thing that all of these instruments have in common is that they are, by design, measures of a preference or propensity for something. They may not accurately predict what respondents will actually do in a specific situation, only their predisposition for a certain behavior or type of behavior.

Self-directed learning is frequently conceptualized as a cognitive process or learning sequence (Jarvis, 1992) wherein the learner exercises choices over a number of elements: "disjuncture, decision to learn, type of participation, aims and objectives, content, method, thought/language, assessment, and action/outcome" (p.134). Jarvis points out that in an actual learning situation, this sequence is not necessarily followed in the order given. These characteristic elements of learning as a self-directed process can also, in the presence of "other-direction," be suggestive of "other-directed learning" (Jarvis, 1992, p.134). Seven of the nine process elements identified by the Jarvis model are:

1. **Decision to Learn:** Learner is motivated to respond to a perceived need or want to learn.

2. **Type of Participation:** Learners decide between learning independently, learning through an organized activity, or some combination.

3. **Aims and Objectives:** Learners choose between learner control, control by others, or negotiated aims and objectives.

4. **Content:** Learner makes a decision regarding the selection of content: learner control, control by others, or negotiated.

5. **Method:** The methodological processes engaged in by the learner: learner controlled, controlled by others, or negotiated.

6. **Thought/Language:** The mode of speech, thought, perception, and so forth, engaged in by the learner: learner chosen, chosen by others, or negotiated.

7. **Assessment:** The process of evaluating how much they have learned, whether their needs or wants have been satisfied, and whether they have achieved their aims and objectives. (Jarvis, 1992, pp.136-141)

Two of the elements of the model were not examined in the present study: disjuncture and action/outcome. Disjuncture, acting on a perceived need or want, precedes the learner's learning process and action/outcome is an evaluation of the results.

PURPOSE OF THE STUDY

The purpose of this study was to determine if there is a relationship between certain personality factors, cognitive style, and self-directed learning among a group of adult learners. This study was designed to answer the following questions:

1. Is there a relationship between learners' cognitive style and their perception of self-directedness?

2. Is there a relationship between learners' personality characteristics and their perception of self-directedness?

HYPOTHESES

The driving assumption in this study was that adults who engage in self-directed learning manifest an identifiable psychological orientation made up of both personality and cognitive style characteristics. For testing purposes, five null hypotheses were examined. One hypothesis examined the relationship between learners' scores on the SLAAP and the GEFT. The remaining four hypotheses examined the relationship between the SLAAP scores and the scores on the four scales of the MBTI.

RESEARCH METHODOLOGY

This study used a correlational design that examined relationships between certain personality factors, cognitive style, and learners' self-perception of self-directed learning as a process. The independent variables were personality and cognitive style and the dependent variable was perception of self-directed learning.

Subjects were adult students enrolled in a baccalaureate level, bachelor's degree-completion program at a small, private college located in the upper mid-west. At the time the study was undertaken there were 464 students enrolled. The sample population was 160, or 34% of the total population. This was a convenience sample; subjects were not randomly selected. Twelve classes were chosen for participation and students enrolled in those classes were invited to participate. There were 85 females and 75 males in the sample. Females averaged 33.9 years of age and males 34.5 years.

INSTRUMENTATION

Participants completed the Myers-Briggs Type Indicator (MBTI) Form K, the Group Embedded Figures Test (GEFT), and a measure of self-directed learning titled Scoring Learning As A Process

(SLAAP). Demographic data was obtained from the instruments. The MBTI items are concerned with four bipolar preferences:

1. Extroversion attitude (E) or Introversion attitude (I)
2. Sensing perception (S) or Intuitive perception (N)
3. Thinking judgement (T) or Feeling judgement (F)
4. Judgement (J) or Perception (P).

In its most common usage, the four scales are combined to produce a "personality type" or preference. For the purposes of this study, the four scales were considered independently. Extensive reliability and validity data exist for the MBTI (Carlson, 1985; McCaully, 1990; Schuerger, Zarrella, & Hotz, 1989; Tzeng, Ware, & Bharadwaj, 1991).

The Group Embedded Figures Test (GEFT) (Witkin, et al., 1971) was used to operationalize cognitive style. Although a number of weaknesses have been noted regarding the GEFT, most notably a possible gender bias, (Bonham, 1988b; Arthur and Day, 1991) it was chosen, for this study, for two reasons. It has been used previously in adult self-directed learning research contexts and confusing and contradictory positions are taken (Brookfield, 1986; Pratt, 1984) concerning its meaning for predicting self-directed behavior. It was thought that additional study might help to establish a clearer relationship between the construct and self-direction in learning.

The SLAAP instrument was designed specifically for this study. It is designed to be a measure of participants' self-perception of their self-directed learning. Developed from the model described by Jarvis (1992), the SLAAP is a self-scoring device that asks the learner to rate him or herself on seven of the nine self-directed learning process elements identified by the model. These elements include:

1. decision to learn
2. type of participation
3. aims and objectives
4. content

5. method
6. thought/language
7. assessment (Jarvis, 1992, pp.136-141)

Responses to the seven items were made on a 7-point Likert scale. A composite score reflecting a learner's perception of his/her self-directed behavior for a chosen activity was computed by summing the scores for the seven items. A pilot test of this instrument established a test-retest correlation of .87.

DATA ANALYSIS

Means and standard deviations were calculated for the dependent and independent variables. Pearson Product Moment correlation coefficients, and analyses of variance were used in hypothesis testing. The frequency distribution, means, standard deviations, and ranges for the sample population are given in Table 13.1.

Table 13.1.	Profile of the Study Participants	
Variable/characteristic	Frequency	Percentage
Age		
22-30	57	35.6
31-40	71	44.4
41-52	32	20.0
Total	160	100.0
Median: 33.0		
Mean: 34.2		
Standard deviation: 7.01		
Range: 22-52		
Gender		
Female	85	53.1
Male	75	46.9

Consistent with the target population, the study participants ranged in age from 22 to 52 years. The mean age was 34.2, with a standard deviation of 7.01. In the study sample, 82 participants, or 53.1%, were female, whereas 71 males represented the remaining

46.9%. This ratio between females and males is similar to that found in the total population.

MBTI

The MBTI was completed by 151 participants. Preference scores are derived from the basic raw scores. Continuous scores are a linear transformation of preference scores for convenience in statistical analysis. Findings based on the MBTI are presented in the form of continuous scores. Descriptive statistics for each of the four MBTI subscales are presented in Table 13.2.

Table 13.2.   **MBTI Descriptive Statistics**

Subscale	Mean	Standard Deviation	Minimum Score	Median Score	Maximum Score
EI	96.19	26.84	49	95	157
SN	97.37	28.84	21	95	141
TF	93.77	25.12	39	93	149
JP	101.38	27.96	45	101	155

GEFT

The GEFT was completed by 148 participants. Table 13.3 provides descriptive statistics for the variable cognitive style as represented by the GEFT scores. The mean (11.46) and standard deviation (4.77) are representative of adult subjects reported in other research using the GEFT (Bernardi, 1993).

SLAAP

The SLAAP instrument was completed by 140 participants. Designed for this study, this instrument is intended to measure learner's self-perception of their self-directedness during one learning project or activity. Because the participant was asked to

Table 13.3. **Pearson Product Moment Correlations and Analysis of Variance for GEFT and MBTI Scores by SLAAP Scores**

Scale	Correlation	F Ratio	p Value	R2
GEFT	-0.0692	0.95	0.33	0.007
MBTI—EI	0.0800	1.04	0.31	0.008
MBTI—SN	0.0113	0.04	0.84	0.000
MBTI—TF	-0.0924	1.25	0.27	0.009
MBTI—JP	0.0345	0.10	0.75	0.001

score only one learning project or activity, the resulting score could have been unrepresentative of the learner's behavior. Consequently, an additional question was asked concerning the representativeness of the learning project. Item D on the SLAAP asked, "How representative is the described learning activity of your typical approach to learning?" Four responses, ranging from "Very untypical" to "Very typical" were possible. These items were scored from 1 to 4, with 1 being least typical and 4 being most typical. The mean for this item was 2.96.

With a mean score of 34.77 and a median score of 36 on the SLAAP, study participants perceived themselves to have engaged in a high degree of self-directed behavior in pursuing their learning projects. Scores ranged from a low of 14 to the maximum of 49. The possible range of scores was 7 to 49; the standard deviation was 7.19. An examination of scores by quartile showed that 75% of the participants had scores of 31 or higher. A composite score reflecting the learner's perception of his or her self-directed learning process for the chosen activity was computed by summing the scores for the seven items. Results of the correlational analysis are presented in Table 13.3. Statistical significance was established at $p < .05$.

DISCUSSION OF THE FINDINGS

The first hypothesis proposed no relationship between participants' scores on the GEFT and the SLAAP. Participants' self-rating on self-direction was found to not be associated with their cognitive style. What this suggests is that the participants' cognitive style was not a significant factor in their pursuit of a self-directed learning activity.

This contradicts the relationships expected by both Brookfield (1986) and Pratt (1984). There was no significant difference in self-perception of self-directedness between FI and FD subjects. This also contradicts other empirical studies (Bitterman, 1988; Shelley, 1991; Tzuk, 1985) that have identified low to moderate correlations between readiness for self-direction and field-independence.

The remaining hypotheses predicted no significant relationship between participants' scores on the four preference scales of the MBTI and the SLAAP. As predicted, the MBTI measures of personality were not correlated with the learners' self-rating on self-direction.

Personality has been generally construed to be a factor in learner self-direction (Candy, 1991; Merriam & Caffarella, 1991; Long, 1996). Previous studies (Johnson, Sample, & Jones, 1988; Myers & McCaully, 1989; Oxford & Ehrman, 1989; Kitsen, Lekan, & Guglielmino, 1995) have produced limited support for this proposition. A preference for Intuition (N) in information processing has been noted (Johnson, Sample, & Jones, 1988; Myers & McCaully, 1989; Oxford & Ehrman, 1989). The present findings when combined with the limited results produced by these other studies (Johnson, Sample, & Jones, 1988; Myers & McCaully, 1989; Oxford & Ehrman, 1989; Kitsen, Lekan, & Guglielmino, 1995) suggest that personality, as with cognitive style, is not a significant factor in learners' pursuit of a self-directed learning activity.

DISCUSSION OF THE RESULTS

The assertion that personality factors and cognitive style are associated with self-direction in learning is based on the assumption that learners' self-directed behavior is influenced by or directed by these factors. Furthermore, it has been generally thought that, when examined, some characteristic set or profile of learner psychological orientation would emerge. These assertions are challenged by the present study.

For this group of learners, their engagement in what they have perceived to be a self-directed learning activity was not the result of psychological orientation but some other factor or factors. Other factors that have been conjectured include ownership of the learning by the learner (Candy, 1991; Long, 1996), learner goal-setting behavior (Schultz, 1991), and the learning situation or context (Candy, 1991). This line of thought supports Danis' (1992) framework in which she submits that learner characteristics directly influence strategies but that "learner characteristics alone do not characterize the self-instructed mode" (p.63).

Perhaps of most importance, considering the findings, is the role of motivation in self-directed learning. In Jarvis' (1992) model, disjuncture precedes the actual process whereby the learner initiates a learning process. In Danis' (1992) framework she characterizes this phase as "reacting to a triggering event or situation" (p.53). More recently, Garrison (1998) has proposed that learner motivation must be an essential part of a comprehensive model of self-directed learning.

Limitations

The methodology followed, for this as well as other studies, partially explains the nature of the disparity and is related to the nature of the instrumentation used. The MBTI and the GEFT are, by design, measures of a preference or propensity for something. They may not accurately predict what a respondent will actually do in a specific situation, only their predisposition for a certain behavior or type of behavior.

One limitation of this study involves the non-random nature of the sample. The participants reflect a highly visible and active element of the non-traditional, higher education population. However, they are also unrepresentative of any broader learner population. Subjects were primarily white and middle-class and all had completed at least two years of higher education. Learners, represented in this study, may have been predisposed to seek formal education resources when engaging in self-directed learning.

CONCLUSIONS

The absence of an identifiable psychological orientation, or profile, derived from this study's participants suggests one unavoidable conclusion. By their own measure, all of the learners in this study were capable of engaging in self-directed learning under some set of circumstances. If self-directed learning is not, as characterized by Tzuk (1985), "an enduring personality trait that would manifest itself regardless" (p.149), then perhaps it is, as Knowles (1990) suggested, a capacity possessed by all.

The psychological orientation of learners may, as Danis (1992) concludes, more directly influence the choice of strategies employed by learners. In this view, learner characteristics, and the distinctive stages or phases of the learning directly affect the strategies used. The implication of this relationship is that, because of individual differences, learners will pursue different strategies (Olgren, 1993) to accomplish their learning goals. Consequently, as supported by the present study results, it can be concluded that no requisite set of skills or set of learner characteristics seem to exist relative to self-directed learning.

IMPLICATIONS FOR PRACTICE

A great deal of attention has been paid to the skills apparently possessed by self-directed learners and to the phases or steps they follow in pursuing their learning. Ideal learner skill profiles or an all-encompassing set of self-directed learning practices have often been reported. Rather than continue to seek out these models of "best practice," more effort should be directed toward recognizing and supporting both individual differences and the contextual nature of adults' self-directed learning.

Recognizing individual learner differences, Bonham (1989) has suggested that self-directed learning is more akin to a learning style. Others (Danis, 1992; Tennant and Pogson, 1995; Tzuk, 1985) have pointed out that a learner's developmental stage may be an important component. Smith (1992), in encouraging a learning-to-learn approach, emphasized that educators must acknowledge learner individual differences and adds, "it is the instructor who is best positioned to assist in enhancing learning abilities, although few instructors have the requisite interest and preparation to take full advantage of this opportunity" (p.176).

Smith's statement gets at the heart of individual differences. Process guidelines and psychological profiles have the primary attraction of ease of application in instructional situations. However, it is more work, and perhaps more challenging work, to engage in facilitating learning for individuals rather than groups. "Instructors who are willing to use a combination of instructor-centered and learner-centered approaches must be capable of assuming a variety of instructional roles and using a range of formats and techniques" (Merriam and Caffarella, 1991, p.26). Knox (1986), Brookfield (1990), Hiemstra and Sisco (1990), and Piskurich (1993) all address the need for individualizing instruction as well as the complexity involved in doing so.

Many authors (Candy, 1991; Spear and Mocker, 1984; Tzuk, 1985; Pratt, 1988) have noted the need to consider the effect of context on learner behavior. This can encompass both the specifics of content and the general learner environment, or life-space. Tennant and Pogson (1995) emphasize the learner's response to the subject matter; "others now acknowledge that autonomous learning is not a general, content-free capacity, and that it only makes sense in relation to a particular subject or domain of inquiry" (p.133). In formal learning situations, Pratt (1988) suggests that the essential variables are the learner's assessment of their competence along with their commitment and confidence to carrying out the learning process autonomously.

At least one difficulty of note arises when contemplating interventions intended to stimulate self-directed learning. In formal
learning contexts, the educator has a dual role of supporting both
individual and institutional objectives. If institutional objectives
and outcomes take precedence, then, in this situation, individual
learners may simply prefer to be "other-directed" (Jarvis, 1992).
According to Cranton (1994), learner empowerment cannot proceed if instructors or facilitators are not in a position to give up
control over learning outcomes.

IMPLICATIONS FOR FURTHER RESEARCH

More needs to be done in investigating the developmental factors
(Tennant and Pogson, 1995), cultural factors, and social factors
influencing self-directed learning. No systematic research has been
conducted on the impact of learner "beliefs and values on their
repertoire of self-regulated learning strategies" (Danis, 1992, p.64).
Such research should specifically examine learners representing
other populations such as minority groups, lower socio-economic
groups, and women (Berger, 1990).

Related to an examination of learner characteristics is the need
to understand self-directed learning from the learner's perspective.
The present study demonstrated that measuring learner self-
perception of self-directedness is a viable undertaking. Far more
needs to be done. Candy (1991) has suggested a number of approaches to assessing the learner's view of autonomous learning.
The developmental implications of self-directedness indicated by
Tennant and Pogson (1995) underscore Candy's recommendations.
Among these is the recommendation to pursue "long-term studies
of individual learners with a view to discovering the components
of their continuing search for personal autonomy" (p.449).

Also of importance is the role of motivation in self-directed
learning. Tennant (1991) points out that while a great deal of research has been conducted in the area of motivation it has been almost exclusively focused on participation in formal learning ac-

tivities. Danis' (1992) has proposed a framework that acknowledges the interplay between learner characteristics, the phases or steps followed by the learner, and the strategies the learner employs. Motivation is implied in these relationships and directly implicated as a sub-component of the phases component: "reacting to a triggering event/situation" (Danis, 1992, p.53).

It also appears useful to examine more fully the critical interplay between disjuncture and motivation. Jarvis (1992), in an extension of the concept established by Lewin (1952), had noted the primary importance of this initial aspect of interpersonal change. As Jarvis (1992) puts it "the potential for learning exists wherever there is a disjuncture between the learner's biography and experience; it provides a catalyst to the questioning process that results in learning" (p.134).

Most studies of learner psychological orientation and self-direction have focused on learner readiness or pre-disposition for self-direction. The present study and others (Berger, 1990; Spear and Mocker, 1984) have examined situations of actual self-directed learning. No studies have addressed the motivational implications of learner response to disjuncture.

Many models of self-directed learning process have been identified (Candy, 1991; Danis, 1992) and most have acknowledged, in some fashion, the disjuncture stage. Spear and Mocker (1984) have characterized this stage as reacting to a triggering event or situation. Understanding this stage could provide valuable insights into learner behavior. Tzuk (1985) suggests "an adult may behave in a self-directed manner in one situation and not so in another" (p.149). Similarly, Atman (1989) has emphasized the significance of conation, or self-striving behavior, in distance learning. If these positions have any merit, then it would seem essential to explore fully the notion of disjuncture and self-directed learning.

SUMMARY

This study examined a group of adult learners who had engaged in independent learning projects. Measures of personality, cognitive style, and self-direction failed to produce an identifiable psychological profile for this group of learners. It can be concluded that no prerequisite set of characteristics exists relative to self-directed learning.

The focus of future research into the area of learner characteristics should continue to be on the learners' assessment of the situation or context. Special attention should be paid to the role of disjuncture in stimulating learner motivation to engage in self-directed activities. It may be that educators can readily influence self-directed learning behavior by establishing a motivating learning environment based on a recognition of individual learner differences and the development of an effective facilitator-learner relationship.

REFERENCES

Arthur, W., & Day, D.V. (1991). Examination of the construct validity of alternative measures of field dependence/independence. Perceptual and Motor Skills, 72, pp.851-859.

Atman, K.S. (1989). The role of conation (striving) in the distance education enterprise. In M.G. Moore, & G. C. Clark (Eds.), Readings in distance learning and instruction, 2 (pp.14-24). University Park, PA: The Pennsylvania State University.

Berger, N.O. (1990). A qualitative study of the process of self-directed learning. Unpublished doctoral dissertation, Virginia Commonwealth University, Richmond, VA.

Bernardi, R.A. (1993). Group Embedded Figures Test: Psychometric data documenting shifts from prior norms in field independence of accountants. Perceptual and Motor Skills, 77, pp.579-586.

Bitterman, J.E. (1988). The relationship between the adult's cognitive style and achieving style to preference for self-directed learning. Proceedings of the 1988 Midwest Research to Practice in Adult and Community Education, Madison, WI.

Bonham, L.A. (1988a). Learning style use: In need of perspective. Lifelong Learning, 11(5), pp.14-17.

Bonham, L.A. (1988b). Learning style instruments: Let the buyer beware. Lifelong Learning, 11(6), pp.12-16.

Bonham, L.A. (1989). Self-directed orientation toward learning: A learning style? In H.B. Long, & Associates (Eds.), Self-directed learning: emerging theory & practice (pp.13-42). Norman, OK: Oklahoma Research Center for Continuing Professional and Higher Education.

Brockett, R.G., & Hiemstra, R. (1991). Self-direction in adult learning: Perspectives on theory, research, and practice. New York: Routledge.

Brookfield, S.D. (1986). Understanding and facilitating adult learning. Milton Keynes, England: Open University Press.

Brookfield, S.D. (1990). The skillful teacher: On technique, trust, and responsiveness in the classroom. San Francisco: Jossey-Bass.

Brookfield, S.D. (1993). Self-directed learning, political clarity, and the critical practice of adult education. Adult Education Quarterly, 43(4), pp.227-242.

Candy, P.C. (1991). Self-direction for lifelong learning. San Francisco: Jossey-Bass.

Carlson, J.G. (1985). Recent assessments of the Myers-Briggs Type Indicator. Journal of Personality Assessment, 49(4), pp.356-365.

Cranton, P. (1994). Understanding and promoting transformative learning: A guide for educators of adults. San Francisco: Jossey-Bass.

Danis, C. (1992). A unifying framework for data-based research into adult self-directed learning. In H.B. Long, & Associates Self-directed learning: application and research (pp.47-72). Norman, OK: Oklahoma Research Center for Continuing Professional and Higher Education.

Garrison, D.R. (1992). Critical thinking and self-directed learning in adult education: An analysis of responsibility and control issues. Adult Education Quarterly, 42(3), pp.136-148.

Guglielmino, L.M. (1977). Development of the Self-Directed Learning Readiness Scale. Unpublished doctoral dissertation, University of Georgia, Athens, GA. Notes: (Dissertation Abstarcts International, 38(11A), 6467.)

Hiemstra, R., & Sisco, B. (1990). Individualizing instruction: making learning, personal, empowering, and successful. San Francisco: Jossey-Bass, Inc.

Jarvis, P. (1992). Paradoxes of learning: On becoming an individual in society. San Francisco: Jossey-Bass.

Johnson, J.A., Sample, J.A., & Jones, W.J. (1988). Self-directed learning and personality type in adult degree students. Psychology: A Journal of Human Behavior, 25(1), pp.32-36.

Kitson, D.L., Lekan, D.F., & Guglielmino, P. (1995). Self-directed learning readiness personality correlates. In H.B. Long, & Associates (Eds.), New dimensions in self-directed learning (pp.39-48). Norman Oklahoma: Public Managers Center, College of Education, University of Oklahoma.

Knowles, M.S. (1990). Fostering competence in self-directed learning. In R.M. Smith, & Associates (Eds.), Learning to learn across the life span (pp.123-136). San Francisco: Jossey-Bass.

Knox, A.B. (1986). Helping adults learn: a guide to planning, implementing, and conducting programs. San Francisco: Jossey-Bass.

Lewin, K. (1952). Group decisions and social change. In G.E. Swanson, T.N. Newcomb, & E.L. Hartley (Eds.), Readings in social psychology (Rev. ed., pp.459-473). New York: Holt.

Long, H.B. (1996). Self-directed learning: Challenges and opportunities. In H.B. Long, & Associates (Eds.), Current developments in self-directed learning (pp.1-10). Norman, OK: Public Managers Center, College of Education, University of Oklahoma.

McCaulley, M.H. (1990). The Myers-Briggs Type Indicator: A measure for individuals and groups. Measurement and Evaluation in Counseling and Development, 22(4), pp.181-195.

Merriam, S.B., & Caffarella, R.S. (1991). Learning in adulthood. San Francisco: Jossey-Bass.

Myers, I.B., & McCaulley, M. (1989). Manual: A guide to the development and use of the Myers-Briggs Type Indicator. Palo Alto, CA: Consulting Psychologists Press.

Oddi, L.F. (1986). Development and validation of an instrument to identify self-directed continuing learners. Adult Education Quarterly, 36(2), pp.97-107.

Oddi, L.F. (1987). Perspectives on self-directed learning. Adult Education Quarterly, 38(1), pp.21-31.

Olgren, C.H. (1993). Cognitive strategies and self-directedness: research into adults' learning processes. In H.B. Long, & Associates (Eds.), Emerging perspectives of self-directed learning (pp.99-116). Norman, OK: Oklahoma Research Center for Continuing Professional and Higher Education.

Oxford, R., & Ehrman, M. (1989). Psychological type and adult language learning strategies: A pilot study. Journal of Psychological Type, 16, pp.22-32.

Piskurich, G.M. (1993). <u>Self-directed learning: A practical guide to design, development, and implementation</u>. San Francisco: Jossey-Bass.

Pratt, D.D. (1984). Andragogical assumptions: Some counter-intuitive logic. <u>Proceedings of the Adult Education Research Conference,</u> Raleigh, NC: North Carolina State University.

Pratt, D.D. (1988). Andragogy as a relational construct. <u>Adut Education Quarterly, 38</u>(3), pp.160-181.

Schuerger, J.M., Zarrella, K.L., & Hotz, A.S. (1989). Factors that influence the temporal stability of personality by questionnaire. <u>Journal of Personality and Social Psychology, 56</u>(5), pp.777-783.

Schutz, P.A. (1991). Goals in self-directed behavior. <u>Educational Psychologist, 26</u>(1), pp.55-67.

Shelley, R. (1991). <u>Relationship of adults' field-dependence-independence and self-directed learning</u>. Unpublished doctoral dissertation, University of Idaho, Boise, ID.

Smith, R.M. (1992). Implementing the learning to learn concept. In A. C. Tuijnman, & M. Van Der Kamp (Eds.), <u>Learning across the lifespan theories, research, policies</u> (pp.173-190). Oxford: Pergamon Press.

Spear, G.E., & Mocker, D.W. (1984). The organizing circumstance: Environmental determinants in self-directed learning. <u>Adult Education Quarterly, 35</u>(1), pp.1-10.

Tennant, M., & Pogson, P. (1995). <u>Learning and change in the adult years: a developmental perspective</u>. San Francisco: Jossey-Bass, Inc.

Tzeng, O.C.S., Ware, R., & Bharadwaj, N. (1991). Comparison between continuous bipolar and unipolar ratings of the Myers-Briggs Type Indicator. <u>Educational and Psychological Measurement, 51</u>, pp.681-690.

Tzuk, R. (1985). <u>The relationship of adults' self-directedness in learning to the cognitive style of field-dependence-independence: An exploratory investigation</u>. Unpublished doctoral dissertation, Concordia University, Montreal, Canada.

Witkin, H.A., Oltman, P.K., Raskin, E., & Karp, S.A. (1971). <u>Manual: Embedded Figures Test, Children's Embedded Figures Test, Group Embedded Figures Test</u>. Palo Alto, CA: Consulting Psychologists Press.

CHAPTER FOURTEEN

THE SDLPS PROFILE: USING THE SDLPS
TO IMPLEMENT SDL

Jane Pilling-Cormick

Discovering the support of the learning environment is crucial when using a self-directed (SD) approach to learning and using the Self-Directed Learning Perception Scale (SDLPS) allows this to happen. The SDLPS is a new tool in the toolbox approach to studying SDL (Pilling-Cormick, 1998b) and the subsequent development of the SDLPS Profile is an addition to this toolbox. The SDLPS Profile is a step towards putting instrument scores into practice by providing detailed feedback about how supportive the scores show specific parts of the environment to be. The profile includes an overall SDLPS score describing how respondents rate the support of the environment as a whole, component scores representing characteristics within that environment, and explanations of how to use these scores. This paper introduces the SDLPS Profile along with an overview of its parts, purpose and uses.

WHAT IS THE SDLPS PROFILE

The SDLPS Profile is a 30 page booklet resulting from SDLPS score calculations. When using the SDLPS, there is the option of developing a SDLPS Profile. To understand the SDLPS Profile, a brief overview of the SDLPS becomes necessary.

The SDLPS is a self-report instrument focusing on perceptions of supportive characteristics in the learning environment for SDL. The unique aspect is that the SDLPS focuses on the learning situation rather than the learner. The basis for the instrument is the Self-Directed Learning Process (SDLP) model (Pilling-Cormick, 1999). The SDLPS uses a Likert type scale, is easy to administer and provides a numerical score (Pilling-Cormick, 1998a). The SDLPS is useful in various settings to discover discrepancies in perceptions, deal with resistance to SDL, develop new techniques, determine what works, encourage participation, promote reflection, provide feedback for planners, explore correlates of helpfulness, and complement current scales (Pilling-Cormick, 1998b). There are currently three versions: educational, training and clinical.

The SDLPS Profile moves beyond providing one overall SDLPS score and reveals in detail how respondents answered items on the SDLPS. It is unique to the sample because its basis is the SDLPS score for a particular study. Inside the profile, there is the overall SDLPS score and five component scores giving an overall picture of how supportive the environment is and specific ways in which it is so. In addition, each SDLPS Profile provides suggestions for further investigation of each component score. One benefit of the SDLPS Profile is that it contains two types of scores: an overall SDLPS score and component scores. By providing both types of scores, it not only becomes possible to discover the overall level of support, but also the existence of supportive characteristics within the learning environment. The SDLPS Profile is practical, population-based and progressive.

Practical

The SDLPS Profile allows the SDLPS scores to be put into practice. Instruments often produce one numerical score which becomes the basis for making judgments about conditions of a learning experience or characteristics of an individual. Rather than provide only a numerical score, the SDLPS Profile explains what the overall SDLPS score means, presents component scores and provides suggestions for future study for each component score. It becomes possible to discover if learners feel they have input into the structure of the learning activity. Do learners feel they freely share ideas? By providing component scores, it becomes possible to go beyond merely stating whether the learning environment is supportive, to determining reasons for rating the learning environment as it is. These detailed findings provide a guideline for users to plan subsequent steps when faced with questions such as: "so what" and "what do I do now"? With this emphasis on practical applications and the SDLPS focusing specifically on the support of the learning environment, the SDLPS Profile is a user-friendly concept.

Population-Based

The basis for the SDLPS Profile is specifically the population or sample used in the individual study; the profile is unique to the sample. By providing sample specific feedback, the results from the SDLPS become especially powerful since the results show how the particular group in question scored. From here, it is possible to make discoveries of how learners feel and how supportive the environment is for learning activities. By being population-based, the profile produced is context-specific making the findings more meaningful and ultimately more useful.

Progressive

The SDLPS Profile is a natural progression in the further development of the SDLPS. Various studies express a need for such a practical application of SDLPS scores. As Pilling-Cormick & Bulik (1999) suggest when studying clinical learning environments, the SDLPS Profile will provide specific feedback about characteristics within the environment that are especially helpful in promoting SDL and may account for overall high SDLPS scores. The SDLPS Profile is a follow-up development stemming from the SDLPS results and a further benefit of using this instrument. The SDLPS Profile is not only a progression in terms of being a practical application, but is also a theoretical progression since it allows researchers to discover more about the characteristics of a supportive SD learning environment.

PROFILE DESCRIPTION

The SDLPS Profile consists of four parts: (1) definitions, (2) overall SDLPS scores, (3) SDLPS component scores, and (4) suggestions for using the component scores.

Definitions

Users of the SDLPS may not be familiar with terminology used in the area of SDL and specifically on the SDLPS. To make interpretation easier, the SDLPS Profile includes a list of definitions representing key players and concepts referred to in the SDLPS. Terminology corresponds to the version of the SDLPS used; the use of the term training site, learning site or rotation site will vary. In a clinical setting, the adoption of the term "preceptor" occurs instead of using "trainer" which is part of the training version. In an educational setting, the term "instructor" emerges. By including situation specific terms, there is a clear presentation of the concepts underlying the use of the instrument in the specific setting making it easy to interpret results. Decisions are subsequently easier to make about how to use the findings.

Overall SDLPS Score

The SDLPS Profile provides one numerical score of the learning environment's overall support showing how the group of respondents rate the presence of supportive characteristics in general. Score level ratings also appear along with the meaning of a high, moderate or low score. By referencing the overall score, it becomes easy to determine at a glance, how supportive the learning environment is. The overall scores allow for comparisons such as those carried out by Pilling-Cormick & Kops (in press) when they look at the overall scores of HR managers and learners in a training environment to determine if the two groups generally agree on the training environment's support for SDL.

SDLPS Component Scores

The SDLPS Profile includes a set of component scores showing how supportive the learning environment is according to specific components, making it easier to discover what the component scores address. In the SDLPS Profile, these component scores appear in numerical and graphical format making it possible to see at a glance which components are most or least supportive. The five environmental components in the SDLP model (Pilling-Cormick, 1998b) are the basis for the SDLPS component scores: institutional characteristics, learning site characteristics, how the institution functions, how the learning activity functions, and climate for building relationships.

Institutional Characteristics

Physical characteristics of the business, university or school, become part of this institutional characteristics component score. To be supportive, the institution should consider if there is a place, be it in a resource center or library, where learners have an opportunity to quietly think about learning; a location within the institution where they can get away from distractions and develop thoughts, plan learning strategies or reflect on what they are learning and the process the learning is taking. This component reveals ways the respondents feel the institution physically supports an SD approach to learning. Are institutional learning resources suitable for SDL? Perhaps not having resources available hinders learning. By using this component to illustrate how learners perceive the support of these institutional characteristics, it becomes possible to discover areas for further investigation. If the institution does provide quiet places to think about learning, why do learners not perceive their existence?

Learning Site Characteristics

The learning location has certain physical features that support a SD approach whether it is a clinic, classroom or training location. For instance, is learner comfort a consideration? Perhaps the structure of the clinic or classroom is not conducive to allowing for learner interaction. Becoming aware of ways the specific learning site is supportive, allows for identification of particular characteristics such as learner comfort which will then be considered for possible change.

How the Institution Functions

Learners must interact with not just the physical resources, but with the processes operating within that school, university or organization. Do learners have the option of choosing what type of learning activities they pursue? Is there an attendance requirement such as spending so many hours per week in a clinic or classroom. When designing learning activities, do institutions consider the effects of having too many learners in one location? As Pilling-Cormick & Bulik (in press) question in their study of clinical learning environments, does the university ask learners about the appropriateness of the rotation length or impact of administrative paperwork.

How the Learning Activity Functions

If the learning environment rating is supportive, it would be expected that the structure of the learning activity should be supportive. Do learners have input into the evaluation scheme? To be supportive, learners should be able to indicate how they are being evaluated. It is possible that the learning activity is presented as being SD and learners encouraged to pursue their own interests, but evaluation may be other-directed such as the instructor marking according to a standard structure or using a standard test. Is the structure of the learning activity flexible enough to allow for the integration of new ideas?

Learners may give ideas for integration into the structure of the learning activity, but when they do offer their thoughts, rarely do they see them actually emerge as part of the structure. Characteristics within the "how the learning activity functions" component score allow for these meaningful details to come to light. If a learning activity is not functioning in a manner consistent with what a SDL approach would promote, then discovering reasons for this misconception are vital.

Climate for Building Relationships
It is possible to overlook building relationships which is a vital part of a SD supportive environment as shown in the SDLPS model (Pilling-Cormick, 1999). Providing a climate where learners feel comfortable sharing ideas and questioning their learning is essential. This component score shows how supportive the climate is for encouraging the development of these relationships. Do learners share thoughts about learning with others? If learners say the environment does not promote this happening, then further investigation about why they feel the climate does not support learners sharing thoughts can take place. Perhaps a presentation by trainers or instructors reviewing the importance of sharing ideas is necessary. A time set aside for specifically promoting this type of interaction may help. Questioning learners further to discover if they share ideas will lead to further revelations of additional factors which were previously unknown. By using the characteristics within the component score for developing a climate for building relationships, a practical way of addressing this vital component of a supportive learning environment comes forth. Is there the development of a non-threatening atmosphere where learners feel free to share their ideas? Ways to develop a more supportive climate appear.

Suggestions for Using the Component Scores
Calculating SDLPS Profile component scores reveals more detail than one numerical indication of the learning environment's support for SDL, allowing for detailed investigation expanding the usefulness of the SDLPS results. Following each component score in the SDLPS Profile, a list of questions appears representing items and subsequently characteristics within the component to consider

for further investigation. As a next step, the profile directs users to choose one of their component scores and refer to the list of questions corresponding to that score. By referencing the questions, it becomes possible to discover especially supportive characteristics within each component and those to consider for further development.

Understand Characteristics of a Successful SDL Learning Activity
The characteristics within the component scores are requirements for successful SDL as outlined in the SDLP model (Pilling-Cormick, 1998b). By providing the five components and accompanying characteristics, it is possible to discover what an ideal supportive environment for SDL looks like. By referencing these lists of questions following each component score, there is an increasing awareness of what characteristics are part of a supportive learning environment. It then becomes possible to try new ideas and techniques to move toward this ideal when there is an awareness of what the ultimate supportive learning environment is like.

Discover if Key Characteristics Exist
Do key characteristics purported in the SDLP model (Pilling-Cormick, 1999) actually exist in the sample being studied and if so, to what extent? The SDLP Profile component scores give a picture of key characteristics found in the individual study. For example, is there freedom for learners to choose what to learn? Is there encouragement of a low threat atmosphere? Do courses of study or rotation structures allow for learner input? Are there opportunities for learners to reflect on their learning? Do learners share thoughts about learning with others? If learners say the environment does not promote this happening, then further investigation about why they feel the climate does not support learners sharing thoughts can take place. Perhaps a presentation by trainers or instructors reviewing the importance of sharing ideas is necessary. A time set aside for specifically promoting this type of interaction may help. In situations where the introduction of SDL into traditional programs is taking place, this type of feedback is essential. In organi-

zations, human resource managers who want to ensure trainers are providing a SD approach will have the opportunity to see what the employee's viewpoints are. Results make it possible to give feedback on training activities, determine learner support and provide feedback for planners.

Increase the Fit of Learning Activities to Learners

By referencing the characteristics within component scores, it becomes possible to discover any discrepancies in opinions and consequently, how well the learning activity fits with the learners. Does the structure of the SD program fit the needs of the learners? It becomes possible to discover more about what those discrepancies actually are and begin to decide how to deal with them. Trainers are able to ensure employees feel there is learner input in business settings where there appears to be resistance to SD in training. Knowledge of component-specific characteristics allows for the development of steps to convert other learners into believing in an SD approach. One study with implications for using these findings to discover fit is in a post-secondary setting using nontraditional and traditional programs where there is the possibility of using these findings as part of counseling techniques to determine course selection (Nuckles, Kachelmyer & Pilling-Cormick, in press). Fitting the learner to the setting becomes possible.

Integrate Learner Feedback

By considering the SDLPS Profile component scores, it becomes possible to utilize learner feedback and allow learners to see the implementation of ideas. Learners will then realize that their input is valuable and that there is integration of learner feedback into the design of the learning activity. Instead of merely stating whether the learning environment is supportive, the profile moves beyond this to say how it is supportive allowing for a practical application of SDLPS scores. In a business setting, employee motivation will increase by incorporating learner feedback into the training plan. By considering the component scores, discoveries about which component characteristics produce motivation emerge. With a profile, there is the option of sharing meaningful findings with learners and they will see that their input is being taken seriously; a key characteristic in a supportive SDL environment.

Develop a Detailed Action Plan

Information from the SDLPS Profile allows for the development of a detailed action plan for a smooth implementation of SDL. Becoming aware of specific supportive component characteristics will make implementation of SDL easier and quicker. It becomes possible to make decisions for planning how to best deal with characteristics which may prevent successful implementation. Identifying possible stumbling blocks allows further investigation of characteristics which are slowing down the successful adoption of SDL. If SDL is the goal, then discovering ways to speed up the progress toward that goal becomes essential. In this way, maximum advantage of SDL opportunities will result and the successful strategies for implementation developed.

Develop Cost-Effective Solutions

The cost of learning is obviously an ongoing issue in almost all learning situations. In medical education, the cost in lost income to all the clinical teaching faculty involved in educating one student for an entire year might average around $43,000. The question becomes in a time of managed care constraints, will the clinical environment "allow" time for medical students to be SD (Pilling-Cormick & Bulik, 1999)? Similarly, money spent on training is a concern in organizations. Since SDL is a desirable way to learn to survive in an ever-changing world of technology, using tools such as the SDLPS Profile will be cost-effective since it enhances the chances of a successful implementation of SDL saving money in the long run. Component characteristics are a starting point for investigating ways to explore alternatives for providing cost-effective learning environments.

CONCLUSION

The development of the SDLPS Profile has both research and practical implications for the study of SDL. The concept of developing a SDLPS Profile is new and as such, provides an additional way of studying the phenomenon of SDL. Profiles appear as part of ongoing studies in clinical (Pilling-Cormick & Bulik, in press), training (Pilling-Cormick & Kops, in press) and educational (Nuckles, Kachelmyer, & Pilling-Cormick, in press) settings. Based on feedback from these studies, the SDLPS Profile will continue to develop.

The SDLPS Profile is a practical way of implementing the SDLPS scores and unique to the sample responding since the SDLPS scores are the basis for its development. The focus is on the learning situation and not the learner. As such, results from the SDLPS differ from other instruments currently being used in SDL research. The SDLPS Profile allows these scores to be put into practice. In the profile, there are suggestions for further investigation for each component score. This allows for immediate identification of components and characteristics within those components which may need work. Similarly, it reveals specific ways the learning environment is supportive providing support for continuing to promote those characteristics.

With the development of the SDLPS Profile, there are now two types of SDLPS scores available: the SDLPS numerical score and component scores. Presenting scores in graphical format enables one to see at a glance how supportive individual components are and makes the SDLPS results more easily understood, comprehensive and detailed allowing for meaningful feedback. The SDLPS Profile moves beyond one numerical score to reveal how respondents rate the support of factors within the environment. Further component analysis will become a large part of further profile development. This will allow specific ways the environment is supportive to emerge from further investigation of the individual components. More detailed feedback such as this will become valuable allowing for identification of specific characteristics within the environment. By moving beyond providing one numerical score, the

SDLPS Profile becomes an invaluable resource and addition to the toolbox approach for assisting learners and educators with SDL.

REFERENCES

Nuckles, C., Kachelmyer, K, & Pilling-Cormick, J. (in press). A validity study of the Self-Directed Learning Perception Scale (SDLPS). In H.B. Long & Associates, <u>New ideas about self-directed learning</u>.

Pilling-Cormick, J. (1998a). <u>SDLPS Guide</u>. Burlington: Professional Learning & Training.

Pilling-Cormick, J. (1998b). The Self-Directed Learning Perception Scale: A step toward a toolbox approach to instrumentation proposed for self-directed learning. In H.B. Long & Associates, <u>Developing paradigms for self-directed learning</u> (pp.159-168). Norman, OK: Public Managers Center, College of Education, University of Oklahoma.

Pilling-Cormick, J. (1999). The Self-Directed Learning Process model: A comparative investigation. In H.B. Long & Associates, <u>Contemporary ideas and practices in SDL</u> (pp.89-102). Norman, OK: Public Managers Center, College of Education, University of Oklahoma.

Pilling-Cormick, J., & Bulik, R. (1999). A preliminary study exploring the use of the Self-Directed Learning Perception Scale in a clinical setting. In H.B. Long & Associates, <u>Contemporay ideas and practices in self-directed learning</u> (pp.102-116). Norman, OK: Public Managers Center, College of Education, University of Oklahoma.

Pilling-Cormick, J. & Bulik, R. (in press). Further investigation into the use of the SDLPS in a clinical setting. In H.B. Long & Associates, <u>New ideas about self-directed learning</u>.

Pilling-Cormick, J., & Kops, W. (in press). Further investigation of organizations identified as supporting a self-directed approach to training. In H.B. Long & Associates, <u>New ideas about self-directed learning</u>.

CHAPTER FIFTEEN

SELF–DIRECTED LEARNING IN THE WORKPLACE: AN EXPLORATORY STUDY TO IDENTIFY ORGANIZATIONS WITH A SDL APPROACH TO TRAINING

Jane Pilling-Cormick
William J. Kops

This paper describes the first phase in a larger research study designed to identify organizations that have adopted a self-directed learning (SDL) orientation to training, and to examine the role of trainers in these organizations. The purpose of this first phase is to identify organizations that provide a supportive environment for self-directed learning. This paper describes the steps taken, the rationale used for the research design, and the use of the Self-Directed Learning Perception Scale (SDLPS) in an organizational setting.

BACKGROUND

An increasing amount of research is being done on SDL in the workplace (Long & Morris, 1995). Several more recent studies examined SDL and training from different perspectives, including training policy and support for SDL (Foucher, 1996; Foucher & Brezot, 1997), intentions of training managers with regard to SDL (Landriault & Gosselin, 1997), and willingness of trainers to endorse SDL (Phelan, 1996). Other studies on SDL (Kops, 1993, 1997; Foucher, 1993, 1995; Carré, 1994), also commented on various aspects of training, training policy, and the role of trainers.

This literature stressed the importance of support from trainers for SDL, and specifically, the contribution that trainers and training policy make to creating a supportive organizational environment for SDL. Kops (1993, 1997) advocated that training departments change their role to provide more resources to learners. In particular, he proposed that trainers become learning facilitators in which their roles are one of coach, consultant, critic, and counsellor to learners. Foucher (1996) claimed that training managers were influential in developing organizational policies that support SDL. In his view, the attitudes and knowledge of trainers with respect to SDL can affect the support for SDL in an organization. Foucher and Brezot (1997) suggested that human resource development (HRD) managers and trainers need to accept SDL as a meaningful approach to staff development, and equip themselves to support self-directed learners. Landriault and Gosselin (1997) indicated that training managers were interested in SDL, and supportive training policy was important to facilitating SDL. On the other hand, Phelan (1996) discovered that trainers were resistant to SDL. He advocated overcoming this resistance through training. Carré (1994) also felt that skill development was important for trainers, specifically to develop their facilitation skills.

One of the objectives of this study is to identify organizations with a SDL approach to training. As Blackwood (1994:51) claims, "group consensus can be reached to define a purpose, pace and method of training ... the objectives, content and evaluation remain prescribed by management or regulation, and not by the consensus of the group." By investigating training with an instrument designed to address supportive SDL environments, the researcher attempted to determine if these characteristics exist. A two-part survey was developed for this purpose.

SURVEY DESIGN

The two-part survey focuses on factors that help learning and approaches to learning in organizations. Part One of the survey includes the training version of the Self-Directed Learning Perception Scale (SDLPS-T), while Part Two addresses more general questions about training and learning in organizations.

The SDLPS is a 57-item, self-report instrument developed over a seven-year period (Pilling-Cormick, 1996). The purpose of the instrument is to investigate perceptions of the factors that help learners with the SDL process. Emphasis is on the learning situation, rather than the learner. The SDLPS produces a numerical score that identifies the degree to which organizations provide environments that are supportive for SDL. In this study, the SDLPS-T was used to identify highly supportive organizations (high scores on the SDLPS-T) that could be included in the second phase of the study.

The SDLPS is based on the Self-Directed Learning Process (SDLP) model. By using the logical construction method, a theoretical chart emerged based on factors identified in the SDLP model. The SDLPS was reviewed in a prepilot study, tried out in a pilot study, revised, and tested again in a field study.

Since the original version of the SDLPS was based on a traditional classroom setting, the SDLPS-T (Self-Directed Learning Perception Scale—Training Version) was developed for use in this study. Wording changes could be made without violating the validity of the original instrument since items are directly based on a theoretical chart derived from the context-based environmental characteristics dimension of the model. The instrument underwent a three-step revision. Initially, all 57 items on the original version were reviewed to identify items that might, because of the original classroom-oriented terminology, be problematic in a training setting. Terminology changes were made to identified items to reflect the training setting. Modifications included, for instance, changing the word "teacher" to "trainer." The original theoretical chart was then consulted for each modified item to ensure that the original meaning of the item was not changed. This entire process was repeated three times until both researchers were satisfied that the items accurately reflected the underlying dimension from the theoretical chart.

The second part of the survey focuses on approaches to training, availability of learning resources, and changes in training activities and programs. The questions about approaches to training and re-sources for learning were developed, based on factors identified in the SDL literature. The question on types of changes in training identified elements of the typical training function, i.e., trainer responsibilities, skill requirements, training methods, staff, and budget. Other ques-tions dealt with training policy, degree of decentralization of authority for training, and type and size of the business/organization. Overall, Part Two of the survey attempted to provide data on the role of train-ing in organizations, which in turn provides a preview to the second phase of the study.

ADMINISTRATIVE PROCEDURE

The survey, along with a cover letter, was sent to 179 member or-ganizations of a provincial (state) association of human resource (HR) management professionals. The selected professional association allowed direct contact with human resource professionals who are generally considered to be well informed in training and HR- related matters. The association membership represented a variety of organi-zations that varied in size and type. The survey was sent to the most senior member, according to position title, in each organization. The term SDL was not defined in the survey materials in order to avoid biasing results. The survey items represent characteristics of a helpful SDL environment, and the researchers wanted to ensure that respon-dents would not answer in a way as to portray their environment as helpful for SDL when, in reality, it was not. A follow-up letter was sent to all nonrespondents two weeks after the initial return deadline date. This increased the response rate from 35% to 50%. Subse-quently, the survey responses were analyzed.

DATA ANALYSIS

Of the 179 surveys distributed, 90 were returned, and 90 were usable. The two parts of the survey were analyzed separately.

For the first part, a standard computer program calculated the SDLPS-T scores for each respondent. A group score of 248 emerged with a standard deviation of 59 and range of 315. The maximum score was 425 and minimum 110. Individual SDLPS-T scores were also calculated. Of the 90 scores, 23 (25%) were high, 59 (65.5%) moderate and 8 (9%) low.

The second part of the survey was analyzed separately from the first. A total of 23 organizations had a high SDLPS-T score, which indicated they had environments that were supportive of SDL. The responses of these organizations were analyzed manually. A mean was calculated for each of the questions requiring a response on a five-point Likert-type scale. Frequency of response was determined for multiple-choice questions, and answers to open-ended questions were sorted by category. The data are reported in Tables 15.1 to 15.3.

FINDINGS

Results of the SDLPS-T give an indication of the supportiveness of the training environments. A more complete picture of training in each organization evolves by considering specific training approaches and availability of identified resources.

Helpfulness of the Environment

The SDLPS-T score indicates how HR managers rate the presence of factors that are helpful in a SDL environment in their organization. These scores can be used to identify organizations with a supportive SDL environment, but need to be interpreted with care since they are based on one person's perception of the learning environment.

The human resource managers' SDLPS-T group score of 248 was moderate. This group score may not be especially significant for the purposes of this study, but it is interesting to note since such a response is not unexpected. As Foucher (1997) claims, few organizations actually adopt a self-directed perspective in their training policies and strategies. Respondents would therefore not be expected to highly rate items representing characteristics that support SDL in such environments. The helpfulness of the environment as indicated by the individual SDLPS-T scores show that of the 90 organizations scored, 65.5% have moderately supportive environments from the HR manager's point of view.

Of the respondents, 9% scored low. This indicates that from the respondent's point of view, characteristics identified in the self-directed learning literature as being helpful are not perceived to be present in the particular learning situation. The small number of low scores suggests that the majority of respondents in the survey indicated at least moderately supportive environments for SDL.

Twenty-five percent of the respondents scored high on the SDLPS-T. Higher levels of helpfulness indicate that factors, identified in the SDL literature as being helpful in a learning environment, have been rated by HR managers as being present in the organization. The presence of these factors in the learning environment should help learners with the SDL process. Findings from the second part of the survey for these organizations can then be examined to develop a broader understanding of training from the HR managers' viewpoint.

Approaches to Training

Items in the second part of the survey dealt with the extent to which specific approaches to training and learning were used in an organization. The data are summarized in Table 15.1.

As may be expected, mean scores varied across items, but overall, the outcome is consistent with organizations that actively promote training and learning. The items with the lower scores are informal mentorship, computer-assisted instruction, reflecting on experience, and visits to other organizations. While these approaches are valued as facilitating learning in organizations, they do not figure prominently in the approaches to training and learning in this group of organizations. Nonetheless, the range of formal and informal approaches that occur is in keeping with a highly supportive learning

200

Table 15.1.   Extent Approaches to Training/Learning are Used

Approach	Mean
Courses by training staff	3.93
Courses by external staff	3.33
Formal coaching – employees	3.26
Informal coaching – employees	3.73
Formal coaching – supervisors	3.40
Informal coaching – supervisors	3.80
Formal mentorship	2.01
Informal mentorship	2.86
Computer – assisted instruction	2.60
Visits to other organizations	1.80
Reflection on experience	2.36
Formal exchange of expertise	3.50
Learn from mistakes	3.73
Constructive criticism & feedback	4.06

environment. In particular, informal coaching, encouraging criticism and feedback, learning from mistakes, and exchange of expertise among co-workers are identified with promoting SDL. As Kops (1993) suggested, a balanced approach to training and development in which a relevant formal program is developed and SDL is encouraged and supported has greatest advantage for organizations and learners. The organizations identified with highly supportive learning environments appear to offer such a balanced approach to training and learning.

Resources for Learning

Respondents were asked to indicate the extent to which various resources were available to learners. These resources are reported in the literature as supporting SDL (e.g., Guglielmino & Guglielmino, 1988; Carré, 1994; Candy, 1991). The data are presented in Table 15.2.

As anticipated in organizations that are supportive of SDL, time in the work schedule for learning is a resource that is most readily available. Networking between employees and, to a lesser extent,

Table 15.2. Extent Resources are Available for Learning	
Resource	Mean
Library	2.20
Learning Center	2.60
Index subject experts	2.53
Connect external experts	2.80
Learning contracts	2.66
Network between employees	3.40
Time in work schedule	3.60
Learn – to learn	2.20

contact with external experts were also rated relatively high as resources that assist learning. Overall, the other resources are rated as being much less available to learners in these organizations, which is somewhat surprising for organizations with apparent supportive environments for SDL. For example, the availability of libraries/reading rooms and programs to develop employee learning skills were rated relatively low, and learning resource centers, information about internal expertise, and the use of learning contracts were not rated much higher.

Changes in Training

All respondents in the selected organizations indicated that changes had occurred in training in their organizations within the last five years. The type of changes that occurred are outlined in Table 15.3.

Of the typical functions performed by trainers, approaches to needs assessment changed the least. Changes of the training department within the organization structure occurred in less than 70% of the organizations, while skill requirements of trainers changed in just under 75% of the cases. All other factors changed in 4 out of 5 of the organizations with highly supportive learning environments. When asked to describe the key changes that occurred, increases in both the number of training staff and training budgets were most frequently mentioned. Change in training policy was mentioned by several

Table 15.3. Changes in Training

Type of change	% of organizations
Number of training staff	80
Training budget	80
Evaluation of training	80
Training methods	80
Needs assessment	60
Trainers skill requirements	73
Trainers responsibilities	80
Training in organization	67

respondents, specifically the development of a training and development policy, policy for reimbursement of external training, and the establishment of minimum employee training requirements. Resources and methods for training were also identified, including creating a skill inventory to track internal experts, and increased training in remote sites. Overall, there appears to be considerable change occurring in training in these organizations, which implies that the role of training is changing in organizations that have a SDL orientation. Further, it suggests that these organizations are adopting a broader view of training and learning.

CONTINUING RESEARCH

As discussed earlier, this initial phase of the study is a starting point leading to further investigation. There are several possibilities for further examination of the survey results.

Developing an SDLPS-T profile would provide more detailed feedback about the way human resource managers responded. This profile would break down the SDLPS-T score into component scores that reveal specific areas for further investigation. This allows determination, with more precision, of how respondents rated the learning environment. As researchers determine which factors were scored high or low, specific comparisons could be made with the second part of the survey.

In-depth interviews could be done to find out if the oral responses of HR managers is consistent with their responses on the survey. This would provide more detail about the organization and would allow for the construction of a more extensive picture of what the training environment is like.

The SDLPS-T could be administered to a group of employees in selected organizations. This would give a more comprehensive view of training and increase the accuracy and amount of data on training in the organization.

Lack of knowledge and resistance toward SDL exists, which may result in discrepancies in the way human resource managers responded to the survey. Lack of support for SDL depends on each organization's specific needs (Foucher, 1998) and varies according to different organizational characteristics, including business strategy, nature of tasks performed, etc. (Foucher, 1995). These types of variations could be investigated further to determine what effect they have on perceptions of the helpfulness of the environment for SDL. The next planned phase of this study is to examine more closely the role of trainers and the training departments in the group of organizations that are highly supportive of SDL. In-depth interviews will be conducted with organizational representatives, including human resource managers, trainers, and selected senior managers in each organization. The interviews will explore several issues in these organizations, including how trainers and training departments adapt in a SDL-oriented setting. What new or different roles and tasks do trainers undertake? What skills and knowledge trainers require to handle new/changed roles?

SUMMARY

The findings in this paper are the first phase of a larger study of the role of trainers in SDL-oriented organizations. The primary purpose of this first phase was to identify organizations that were supportive of SDL. The modified version of the SDLPS-T was used for this purpose. Further examination may be done, as indicated above, to increase the level of confidence that organizations with highly supportive learning environments are included in the second phase of the study. The results of Part Two of the survey provided insight into the training approaches and learning resources used in these organizations. As well, there is evidence that change in training has occurred in these organizations. These findings indicate that these issues are worth exploring further as planned.

REFERENCES

Blackwood, C.C. (1994). Applying self-directed learning principles in the technical training of a high-risk industry. In R. Hiemstra & R. Brockett (Eds.), Overcoming resistance to self-direction in adult learning, New Directions for Adult and Continuing Education, No. 64, pp.47-54. San Francisco (California): Jossey-Bass.

Candy, P. (1991). Self-direction for lifelong learning. San Francisco: Jossey-Bass.

Carré, P. (1994). Self-directed learning in French professional education. In H.B. Long & Associates, New ideas about self-directed learning. Norman, OK: University of Oklahoma, pp.139-148.

Foucher, R. (1995). Factors affecting organizational policies and practices regarding self-directed learning. In H.B. Long & Associates, New dimensions in self-directed learning. Norman, OK: University of Oklahoma, pp.293-314.

Foucher, R. (1996). Enhancing self-directed learning in the workplace: A model and a research agenda. In H.B. Long & Associates, Current developments in self-directed learning. Norman, OK: University of Oklahoma, pp.23-35.

Foucher, R. (1997). Self-directed learning in the workplace: Summary report on research and practice in Quebec. In H.B. Long & Associates Expanding horizons in self-directed learning. Norman: Public Managers Center, University of Oklahoma, pp.129-138.

Foucher, R. (1998). Self-directed learning in the workplace: Data on the gap between individual and organizational practices. In H.B. Long & Associates Developing paradigms for self-directed learning. Norman: Public Managers Center, University of Oklahoma, pp.169-177.

Foucher, R. & Brezot, F. (1997). Self-directed learning in health care institutions: An analysis of policies and practices. In H. B. Long & Associates, Expanding horizons in self-directed learning. Norman, OK: University of Oklahoma, 101-116.

Guglielmino, L., & Guglielmino, P. (1988). Self-directed learning in business and industry: An information age imperative. In H. B. Long & Associates, Self-directed learning: Application and theory. Athens: University of Georgia, 125-148.

Kops, W. (1993). Self-planned learning of managers in an organizational context. In H. B. Long & Associates, Emerging perspectives of self-directed learning. Norman, OK: University of Oklahoma, 247-261.

Kops, W. (1997). Managers as self-directed learners: Comparing findings of studies in private and public sector organizations. In H. B. Long & Associates, Expanding horizons in Self-directed learning. Norman, OK: University of Oklahoma, 71-86.

Landriault, J., & Gosselin, A. (1997). Perceptions and intentions of training managers regarding self-directed learning. In H. B. Long & Associates, Expanding horizons in self-directed learning. Norman OK: University of Oklahoma, 117-128.

Long, H.B. & Morris, S. (1995). Self-directed learning in business and industry: A review of the literature, 1983-1993. In H. B. Long & Associates (Eds.), <u>New dimensions in self- directed learning</u>. Norman, OK: University of Oklahoma, 367-381.

Phelan, T.D. (1996). Interests of corporate trainers in application of self-directed learning techniques in training. In H. B. Long & Associates, <u>Current developments in self-directed learning</u>. Norman, OK: University of Oklahoma, 51-64.

Pilling-Cormick, J. (1996). Development of the self-directed learning perception scale. (Doctoral dissertation, University of Toronto).

CHAPTER SIXTEEN

FURTHER INVESTIGATION OF ORGANIZATIONS IDENTIFIED AS SUPPORTING A SELF–DIRECTED APPROACH TO TRAINING

Jane Pilling-Cormick & William J. Kops

The overall purpose of the study is to examine the changing role of trainers in organizations that support a self-directed (SD) approach to training. The study consists of two phases: (1) identifying organizations with supportive SD training environments suggesting there is support for self-directed learning (SDL) and (2) within those organizations examining the changing role of trainers. The purpose of the first phase is to identify organizations that support an SD approach to training by: a) initially identifying such organizations based on human resource managers' viewpoints (Pilling-Cormick & Kops, in press) and b) determining learners' viewpoints of training environments in those same organizations. This paper reports the results of the identification process from the learners' perceptions of the nature of the training environment. Results indicate learners similarly rate organizations initially identified by human resource (HR) managers as being supportive of an SD approach to training.

IDENTIFYING ORGANIZATIONS: THE HR MANAGER'S PERSPECTIVE

Initially, the Self-Directed Learning Perception Scale (SDLPS-T), a 57 item self-report instrument designed to identify the existence of characteristics that support self-directed learning (SDL) was administered to HR managers in 90 organizations. Based on the SDLPS-T scores, twenty-three organizations were initially identified with training environments that support a self-directed approach to training (Pilling-Cormick & Kops, in press). In reporting these results at the 1997 International Symposium on Self-Directed Learning, there were suggestions that a more comprehensive perspective of these training environments be determined in order to ensure the appropriateness of the SDLPS-T to identify organizations with a SD approach to training. Further, it was suggested that a learner's perspective of the training environment be considered.

USING THE SDLPS-T IN THIS STUDY

Since the original version of the SDLPS was based on a traditional classroom setting, modifications were made to produce the SDLPS-T, training version (Pilling-Cormick & Kops, in press). Wording changes did not violate the validity of the original instrument since items were directly based on a theoretical chart derived from the context-based environmental characteristics dimension of the Self-Directed Learning Process model (Pilling-Cormick, 1998). The SDLPS-T is used in this part of the study to determine employees'/learners' perceptions of the training environment. Key definitions used in the SDLPS-T and the study appear below to clarify and ease interpretation.

- *Self-directed learning* is an approach to learning in which individuals determine their priorities (what to learn) and choose from various resources available (how to learn). Individuals play an active role in developing a system of meaning to interpret events, ideas and circumstances.

208

- *Trainer* is the person(s) in the organization who helps individuals improve performance in their job normally by providing organized learning experiences. The trainer is typically responsible for determining what is to be learned and how it will be learned.

- *Training* is planned learning (education) offered by an organization that helps learners to acquire new knowledge, information, and skills in order to better perform their jobs.

- *Training activity* is an event where learners either formally or informally participate in training.

- *Training environment* is the physical and affective conditions specific to training that influence training activities. Physical conditions include anything that can be perceived by the five senses and described objectively, e.g. training policy manual, room temperature. Affective conditions are sensed emotionally by those participating in training, e.g. psychological climate in the training setting, perceived support for new ideas.

- *Training site* is the location where the training activity takes place. Typically the training activity takes place in a classroom (formal course), but may occur elsewhere in the organization (informal training), such as at a learner's desk/office (computer-assisted learning package).

- *Organizational environment* includes the conditions in the organization that generally influence training, e.g. organizational goals, resource availability, management style.

- *Learners* refers to employees of the organization who participate in training activities.

IDENTIFYING ORGANIZATIONS: THE LEARNERS' PERSPECTIVE

By surveying learners who recently participated in a training activity, it is expected that a broader perspective of the training environment in organizations initially identified as having a SD approach to training "will emerge." This should provide more assurance in identifying organizations that are supportive of a SD approach to training. This is important for the next phase of the study that will examine the role of trainers in organizations that are supportive of SDL.

Administrative Procedure

In the initial survey, 23 of the 90 organizations indicated a highly supportive training environment exists. The respondents were senior HR managers in member organizations of a provincial association of human resource professionals. The association membership represented a variety of organizations in terms of both size and type. The follow-up survey was conducted with learners from the highly supportive organizations. These organizations received an initial letter requesting their participation. Six of the original 23 organizations agreed to participate in the follow-up survey. Participating organizations agreed to have 10 to 15 employees who had recently completed a training activity or event respond to the SDLPS-T. Each participating organization received copies of the SDLPS-T and modified administration instructions emphasizing that responses should focus on experiences in training activities. Five of the six organizations completed the SDLPS-T with respondent numbers of 10, 7, 8, 9, and 12 respectively for a total of 46 learner/respondents. A standard computer program calculated the SDLPS-T scores for each respondent.

Results

The focus of the SDLPS-T is the physical and affective conditions specific to training that influence training activities. Organizations with high SDLPS-T scores have supportive training environments for SDL. As well as an overall score, a SDLPS-T Profile was developed for each organization that produces five component scores. The profile component scores show in detail the extent of support of the training environment within an organization. Each profile component score represents an environmental component of the SDLP model (Pilling-Cormick, in press). The SDLPS-T overall scores are outlined in Table 16.1 and the SDLPS-T component scores for each organization are in Table 16.2. The scores indicate how learners in each organization rate the support of the training environment in their organization and allow for comparisons between the scores of learners and HR managers.

Similarities Between SDLPS-T Overall Scores

When considering scores from each organization (Table 16.1), both HR managers or learners score the environment as being supportive of SDL. This finding is not surprising since these organizations were initially identified as having supportive training environments, nonetheless it is reassuring that both groups score as they do.

The SDLPS-T learners' scores are all in the middle to high moderate range while the managers' scores are in the high range. In part, the overall lower scores of learners may be explained because HR managers tend to perceive things about the organization more positively; for example, the learning environment as more supportive than learners. The fact that overall scores from both groups are in the higher ranges provides support that the SDLPS-T is a useful indicator of the extent to which the training environment is supportive.

Table 16.1.   Overall SDLPS-T Overall Scores

Organization	Learner	HR Manager
1	290	361
2	266	361
3	252	346
4	311	359
5	269	356
Group Score	278	357

Patterns Among Group Profile Component Scores

By examining group profile component scores, interesting patterns emerge in the HR managers' and learners' scores (see Table 16.2). There are similarities in the rankings of the two group profile component scores providing additional support for the SDLPS-T as a means for identifying organizations with supportive training environments. For the purposes of this phase of the study, comparisons of group profile component scores for managers and learners will help explain differences in perspectives of the training environment.

Group profile component scores were ranked separately in Table 16.2 to simplify pattern identification. Even though all group profile component scores are in the supportive range, the rankings make it possible to determine if components were similarly ranked in terms of support. It is then possible to determine if organizations scored highly supportive by the managers are similarly scored by learners.

Table 16.2. SDLPS-T Scores and Profile Component Scores

Organization	Learner Scores				
	C1	C2	C3	C4	C5
1	314	327	283	262	310
2	275	294	272	241	281
3	243	295	243	241	261
4	312	299	281	307	331
5	271	312	246	252	287
Group Profile Component Scores	283	305	265	261	294
Group Profile Component Score Ranking	3	1	4	5	2

Organization	HR Manager Scores				
	C1	C2	C3	C4	C5
1	411	421	364	341	354
2	374	374	384	355	349
3	299	327	364	346	354
4	224	397	353	337	413
5	318	374	312	341	399
Group Profile Component Scores	325	379	355	344	374
Group Component Score Ranking	5	1	3	4	2

C1 = Organizational Characteristics
C2 = Training Site Characteristics
C3 = Way the Organization Functions
C4 = Way the Training Activity Functions
C5 = Climate for Building Relationships

While the total learners' component scores are lower in almost every instance, the rankings of component scores are very similar between learners and HR managers suggesting that learners and managers have similar perceptions of the training environment (Table 16.1). Based on the group SDLPS-T scores, both learners and HR managers rank "training site characteristics" (C2) highest. Both learners and HR managers rank "climate for building relationships" (C5) as the second highest component. "The way the training activity functions" (C4) had the lowest ranking by learners, and only slightly higher by HR managers. The remaining two components (C1 and C3) rank between the other components. The comparable rankings support the claim that the SDLPS-T is meaningful in assessing the training environment in organizations.

Component Score Comparison Within Organizations
The overall SDLPS-T score is broken down into five component profile scores, each representing a component of a supportive SDL training environment found in the Self-Directed Learning Process model. Each of these profile component scores is based on a specific set of supportive characteristics. By studying the profile component scores of HR managers and learners within each of the five organizations (Table 16.2), additional evidence is available about the support in the training environments. These findings are a starting point for further investigation of training environments in future stages of the study; particularly the trainers' roles within these environments.

Many of the SDLPS-T items within the components refer specifically to trainers. Further component score analysis will assist in providing details about the role trainers play in organizations identified as having supportive training environments for SDL. Comparisons between these component scores indicate any major discrepancies between the perceptions of learners and HR managers on specific characteristics within the environment. Organization specific patterns among profile component scores emerge giving a broader understanding of what constitutes a supportive training environment in organizations scoring high on the SDLPS-T. For the purposes of this stage of the study, considering these types of comparisons provides further evidence that the SDLPS-T is a good indicator of supportive training environments because there were not only similarities among HR managers' and learners' overall SDLPS-T scores, but also similar patterns in the profile component scores. To illustrate this additional support, comparisons for the five organizations follow with suggestions of how additional component score analysis will allow for further discoveries.

Organization 1. Both learners and the HR manager consider "training site characteristics" (C2) to be the most supportive component, followed by "organizational characteristics" (C1). They agree on the support of physical characteristics. They both consider "way the training activity functions" (C4) to be least supportive. There appears to be agreement between three of the five components ratings.

Where the HR manager and learners differ is in terms of "climate for building relationships" (C5). Learners rate C5 lower than the HR manager. This leads to questions for further investigation including: In what ways do the learners rate the climate lower? Is the trainer in this organization in a position to make changes to these specific training environment characteristics?

Organization 2. Even though overall component scores indicated support for SDL, one of the largest differences between learners' and the HR manager's overall SDLPS-T scores appears for organization 2 (Table 16.1). The profile component scores are a good starting point to begin this type of investigation to determine why the difference exists. The component scores and the ranking of these scores do not correspond. For example, the learners did not rate "way the organization functions" as high as the HR manager did. It would be useful to determine in what ways the HR manager feels the organization is supportive in this component. What is the role of the trainer in determining how the organization structures training activities? Are learners' needs considered when scheduling training activities and what role does the trainer play in this scheduling?

Organization 3. This organization also has one of the largest differences between learners' and HR manager's scores. However, unlike organization 2, both learners and the HR manager agree on the rating of the "climate for building relationships" (C5). "Organizational characteristics" are ranked relatively lower by the HR manager when compared to the other HR managers' component rankings. This is surprising because HR managers could be expected to rate organizational characteristics higher. Questions then arise such as: Is there suitable access to organizational learning resources? Can learners find the information they need?

Organization 4. In the overall SDLPS-T scores, organization 4 has the highest agreement between learners' and the HR manager's scores. This would indicate that there are more similarities between perceptions in this organization. Patterns among the rankings of the profile component scores may be typical of a truly highly supportive environment. In future studies, comparisons of profile component scores should be carried out to determine if over time, there is repetition of the patterns among rankings.

Organization 5. This organization also has high agreement between learners' and the HR manager's scores. In particular, both agree that the "way the organization functions" (C3) is the least supportive of the component scores leading to questions such as: Does the organization consider individual needs when scheduling training activities? Are various training activities promoted as being SD? Further component score analysis would determine reasons for this rating.

FUTURE RESEARCH

To discover more about the supportive characteristics of the training environments and in particular, the role of trainers within these organizations, future research will include: additional profile development, profile component score analysis and in-depth interviews.

Additional Profile Development

Since overall SDLPS-T scores and patterns among profile component scores of the five organizations involved in this phase of the study suggest the SDLPS-T is a good indicator of supportive SDL training environments, development of SDLPS-T profiles for the HR managers in the remaining 18 supportive organizations would reveal useful patterns in the components. Some components may appear more consistently in training environments. By discovering patterns among component scores, it becomes possible to determine which characteristics appear to be difficult to foster. Further investigation of these components could lead to the development of supportive training environments for SDL.

Profile Component Score Analysis

A more detailed profile component score analysis will reveal the degree to which characteristics within each of the components exists. An indication of this type of investigation appears in the results from the five profiles developed in this phase of the study. By examining specific components, further information such as the role the trainer plays within each component will emerge as responses to SDLPS-T items about trainers are analyzed. For instance, is the trainer seen as a resource available upon request? Are there times established for learners to approach trainers to ask questions? By using a component score analysis, it becomes possible to learn more about component specific characteristics scored as supportive.

In-Depth Interviews

In the literature, a number of researchers (Kops, 1993; Foucher and Brezot, 1997; Hatcher, 1997) advocate that trainers need to revise their role in order to better provide resources for learning. More specifically, they suggest that trainers become learning facilitators with varied roles such as coach, consultant and critical reactor. Based on the response of HR managers to the initial survey, it is evident that there is considerable change happening in training approaches in organizations with supportive environments for SDL. Among other changes, organizations are adopting a broader view of training and learning, which implies the role of trainers is changing. Further phases of this study will attempt to document these changes.

As well as being influenced by training environments, trainers play a part in shaping the environment. Foucher (1996) attributes a good deal of importance to the role played by training managers in the support of SDL because they have a strong influence on the policies and practices that affect training in organizations. The SDLPS-T Profile component scores developed in this study are a starting point for revealing supportive characteristics which are often directly influenced by the trainer, and it is anticipated the in-depth interviews will reveal more details.

In-depth interviews will explore several main issues, including how trainers and training departments adapt in a SDL setting? What new or different roles and tasks do trainers undertake? What skills and knowledge do trainers need to handle their new/changed roles? By combining findings from the SDLPS-T Profiles and in-depth interviews, an overall picture of the changing role of trainers in training environments and the organization will emerge.

SUMMARY

In this part of the study, the SDLPS-T overall and profile component scores of learners were consistent with those of HR managers in the same organizations suggesting the SDLPS-T is useful in assessing the training environment in organizations. Both HR managers and learners indicated a supportive environment for SDL based on their respective SDLPS-T scores. These results give confidence to the selection of organizations for future phases of the study. Patterns among SDLPS-T profile component scores also confirm the use of the SDLPS-T as an indicator of supportive SD training environments and point to further research opportunities about each of these environments and the role of trainers within them.

REFERENCES

Hatcher, T.G. (1997). The ins and outs of self-directed learning. Training & development, 51(2), pp.34-39.

Foucher, R. (1996). Enhancing self-directed learning in the workplace: A model and research agenda. In H.B. Long & Associates. Current developments in self-directed learning (pp.23-35). Norman: Public Managers Center, College of Education, University of Oklahoma.

Foucher, R., & Brezot, F. (1997). Self-directed learning in health care institutions: An analysis of policies and practices. In H.B. Long & Associates. Expanding horizons in self-directed learning (pp.106-116). Norman: Public Managers Center, College of Education, University of Oklahoma.

Kops, W. J. (1993). Self-planned learning efforts of managers in an organizational context. In H.B. Long & Associates. Emerging perspectives of self-directed learning (pp.247-261) Norman: Public Managers Center, College of Education, University of Oklahoma.

Pilling-Cormick, J. (1998). The self-directed learning process model. In H.B. Long & Associates. Contemporary ideas and practices in self-directed learning (pp.89-102). Norman: Public Managers Center, University of Oklahoma.

Pilling-Cormick, J. (in press). The SDLPS profile: Using the SDLPS to implement SDL. In H.B. Long & Associates. New ideas about self-directed learning.

Pilling-Cormick, J., & Kops, W. J. (in press). Self-directed learning in the workplace: An exploratory study to identify organizations with a self-directed learning approach to training. In H.B. Long & Associates. New ideas about self-directed learning.

CHAPTER SEVENTEEN

FURTHER INVESTIGATION INTO THE USE OF THE SDLPS IN A CLINICAL SETTING

Jane Pilling-Cormick
Robert J. Bulik

This chapter presents the findings from the second phase of an ongoing study investigating the use of the Self-Directed Learning Perception Scale (SDLPS-C), a 57 item self-report instrument designed to identify factors that support self-directed learning (SDL), in a community-based clinical setting with third year medical students. The overall purpose of the second phase was to continue to examine the support of learning environments for medical students when they are away from the university campus in community-based clinical rotation sites. Similar to the results reported from Phase One of our study (Pilling-Cormick & Bulik, 1999), results of Phase Two again point to the key role the SDLPS plays in evaluating the community-based, clinical aspect of medical education in terms of SDL, and reinforces the results of the initial study.

An indication of the importance for encouraging the development of SDL skills in medical students was previously documented in our Phase One study report. This topic continues to be so central to the medical profession that the <u>Journal of the American Medical Association</u> (<u>JAMA</u>) will dedicate their 1999 Educational issue to professional development across the medical education continuum. One of the central research questions the journal asks in its Call for Papers is this: "What can learning theories tell us about how to stimulate self-directed learning?" (JAMA, 1998: 1786) While new approaches to teaching medical students, such as the problem-based learning (PBL) curriculum, have evolved on campuses across the country, little attention has been focused on the training that occurs away from the university at community-based clinics. This chapter draws attention to the need to monitor clinical sites, and the effectiveness of the SDLPS to provide valuable feedback in terms of how supportive sites are in relation to SDL.

INITIAL INVESTIGATION

The preliminary exploration of using a clinical version of the SDLPS provides the background and initial argument for monitoring medical students as they progress through their community-based, clinical training; recommendations for future research that included a larger administration of the clinical-SDLPS were also made (Pilling-Cormick & Bulik, 1999). Since the basis for the original version of the SDLPS was a formal education or classroom setting, this first phase provided an indication of the applicability of the design of this instrument for a clinical setting. In Phase One, a group of third year medical students from Ohio University - College of Osteopathic Medicine (OU-COM) completed the SDLPS. This initial phase of the study was the first time the instrument was used in a clinical setting and as such, provided invaluable input for modifications. From the results of Phase One, four research objectives appeared.

1. Further exploration of resistance to SDL to determine if similarities occur with other samples.

2. Development of instructions to ease the administration of the SDLPS in a clinical setting, without biasing responses.

3. Administration of the SDLPS to several groups to discover similarities in the way they respond.

4. Profile development to provide information about specific clinics and explore the practical implications of the SDLPS results.

SAMPLE

Similar to the Phase One study, the medical students involved in Phase Two of this study were in their third year of medical school at the University of Texas Medical Branch (UTMB) in Galveston, Texas. Approximately two hundred medical students were involved in each of the four years of medical school at UTMB. Each month, fifteen to twenty students in their third year of medical school training participate in the Family Medicine course, which utilizes community-based, clinical sites spread across the State of Texas.

Upon returning to the university campus from their four-week community-based clinical rotations, students were asked about their experiences through the format of a focus group; the SDLPS was added to the list of topics covered during this session.

METHODOLOGY

The methodology for Phase Two involved three pilot administrations during three focus groups of the SDLPS with the purpose of collecting additional feedback on semantics and conducting an actual administration using revised survey instructions. Additionally, each pilot administration was considered progressive in nature; what was learned from the previous administration was applied to subsequent groups.

First Pilot
Because of the change in venue, a preliminary investigation of wording of the SDLPS occurred prior to the first pilot. In order to further explore resistance, clarification of the wording and corresponding definitions emphasized how and why the instrument is suitable for use in a clinical setting. For example: (1) Rotation site is the location where learning takes place in a clinical setting, be it a medical clinic, office, or hospital; and (2) Learner is a medical student or intern. The definitions reinforce the intent and applica-

bility of using the SDLPS, but the wording of the questions was made specific for a clinical setting. This first pilot group of 20 third year medical students from UTMB did not complete the SDLPS but instead, provided feedback on wording of the survey questions. The intent of this first pilot study was to identify any semantic concerns.

Second Pilot

In the second pilot, 14 third year medical students from UTMB completed the SDLPS. No learner opinions were sought prior to administration of the SDLPS; new administration instructions that more clearly define the intent of the survey in terms of clinical education were used. The intent of this second pilot study was to conduct an administration of the SDLPS with the possibility of scoring the survey and beginning to develop a clinical profile. Medical student opinions on the wording of the survey questions occurred after the SDLPS was completed.

Third Pilot

Full implementation of the SDLPS occurred with 13 third year medical students from UTMB. Administration instructions were provided to the students, but no other guidelines or discussions occurred. After the medical students completed the instrument, their opinions were again solicited in a focus group format. At this stage in the study, development of profiles allowed for the discovery of how learners respond in general and to discover if trends appear in this preliminary investigation.

RESULTS

Two forms of results appear: Learner reactions and data analysis. Learner reactions for each pilot led to modifications for the subsequent administrations. After the third pilot, SDLPS scores and profiles were established.

Learner Reactions

One objective of Phase Two was to see if the SDLPS could be changed, but not modified drastically from its original form, in order to reduce terminology problems identified during Phase One. Reactions from the three pilots aided in the development of a SDLPS version suitable for use in a clinical setting.

First Pilot

Results from the first pilot in Phase Two determined any terminology problems with a sample (n = 20) from a different medical school. Concerns centered on how to ask questions that included references to the university. For example, do learners even consider using university resources when in a clinical setting. Learners appeared to see themselves outside the control of the university when they were at their clinical sites. Interestingly, while there was a sense of being in the community and free of the constraints of the university, students showed a preference for the term "student" to that of "learner". This finding contradicted what OU-COM students in Phase One reported. It was decided to go back again to the theoretical chart to reword items so that there were few changes from the original educational version and that those changes would appear consistently among items. The words "office/clinic" were used throughout along with "preceptor". The term "learner" remained. Wording standardization across items ensured that each question matched the purpose on the theoretical chart from the original SDLP model.

Second Pilot

The second group to complete the SDLPS (n = 14), showed less resistance to examining SDL as the change in the wording of the questions clarified some issues. Similar to the first sample group, these third year medical students participated in a focus group immediately following their month-long Family Medicine rotation. A new set of administrative instructions also appeared to aid the students in understanding the intent of the survey, and resulted in less concern about item wording. When using the new administration instructions, it was easier for students to complete the SDLPS since only 2 of the 14 surveys were incomplete and each had only one missing response.

Additionally, in this second pilot, there were not as many specific concerns about wording and the learners report that overall, the instrument is "good." Questions dealing with university characteristics appeared to still cause some minor concern since some learners were actually completing their rotations on campus. For instance, there was concern that asking about having access to university resources would lead to a different response if learners were on campus. Even if learners bring resources with them to their community-based preceptor's location, the question still remains one of whether they have access to further university resources from the distant office/clinic.

Just as the first pilot study in Phase Two influenced the second study, findings from the second pilot study were a stimulus for changes for the third pilot in two areas: (1) Interacting with the university; and (2) Characteristics of the office/clinic. Modifications took place to five items dealing with physical characteristics of the university to emphasize the interactions learners have with the university while in their clinical placements, including reference to electronic and traditional learning resources. For example, students were asked if the university provides up to date electronic and traditional learning resources. Another item asked if there was access to electronic and other university learning resources in addition to learning resources in the office/clinic.

Third Pilot

The third and final pilot study in Phase Two yielded an overwhelmingly positive response to the item wording. Similar to the first and second sample groups in Phase Two of the study, the third group of third year medical students participated in a focus group immediately following their month-long Family Medicine rotation. The learners felt that the wording of the questions was "good," and that the SDLPS-C would be suitable for use in a clinical setting. Based on these findings from the third pilot, SDLPS score calculations and pilot profile development were generated for each of the community-based clinics.

Data Analysis

Calculation of the overall scores allowed for the discovery of how learners rated the support of community-based clinics in general terms. More specific responses evolved with the SDLPS profile development, which provided details of how students in a certain group or setting responded and revealed information specifically relevant to the clinics being surveyed. A more comprehensive view evolved of characteristics rated as supportive. From this data analysis both general and clinic specific trends appeared.

Table 17.1.   SDLPS Scores and Profile Component Scores

Clinic	SDLPS Score	Component Scores				
		C1	C2	C3	C4	C5
1	277	299	421	166	252	320
2	238	411	374	166	210	226
3	277	187	281	218	285	320
4	307	374	444	239	281	320
5	213	131	374	208	187	231
6	315	281	397	260	295	354
7	310	337	468	229	299	320
8	322	94	468	301	323	359
9	243	131	421	197	229	271
10	353	281	468	343	341	364
11	410	281	444	395	411	443

C1 = University Characteristics   C4 = Way the Rotation Functions
C2 = Clinical Site Characteristics   C5 = Climate for Building Relationships
C3 = Way the University Functions

General Trends

General trends in the SDLPS scores are interesting to note, but interpretation must be done with care since one individual's perceptions of an independent clinic is the basis for the SDLPS score reported above. Results indicate that characteristics supportive of SDL do exist.

The overall sample score is in the high moderate range (297) indicating that the group, as a whole, felt their learning environments supported a self-directed approach, but not excessively so. The standard deviation is higher, so there may not be a high consensus among the group; however, that is not surprising since each student is basing his or her responses on a separate clinic and experiences in that clinic. Still, it is useful to see that generally, the group feels community-based clinical learning environments are supportive.

From here, determining what ways the individual learning environments are supportive becomes crucial and the profile component scores allow for these comparisons. Each profile is specific to the individual clinic, meaning comparisons between scores must be done with caution. Yet scores reflect the experiences of the learner in the clinical setting and provide a starting point for further exploration.

University Physical Characteristics (C1). Four students felt the physical characteristics of the university were not supportive. Is access to university resources limited when learners are in a clinical setting? Perhaps encouragement for learners to interact with the university does not occur? Should this type of interaction be encouraged or do learners see themselves as being disassociated from the university? Is this what the medical program is designed to do or should faculty developers be investigating ways for learners not to feel cut off from the university? Traditionally, in a supportive SDL environment, interaction with the university or institution would be desirable. But if the intent is to provide space and not emphasize this component, then a lower score for the university being supportive while learners are in clinical settings would be sought. Further component analysis will reveal how learners feel about the support of characteristics in this component and if a trend develops.

Clinical Characteristics (C2). Ten of the 11 scores rated C2 as high, indicating clinical site characteristics are supportive. This is a positive finding since clinics appear to be physically structured to support a SDL approach. Survey questions centered on providing "personal comfort" and providing a "place for learners to think about learning while at the clinic," are two examples. Component analysis will indicate ways learners in specific clinics feel their particular environments provide support. There will obviously be variations according to the clinic, but being aware that clinical characteristics are generally supportive across the group is encouraging.

How the University Functions (C3). There were few components with "never happens" scores. Yet four students rate C3, the way the university functions, as low. Does the university consider the impact of administrative paperwork? Are learners asked about the appropriateness of the rotation length? Further investigation into ways that these students feel the university is not supportive would reveal areas to monitor in future administrations.

How the Rotation Functions (C4). For the most part, this component's rating fell in the moderate range. Of course each clinic operates or functions in a different way, but it is interesting to note that as a group, the learners perceived the rotation structure to be moderately supportive. There still may be room for improvement in this area. Component analysis of specific profiles will reveal in what ways students feel the rotation is not as supportive as it possibly may be. Perhaps there is not a lot of learner input into the rotation design. It will be interesting to see if future administrations produce similar moderate scores for this component.

Climate for Building Relationships (C5). Only two of the 11 rated the climate for building relationships in the lower part of the moderate range. The remaining scores were in the upper section of the moderate or the highly supportive range implying that providing support for interacting with others may not be high in all clinics, but certainly does not rank low or as not happening. Providing a climate where the learner feels secure and interacts with others is an important part of a SDL approach. Component analysis will reveal trends in the way the climate for building relationships is specifically supportive.

Clinic Specific Trends

Clinic specific trends reveal learner perceptions of individual clinics. Even though these clinic specific component scores are based on one student's perceptions, they do suggest ways the clinic is supportive and become a starting point for further investigation within that specific clinic. A selection of clinics were chosen here to illustrate potential uses for the profile.

Clinic Five. This clinic had the lowest SDLPS overall score. Clinic 5's rating was low in C1, C3 and C4. Are there trends within these three lower components that would point to a specific area for further investigation? The two lowest of the three deal with opinions about how the university functions and physical characteristics of the university. As seen in earlier pilots, this rating could reflect learners as seeing themselves as not part of the university environment. Further investigation of the role the university plays while learners are in a clinical environment will reveal why learners do not perceive the university to be supportive. Perhaps this learner felt some hostility toward the university. This clinic would be one to possibly target in future studies because of the lower scores in components relating to the university.

Clinics 10 and 11. These two clinics had the highest SDLPS overall scores. Both clinic scores indicated a highly supportive learning environment for C2 through C5. Interestingly, both rated C1 identically and as moderate. Since these were the strongest profiles, investigation will indicate what seems to be working for these learners. Component analysis will determine comparisons between similarly rated high items in the two clinics and allow the investigation to begin about why C1, university characteristics, is lower.

Clinic 2. Highly supportive scores appeared for C1 and C2, while C3 and C4 were lower. The physical characteristics of both the university and clinic were supportive while the way the rotation and university functions was lower. The physical surroundings may be present to support a SDL approach, but the way the university and the rotation operates is not consistent with the physical characteristics. The ways in which the functioning appears lower, will reveal areas for further investigation and possible changes.

RECOMMENDATIONS FOR FUTURE RESEARCH

The continued investigation using the SDLPS in a clinical setting provides invaluable feedback for use of this instrument in diverse settings. The SDLPS is indeed a good instrument for studying the learning environment in a clinical rotation. Future research will provide numerous practical implications for improving the support of learning environments within clinical settings for SDL. Recommendations include:

1. Completing a profile component analysis to reveal the ratings of particular items. One learner's experiences is the basis for the profile in this study. It would be interesting to compare scores from various learners over time. This will allow for identification of specific supportive characteristics within the learning environment. Similarly, targeting characteristics for faculty development and change become possible. Acquiring a quasi-autonomous art of clinical practice, as with learning to apply research-based theory, becomes a concern of the medical practicum (Schon, 1987). Results from the SDLPS profile enable educators to ensure that the learning environment supports this quasi-autonomous approach.

2. Gathering responses according to clinic would become possible. In this way, comparisons of learner responses will help the university identify office/clinics with supportive SDL learning environments. Educators express dissatisfaction with a professional curriculum that cannot prepare students for competence in the indeterminate zones of practice (Schon, 1987:11) and using the SDLPS in clinical settings will help deal with this concern. Discovering discrepancies between preceptors and learners' views would be useful. Do preceptors rate the environment as being supportive when learners do not? If a particular clinic consistently has a lower rating in one component, this may be an area for future investigation.

3. Continuing to administer the SDLPS to different groups of learners. Administering the SDLPS-C in other clinical settings, such as nursing, would present interesting comparisons. Plans for additional administrations with groups of 20 for this study are underway. As larger administrations occur, SDLPS scores will build for specific groups or office/clinics and profile development will continue.

4. Collection of more responses allowing for item analysis to statistically identify problem items for monitoring in future administrations. This may be a more accurate method than merely depending on subjective comments from students. Exploring items missed and calculating Cronbach-alpha correlations with a larger sample would be useful.

5. Using the SDLPS as a stimulus to encourage learners to think of themselves as learning in the clinical environment and about how effective their learning is. It appears that some learners in a clinical setting do not like to view themselves as "students" interacting with the university and others. Further exploration will indicate possible reasons for these thoughts.

6. Administering the SDLPS-E (educational version) to learners prior to leaving the university for clinical placements. Traditionally, physicians are thought to be trained as biotechnical problem-solvers by immersion, first in medical science and

then in supervised clinical practice where they learn to apply research-based techniques (Schon, 1987). But how does the learning environment support using a SDL approach to this problem solving in the clinical setting. This type of administration will indicate if there are vast differences between learning at the university and in a clinical setting. Similarly, it is possible for administration to take place in a clinical type of course before leaving the university. Comparisons between the learning environment prior to and while in clinical training become possible.

SUMMARY

Phase Two of this ongoing study exploring the use of the SDLPS in clinical settings provides support for the continued use of the modified SDLPS-C. Initial resistance toward responding to such an instrument is decreasing with each administration. Minor modifications to wording changes make students feel more comfortable since terms such as "preceptor" and "office/clinic" appear to which students will better relate. Larger administrations will produce more SDLPS scores allowing for more comparisons to be made between clinics, offices or specific groups. Developing SDLPS Profiles for individual rotation sites has the potential of providing invaluable insight into ways an individual office or clinic is supportive. Component analysis of profile scores is a promising step for future research. With the development of the SDLPS profile, practical application of SDLPS scores becomes easy. This second phase of the study provides another stepping stone toward enabling individuals to successfully use the SDLPS in clinical settings.

REFERENCES

JAMA. (1998). Encouraging lifelong professional development across the medical education continuum: Call for papers in medical education. JAMA, 280(20), 1786.

Pilling-Cormick, J., & Bulik, R. (1999). A preliminary study exploring the use of the Self-Directed Learning Perception Scale in a clinical setting. In H.B. Long & Associates, Contemporary ideas and practices in self-directed learning (pp.103-116). Norman, OK: Public Manager's Center, College of Education, University of Oklahoma.

Schon, D.A. (1987). Educating the reflective practitioner. San Francisco: Jossey-Bass.

CHAPTER EIGHTEEN

TEACHERS, SELF–DIRECTED LEARNING AND TEACHER INVOLVEMENT IN SCHOOL REFORM

Vickie Dodds Urban

CONCEPTUAL FRAMEWORK

While there has been talk about the empowerment of teachers (Blase & Blase, 1994; Byham, 1992; Maeroff, 1988), shared decision making (Clift, Veal, Holland, Johnson, & McCarthy, 1995) and site-based management (Blase, Blase, Anderson, & Dugan, 1995; Glickman, 1993), schools have not really changed. Instead, not only are schools run essentially the same way they have always been run, but also the majority of teachers continue to teach the same way they have always taught. There has been little motivation, either internally or externally, for teachers to reform (Evans, 1996). Most teachers believe that the current school reform efforts will be just as short-lived as previous school reform efforts, and the only action they need to take is inaction (Sarason, 1990). So, even though teachers have been asked to reflect upon current conditions, learn new methods, collaborate with others and take on new roles (Fullan, 1993b; Leiberman, 1988; Smylie & Denny, 1990), and even though there are some teachers who have actively taken on and embraced these new challenges (Hart, 1994), the majority of teachers have been resistant (Smylie & Denny, 1990). It is estimated that only 25% of the current teaching population is actively involved in school reform (Evans, 1996). Since school reform efforts need all teachers as active participants (Schlechty, 1997), schools must find a way to engage much greater teacher participation (Sergiovanni, 1996).

There has been some controversy over the comparison of businesses to schools (Schlechty, 1997), but schools could certainly benefit from some of the lessons learned in the business world. When businesses realized the need to implement major changes in their organizational structure, one of the first steps they took before they began to implement any change at all was to study those people in their organizations who already played key roles in the change process, and one of the areas chosen for study was that of self-directedness in learning. The purpose of these studies was to determine whether a link existed between performance on the job and the personality traits found in self-directed learners, that is, people who exhibit initiative, independence and persistence in learning; people who accept responsibility for their own learning and view problems as challenges, not obstacles; people who are capable of self-discipline and have a high degree of curiosity; people who have a strong desire to learn or change; and people who are self-confident (Guglielmino, 1977/1978). Guglielmino and Guglielmino (1992) administered the *Self-Directed Learning Readiness Scale (Form A),* an instrument designed by Guglielmino, to 753 managers and nonmanagers of a large utility company. It was found that those individuals who rated as "outstanding performers" in jobs requiring high levels of creativity, problem-solving ability, and/or a high degree of change scored significantly higher on the *SDLRS* than the remainder of the subjects in the sample. Roberts (1986) and Durr (1992) found similar results.

Research indicates that people who are highly self-directed also possess other personality characteristics associated with self-directedness, such as positive self-concept (Sabbaghian, 1979), high motivational orientation (Reynolds, 1986), greater life satisfaction (Brockett, 1982) and a stronger desire for intellectual development (Shaw, 1987); and the information gained from this research has provided a base that has helped to implement change in the workplace (Durr, 1994). These studies of self-directed learning and the characteristics associated with self-directed learning were timely when considering the later movements of the business world towards empowerment (Wellins, Byham & Wilson, 1991) and self-directed work teams (Fisher, 1993). Interestingly enough, while many groups have been studied for the characteristic of self-directedness in learning, few studies have focused on K-12 teachers.

Just as businesses have had to assess, evaluate and develop new ways to conduct business (Bolman & Deal, 1991; Watkins & Marsick, 1993), schools need to assess, evaluate and develop new ways to conduct the "business of education," but the majority of schools have not done this. Since there has been much written about the necessity of teacher involvement in school reform (Barth, 1990; Fullan, 1993a; Glickman, 1993; Schlechty, 1997; Sizer, 1992), one possible way to increase teacher involvement in school restructuring is to follow the example of business and study those people in schools who already play key roles in the change process. This knowledge can then be used to further develop both the theory and the implementation of teacher involvement in school reform as well as provide clues as to how to reach those teachers who are not currently involved in school reform.

THE STUDY

The research conducted was an exploratory and descriptive case study of a specific cadre of teachers, focusing on their involvement in school reform. The purpose of the research conducted was to try to discover characteristics common to this cadre and to explore the experiences and attitudes of this cadre in regard to their school reform efforts. The primary questions in this study were (a) What are the characteristics common to teachers who become involved in school reform which influence them to become involved? and (b) Is self-directedness in learning among those characteristics?

RESEARCH SAMPLE AND DESIGN

The School District of Broward County, Florida, was chosen as the site for this research. The Coalition of Essential Schools, a national school reform initiative founded by Ted Sizer at Brown University, has been supported by Broward County since 1985. At present, over 60 schools are actively participating in the Coalition and one of the most important components of the support for the Coalition of Essential Schools has been Broward County's development of a cadre of teacher coordinators and facilitators, from whom the sample for this study was drawn.

Fifty-seven facilitators and coordinators were contacted in regard to their possible participation in the research project, and of these a total of 37 coordinators and facilitators completed the quantatative portion of the research. Thirty-five of the 37 volunteered to be interviewed and a total of 13 interviews with participants was completed. As was cautioned by Houle (1961), this group should in no sense be considered a statistical sample as it is too small in size and geographical area to be considered representative of the total population of educators involved in school reform. It should, however, be considered a purposeful sampling (Patton, 1990).

Data were obtained through the use of a General Background Information Form, a Teacher Questionnaire Survey, Guglielmino's *Self-Directed Learning Readiness Scale (Form A)*, and individual teacher interviews. Data collection was completed in two phases. In the first phase, participants completed the General Background Information Form, the Teacher Questionnaire Survey and Guglielmino's *Self-Directed Learning Readiness Scale (Form A)*. In the second phase, selected participants were interviewed. The actual data collection instruments are described below.

Guglielmino's *Self-Directed Learning Readiness Scale (Form A)*
The *SDLRS* is a self-report questionnaire with 58 Likert-type items described to subjects as "a questionnaire designed to gather data on learning preferences and attitudes toward learning" (Guglielmino,

1977/1978). Guglielmino's *Self-Directed Learning Readiness Scale (Form A)* was chosen in order to identify characteristics of Coalition facilitators and coordinators and find out whether the characteristic of readiness for self-directed learning and the characteristics associated with readiness for self-directed learning were common to this group.

General Background Information Form

A General Background Information Form was created to obtain information concerning the participants' age, sex, and ethnic background. Also included on the form were questions concerning the participants' martial status, whether the participants had any children, and if so, whether the children were still living at home.

Teacher Questionnaire Survey

A teacher survey was designed by the researcher to obtain general background information about the Coalition coordinators and facilitators participating in the study. The survey also asked coordinators and facilitators about their present practices in regard to "keeping up" with the current literature and developments in the field of school reform.

Interviews

Phase Two of the study consisted of individual interviews. Building on the data obtained in Phase One, participants were asked to further detail their self-directed learning activities as well as discuss their involvement in school reform efforts in Broward County. After giving a brief description of their professional background, participants were asked to explain their reasons for becoming involved in school reform.

FINDINGS

It was from the analysis of the data obtained from the three instruments and the interview data that the following observations were drawn. The profile that emerged was that of an older, white, married female who is not involved with the responsibilities of child rearing. Also, this female is a highly self-directed learner who actively pursues a wide variety of educational activities.

General Background Information Form Results
Analysis showed that 35 of the 37 participants were white women. Analysis also showed that of those 37 people, 78% (29 people) were coordinators for their schools and 41% (15 people) were both coordinators and facilitators. Analysis of the instrument further showed that 70% (26 people) of participants were 45 years of age or older, 78% (29 people) were married and 76% (28 people) either had no children or had children who were grown and no longer living at home.

Teacher Questionnaire Survey Results
The Teacher Questionnaire Survey was used to obtain information concerning the participants' pursuit of further educational activities, both formal and informal. The data obtained showed that all participants were actively engaged in some kind of learning activity and that all were actively engaged in more than one kind of activity. All 37 participants had attended three or more workshops, conventions, and/or training sessions within the last six months. All 37 had also engaged in what they considered to be educational conversations, that is, conversations concerning education, educational reform or educational teaching strategies, within the last six months, and 31 of the participants (84%) had had 10 or more educational conversations. While only 17 of the 37 participants (46%) had taken formal educational classes within the past six months, all but two participants (95%) had read one or more educational articles; 30 participants (81%) had read at least six articles and 24 participants (65%) had read 10 or more educational articles. Finally, all but 3 of the 37 participants (92%) had read between one and five educational books within the last six months and three participants (8%) had read six or more educational books. Preliminary indications suggest that this group of participants is highly

motivated to pursue additional educational activities in both formal and informal settings, and that these teachers pursue further educational activities on a regular basis.

Guglielmino's Self-Directed Learning Readiness Scale Results
The third instrument used by the researcher was the Self-Directed Learning Readiness Scale; 37 participants completed this survey. An interpretation of the *SDLRS* score has been developed and according to this interpretation sheet, the average *SDLRS* score for adults completing the questionnaire is 214, and the standard deviation is 25.59. Of the 37 participants who took the *SDLRS*, no participant scored lower than 216. For the 13 participants interviewed, no participant scored lower than 221.

Scoring "ranges" of *low, below average, average, above average* and *high* have also been developed for the *SDLRS*. Table 18.3 shows that when looking at all the scores of the participants, only three participants scored in the *average range*, 16 participants scored in the *above average range* and 18 scored in the *high range*. The range from the lowest score to the highest was 63, and all but three of the people scored above the 65th percentile. Also, 21 of the 37 scored in the 90th percentile or above. The mean score of all the participants completing the questionnaire was 250.297, and the standard deviation was 16.548. The participants who were interviewed scored an even higher average of 255.769, and had a standard deviation of 16.589. The range from the lowest score to the highest was 58. Table 18.4 shows that this group also had a higher percentage of people (61%) score in the *high range*.

Table 18.5 shows a comparison of the means of these two groups to the means of other teachers and similarly educated groups as well as a comparison of the low and high scores of the different groups (Guglielmino and Nowocien, 1998). It is interesting to note that only the female executive group had a higher mean score. It is also interesting to note that the lowest score scored by a participant (216) was still higher than the low scores for participants of all the other studies.

Table 18.1.		SPSS Output: SDLRS Scores and Frequencies for all Participants (Valid Cases: 37 — Missing Cases: 0)		
Value	Frequency	Percent	Valid Percent	Cum Percent
216	1	2.7	2.7	2.7
221	1	2.7	2.7	5.4
224	1	2.7	2.7	8.1
227	1	2.7	2.7	10.8
229	1	2.7	2.7	13.5
230	1	2.7	2.7	16.2
235	2	5.4	5.4	21.6
236	1	2.7	2.7	24.3
238	1	2.7	2.7	27.0
239	1	2.7	2.7	29.7
244	1	2.7	2.7	32.4
246	1	2.7	2.7	35.1
247	2	5.4	5.4	40.5
248	1	2.7	2.7	43.2
249	1	2.7	2.7	45.9
250	1	2.7	2.7	48.6
251	1	2.7	2.7	51.4
252	2	5.4	5.4	56.8
253	2	5.4	5.4	62.2
256	1	2.7	2.7	64.9
257	1	2.7	2.7	67.6
259	1	2.7	2.7	70.3
262	2	5.4	5.4	75.7
266	2	5.4	5.4	81.1
268	1	2.7	2.7	83.8
269	1	2.7	2.7	86.5
270	2	5.4	5.4	91.9
277	1	2.7	2.7	94.6
279	1	2.7	2.7	97.3
279	1	2.7	2.7	100.0
TOTAL	37	100.0	100.0	

Table 18.2.		SPSS Output: SDLRS Scores and Frequencies for Interviewed Participants (Valid Cases: 13 — Missing Cases: 0)		
Value	Frequency	Percent	Valid Percent	Cum Percent
221	1	7.7	7.7	7.7
235	1	7.7	7.7	15.4
246	1	7.7	7.7	23.1
247	1	7.7	7.7	30.8
250	1	7.7	7.7	38.5
253	2	15.4	15.4	53.8
262	1	7.7	7.7	61.5
266	2	15.4	15.4	76.9
270	1	7.7	7.7	84.6
277	1	7.7	7.7	92.3
279	1	7.7	7.7	100.0
TOTAL	13	100.0	100.0	

Table 18.3.   Ranking of all Participants *SDLRS* Scores

Ranking	Range	Participants	Percentage
Low	58 – 176	0	0
Below Average	177 – 201	0	0
Average	202 – 226	3	.08
Above Average	227 – 251	16	.43
High	252 – 290	18	.49

Table 18.4.   Ranking of Participants Interviewed *SDLRS* Scores

Ranking	Range	Participants	Percentage
Low	58 – 176	0	0
Below Average	177 – 201	0	0
Average	202 – 226	1	.08
Above Average	227 – 251	4	.31
High	252 – 290	8	.61

Table 18.5.   Comparison of Mean SDLRS Scores of Study Participants with Scores of Other Groups

Groups	N	Mean	Low Score	High Score
All Study Participants	37	250.297	216	279
Only Study Participants Interviewed	13	255.769	221	279
Teachers	54	242.89	181	288
Meta-analytic	4596	227.7	185	247
Entrepreneurs	162	248.6	195	279
Female Executives	19	257.8	210	282

The quantitative research conducted was not used for purposes of in depth analysis and/or interpretation. It was used, however, both to gain more background information about this unique sampling and to look for indications of possible trends found within the sample. Besides developing a more complete picture of the participants interviewed, information gained from the analysis of quantitative data was used to develop questions for the in depth interviews.

Interviews

Research has suggested that individuals who have high scores on the SDLRS tend to perform better in jobs requiring a high degree of problem-solving ability, a high degree of creativity and involving a high degree of change (Brockett & Hiemstra, 1991). Since individuals involved in school reform efforts require a high degree of problem-solving ability, a high degree of creativity and are faced with a high degree of change, evidence of these skills and traits was sought not only through analysis of the *SDLRS*, but also through analysis of the individual interviews.

Interview data gathered as a result of the questions developed from analysis of quantitative data corroborated the fact that participants were truly self-directed, lifelong learners who have been and continue to be attracted to further education and inservice. All the participants expressed the need to pursue additional educational activities in their interviews. Analysis of the interview data also showed that the participants were people who, over the course of their professional careers, looked at current developments in education, took what they learned and then applied that knowledge to their own classroom experiences.

Participants also continued to show evidence of a positive orientation towards change. Not only did the participants not fear change, they actively sought it out. In fact, when change did not occur, the participants became restless and sought to bring about change, even if it meant going so far as to change schools. One participant interviewed transferred to another school so that she might have new experiences. Another participant considered leaving her school and the teaching profession, but then changes started taking place in her school and she decided to "stick it out" and see what was going to happen. When asked why change was so important, one of the reasons given was the belief of the participants that they needed to grow—that circumstances were constantly changing and that they needed to be a part of those changing circumstances. That belief was also a contributing factor to their involvement in school reform.

Part of the appeal that change holds is the challenge it presents and many of the challenges presented to the participants occurred in their classrooms. The participants faced these challenges by using a variety of teaching methods and teaching techniques. Conventions and inservice trainings further helped the participants to meet these challenges by providing the most current and up to date information about changes occurring in the field of education.

CONCLUSIONS

The information gained from the analysis of the three instruments and the interview data does indicate that the participants are highly self-directed learners. Throughout their professional careers the participants have always been interested in changing education, but that interest in change has varied in both form and substance. For most participants, interest in changing education was an outgrowth of their own school experiences, as well as a growing realization that while times and students had changed, teachers and education had not. The qualitative data also indicate that their self-directedness in learning was a factor in their initial involvement in school reform (Urban, 1997).

Because the Coalition of Essential Schools is a loosely structured reform movement that allows for a high degree of ambiguity and encourages risk taking, their choice of reform movement matched both their philosophical and educational practices. Also, because of their experiences in the classroom, both as students and as teachers, because of their commitment to teaching, and because of their belief that schools needed to change, the participants interviewed were among the first people to become involved in the Coalition of Essential Schools.

Their self-directedness is also a factor in their continuing involvement in school reform. The participants interviewed were constantly learning, growing and evolving, and these characteristics contributed to their becoming involved and staying involved in school reform. Further, the characteristics found and discussed in this paper contributed to the participants' taking on the roles of Coalition coordinators and facilitators when their schools became involved with the Coalition of Essential Schools. As a result of their educational pursuits and their involvement in school reform, these teachers had found a renewed commitment to teaching and were happier in their profession.

RECOMMENDATIONS

When Houle wrote *The Inquiring Mind* (1961), he suggested that while our society supports enclaves of people who advocate and promote continuing education, many of the attitudes and values of American society are directly and specifically opposed to the idea of lifelong learning. He believed that there was a need for a concerted effort to express the importance of lifelong learning and get people to support the idea that learning is a natural way of life. Many educational leaders in today's society have come to the same conclusion as Houle. The references in educational literature to lifelong learning, the need for continual dialogue concerning classroom beliefs and practices, and the call for the development of learning communities all illustrate this support.

Even more important, however, is discovering how to get people involved in the pursuit of lifelong learning. Houle suggests that for people to get involved, three critical elements must first come together: (a) the recognition of a need or an interest (b) the will to do something about it and (c) the opportunity to do so. He also suggests that once the learner decides to learn, that decision needs to be reinforced by several other factors before one becomes a continuing learner. Those factors are (a) a successful initial experience (b) a variety of offerings at different levels of depth, so that the individual has the opportunity—even the enticement—to go on and (c) skillful and subtle guidance.

The key to school reform is helping all teachers become self-directed learners and getting all teachers involved in the study of school reform. For this to occur, teachers must recognize the need for and become interested in school reform. They must also develop the will to become involved in school reform and be provided with a variety of opportunities to participate in learning activities and school reform. Once involved with school reform, teachers must have successful initial experiences with school reform, be given a wide variety of offerings concerning school reform that are at different levels of depth, and finally, teachers must be given skillful and subtle guidance. By having all teachers examine their own classroom beliefs and practices, by having all teachers try new strategies in their own classroom, and by having all teachers evaluate the results of those new strategies in their classrooms, not only will most teachers find a renewed commitment to teaching, they will be happier in their classrooms.

Even more important, and as recommended by Peters (1987), support for teachers to pursue professional development, both individually and in group settings, will become a central part of the school's strategic plan and continuous learning will become an accepted part of the school's organizational culture. Learning will be considered a part of every job and there will be an interaction among all the stakeholders of the school which will allow for information to be transmitted across lines, as well as up and down the organizational structure. School reform will be looked at as an ongoing process and the reforms that are implemented will be reforms that have come from within the school rather than being mandated from without. Finally, not only will these reforms meet the needs of the individual school, they will be reforms that have been developed and agreed upon by those most involved in the implementation process and by those who most need to be involved in the school reform process—the teachers.

REFERENCES

Barth, R.S. (1990). Improving schools from within: Teachers, parents and principals can make the difference. San Francisco: Jossey Bass.

Blase, J., & Blase, J. (1994). Empowering teachers: What successful principals do. Thousand Oaks, CA: Corwin Press.

Blase, J., Blase, J., Anderson, G.L., & Dugan, S. (1995). Democratic principals in action: Eight pioneers. Thousand Oaks, CA: Corwin Press.

Bolman, L.G., & Deal, T.E. (1991). Reframing organizations: Artistry, choice and leadership. San Francisco: Jossey Bass.

Brockett, R.H., & Hiemstra, R. (1991). Self-direction in adult learning: Perspectives on theory, research, and practice. New York: Routledge.

Byham, W.C. (1992). Zapp! in education. New York: Fawcett Columbine.

Clift, R.T., Veal, M.L., Holland, P., Johnson, M., & McCarthy, J. (1995). Collaborative leadership and shared decision making: Teachers, principals and university professors. New York: Teachers College Press.

Durr, R.E. An examination of readiness for self-directed learning andselected personnel variables at a large midwestern electronics development and manufacturing corporation. Doctoral dissertation, Florida Atlantic University, 1992.

Durr, R.E. (1994, February). Integration of self-directed learning into the training and educational process at Motorola. West Palm Beach, FL: Eighth International Symposium on Self-Directed Learning.

Evans, R. (1996). The human face of school reform. San Francisco: Jossey Bass.

Fisher, K. (1993). Leading self-directed work teams: A guide to developing new team leadership skills. New York: McGraw Hill.

Fullan, M. (1993a). Change forces: Probing the depths of educational reform. New York: Falmer.

Fullan, M. (1993b, March). Why teachers must become change agents. Educational Leadership 51(6), pp.12-17.

Glickman, C.D. (1993). Renewing America's schools: A guide for school-based action. San Francisco: Jossey Bass.

Guglielmino, L.M. (1978). Development of the Self-Directed Learning Readiness Scale (Doctoral dissertation, University of Georgia, 1977). Dissertation Abstracts International, 38, 6467A.

Guglielmino, P.J., & Guglielmino, L.M. (1992). The self-directed learner: A valued human resource of the 21st century. Sundridge Park Management Review, 5(4), pp.32-39.

Guglielmino, L.M., & Nowocien, D. (1998). Self-directed learning and teachers' professional development. In H.B. Long & Associates, Developing paradigms for self-directed learning (pp.91-106). Norman, OK: Public Managers Center, College of Education, University of Oklahoma.

Hart, A.W. (1994, November). Creating teacher leadership roles. Educational Administration Quarterly, 30(4), pp.472-497.

Houle, C.O. (1961/1988). The inquiring mind. Norman, OK: Oklahoma Research Center for Continuing Professional and Higher Education.

Johnson, S.M. (1996). Leading to change: The challenge of the new superintendency. San Francisco: Jossey Bass.

Leiberman, A. (1988, February). Expanding the leadership team. Educational Leadership, 45(5), pp.4-8.

Lightfoot, S.L. (1983). The good high school. New York: Basic Books.

Maeroff, G. (1988). The empowerment of teachers. Overcoming the crisis of confidence. New York: Teachers College Press.

Patton, M.Q. (1990). Qualitative evaluation and research methods. Newbury Park, CA: Sage.

Peters, T. (1987). Thriving on chaos. NY: Alfred A. Knopf.

Reynolds. M.M. (1986). The self-directedness and motivational orientations of adult part-time students at a community college (Doctoral Dissertation, Syracuse University, 1984). Dissertation Abstracts International, 46, 571A.

Roberts, D. G. (1986). A study of the use of the Self-Directed Learning Readiness Scale as related to selected organization variables (Doctoral dissertation, George Washington University, 1986). Dissertation Abstracts International, 47, 1218A.

Sabbaghian, Z. (1979). Adult self-directedness and self concept: An exploration of relationship. (Doctoral dissertation, Iowa State University). Dissertation Abstracts International, 40, 3701A.

Sarason, S. B. (1990). The predictable failure of educational reform. San Francisco: Jossey Bass.

Schlechty, P.C. (1997). Inventing better schools: An action plan for educational reform. San Francisco: Jossey Bass.

Sergiovanni, T.J. (1996). Leadership for the schoolhouse: How is it different? Why is it important? San Francisco: Jossey-Bass.

Sizer, T. (1992). Horace's school. Boston: Houghton Mifflin Company.

Smylie, M.A., & Denny, J.W. (1990, August). Teacher leadership: Tensions and ambiguities in organizational perspective. Educational Administration Quarterly. 26(3), pp.235-259.

Urban, V.D. Teacher Involvement in School Reform. Doctoral dissertation, Florida Atlantic University, 1997.

Watkins, K.E., & Marsick, V.J. (1993). Sculpting the learning organization. San Francisco: Jossey Bass.

Wellins, R.S., Byham, W.C., & Wilson, J. M. (1991). Empowered teams. San Francisco: Jossey Bass.

CHAPTER NINETEEN

LEADER READINESS FOR SELF–DIRECTED LEARNING AND PERCEPTIONS OF ORGANIZATIONAL CULTURE IN SCHOOLS ENGAGED IN IMPROVEMENT INITIATIVES

Lucy M. Guglielmino & Kimberly Knutson

Schools that serve K-12 learners are struggling to meet the needs of a society undergoing unprecedented levels of change, including a shift in organizational values and expectations. Students in these schools, if they are to function in this new society, must be prepared not only to continue learning, but to assess their own learning needs and devise ways of addressing them. They must become self-directed learners, prepared to function in organizations in which continuous individual and collaborative learning is the norm. As society changes, therefore, the need for facilitating self-direction in learning in schools, not only among the students, but also among teachers and administrators, becomes increasingly important (Guglielmino, Alligood, & Nowocien, 1999). Concurrently, it is becoming evident that the level of shared learning among educators essential to providing effective educational experiences in a rapidly changing environment is impeded by the highly bureaucratic structures and restrictive cultures which traditionally characterize educational institutions. Many are calling for schools to initiate changes that would move them toward becoming learning organizations (Senge in O'Neil, 1995).

READINESS FOR SELF–DIRECTED LEARNING AND PERFORMANCE IN CHANGING ENVIRONMENTS

The link between readiness for self-direction in learning and performance in rapidly changing environments was first explored in 1982 in a business setting (Guglielmino, P. & Guglielmino, L.), and a number of subsequent studies have verified a positive relationship. High performers in organizations have been found to have significantly higher SDLRS scores than the average worker (Durr, 1992; Guglielmino & Guglielmino, 1982; Roberts, 1986), as have managers (Durr, 1992; Roberts, 1986). Studies of top entrepreneurs (Guglielmino, P., & Klatt, 1994) and top female executives (Guglielmino, L., 1996) have revealed even higher SDLRS scores. In 1988, Guglielmino and Guglielmino, focusing on business and industry, commented,

> The information explosion and the rapidly accelerating rate of change create the need for increased encouragement and facilitation of self-directed learning....[and] the focus on developing human potential in order to increase... productivity provide[s] an environment in which self-directed learning will thrive. (p.130)

It appears likely that conditions in the larger environment may not only increase the individual's need for readiness for self-direction in learning, but can also promote its development. When the old procedures and solutions no longer work, and there is no authority offering new ones because the change is rapid and constant, it becomes necessary to reflect, gather data, experiment, analyze, and develop one's own new solutions—in short, it becomes necessary to become a self-directed learner. Testing this line of thought, an exploratory study (Guglielmino & Guglielmino, 1998) was done in Nanjing, China, with three samples of workers and managers drawn at two-year intervals. Because the area was undergoing rapid change and growth, it was hypothesized that an increase in levels of readiness for self-direction in learning might be measured. While the study was hampered by the difficulties of obtaining representative samples in another country and the results cannot be considered conclusive, there was a significant increase in

248

mean scores on the SDLRS for the samples examined after two years and after four years, during the period of exceptionally rapid change.

If changes in the larger environment can be assumed to promote or discourage the development of readiness for self-direction in learning, it seems likely that the climate within an organization can also. In a business setting, York (1991) investigated the relationship between organizational learning climate, self-directed learning, and performance at work and found that self-directed learning is encouraged when resources are provided to support it, when learning is reinforced with acknowledgment and encouragement, and when the work environment is flexible and allows for transfer of learning and behavior change. Similarly, Kops (1997) found that a group of managers who were active self-directed learners reported an organizational climate encouraged learning enhanced their self-directed learning. The managers cited the importance of leaders who constructed supportive learning climates through open communication, high expectations of staff, recognition of staff contributions, and creation of a vision for the organization.

READINESS FOR SDL IN K–12 SETTINGS

While more than 15 years of research efforts have been directed toward the examination of readiness for self-directed learning in business and industry, use of the SDLRS with K-12 teachers has been relatively recent. Guglielmino and Nowocien (1998) and Guglielmino and Urban (1997), examining samples from two of the largest school districts in the US, found levels of readiness for self-direction in learning among teachers to be high, with the mean scores of teachers selected as mentors for other teachers being the highest (Guglielmino & Nowocien, 1998). In the past five years, reference to the importance of developing self-direction in students has begun to appear in professional journals in education (for example, Posner, 1991) and in the mission statements of many educational institutions at all levels; and some have noted that if teachers are to foster self-direction in their students, important changes must be made in their professional preparation programs and in the way their continuing professional education is addressed (Guglielmino, Alligood, & Nowocien, 1999).

DEVELOPMENT OF LEARNING ORGANIZATIONS IN K–12 SETTINGS

Schools seeking to become learning organizations can benefit from the research and thinking on this topic, which has been largely based in business and industry. In learning organizations, individual and collective engagement in the learning organization is facilitated "...in such activities as shared vision development, problem identification, learning, and problem resolution" (Hord, 1997, p.4). Organizational culture is based on collaboration and continuous problem solving, and critical reflection and self-management are valued. Leaders are found at all levels of the organization; and they behave as designers, stewards, and teachers (Senge, 1990; Watkins & Marsick, 1993).

It appears that the conditions reported to support self-directed learning in individuals are remarkably similar to those reported to support the development of the learning organization. Noting this, Guglielmino and Guglielmino (1997) contended that the learning organization is based in self-directed learning by individuals and groups and the sharing of that learning throughout the organization; that, in fact, "...self-directed learning is the keystone of the learning organization" (p.1).

As schools move toward becoming learning organizations, many important questions emerge. The research findings cited suggest an examination of readiness for self-directed learning and perceptions of organizational culture among school personnel, preferably in schools engaged in improvement initiatives designed to move them toward a learning organization model.

PURPOSE

The purpose of this study is to explore possible relationships between and among school culture; school involvement in various approaches to school reform; and teacher, teacher leader, and administrator readiness for self-direction in learning. Through examination of a number of schools engaged in two types of intensive staff development efforts designed to move them toward becoming learning communities, the following questions will be explored:

1. Are there relationships among levels of readiness for self-directed learning of school personnel and their perceptions of the cultures of the schools in which they work?

2. Is there a relationship at the school level between mean levels of levels of readiness for self directed learning of school personnel and mean school culture scores?

3. Do levels of readiness for self directed learning of teachers, teacher leaders and administrators differ among schools which have committed to varying levels of school reform efforts (extensive staff development only, as opposed to staff development combined with a school-wide action research model)?

4. Do perceptions of school culture of teachers, teacher leaders and administrators differ among schools which have committed to varying levels of school reform efforts (extensive staff development only, as opposed to staff development combined with a school-wide action research model)?

5. Do levels of readiness for self-directed learning differ among school administrators, teacher leaders, and teachers who have not taken leadership roles in school reform initiatives?

One of the most promising approaches to meaningful school reform that results in improved outcomes for students is the engagement of faculty and administrators in efforts to develop learning communities in their schools (Dale, 1997; Hodges, 1996; Leithwood, Leonard, & Sharratt, in press). This study explores the relationships between perceptions of school culture as supportive of a learning community and readiness for self-directed learning of teachers, teacher leaders, and administrators; it may lend insight into the evolving nature of continuous learning and how it responds to and/or shapes organizational cultures and develops personal capacity to be self-directed.

METHODOLOGY

<u>Population and Sample</u>
The population from which the sample for this study was drawn includes personnel from two groups of schools that are members of the South Florida Center for Educational Leaders (SFCEL) Consortium of Schools. The Consortium includes 44 schools from five South Florida counties: Broward, Collier, Dade, Monroe and Palm Beach. The mission of the SFCEL Consortium of Schools is to improve student achievement through a comprehensive program of professional staff development. The organization provides resources and training to groups of teacher leaders and administrators from member schools and promotes inter- and intra-school collaboration to help them meet the needs of their students.

Of the 44 schools, 19 have gone beyond the commitment to an extensive program of professional development; they have chosen to participate in a schoolwide action research initiative to improve student achievement. In addition to regular member activities, the schools have formed learning groups of teachers and administrators, known as cadres, which have been engaged for approximately one year in learning to conduct collaborative schoolwide action research and sharing what they have learned with others at their schools. Because of the highly collaborative nature of schoolwide action research related to planning, data collection, and sharing of information, these schools are expected to move more rapidly toward a culture which could be described as a learning organization. Both groups are interested in supporting student achievement, yet have the potential of representing different organizational climates. The two groups of schools examined in this study will be designated as schools that have committed to extensive professional development (EPD) and those that have committed to extensive professional development and schoolwide action research (EPD+SAR). It must be noted that while most of the EPD schools have been involved in the consortium for several years, the EPD+SAR schools were just beginning the schoolwide action research process at the time the data were collected; principals and one teacher leader had attended an orientation in March 1998 and principals and 2-3 teacher leaders had attended a three-day workshop in June 1998, with instructions to begin forming research groups at their schools in Fall 1998. While there may be some differences in the two groups of schools related to their *commitment* to EPD only or to EPD+SAR, there had been no difference in the level or type of total school involvement at the time these data were collected in Fall 1998, other than a possible awareness among teachers that their schools had elected to continue with EPD only or to add the SAR option. Therefore, there had been little opportunity for differentiation based on the approaches to staff development by Fall 1998 when the data were collected, and the results of this study will be most useful as a baseline for later comparisons.

All of the schools in the SFCEL Consortium were invited to participate in this study. A total of nine schools volunteered to participate through self-selection. The sample that self-selected to participate in the study was composed of three schools engaged in extensive professional development only (EPD) and six schools involved in EPD and schoolwide action research (EPD+SAR). Representation by group and county is detailed in Table 19.1.

Table 19.1.   Sample by County and Group

	Broward County	Collier County	Dade County	Monroe County	Palm Beach County	Total
EPD+SAR	4	0	1	0	1	6
EPD Only	2	1	0	0	0	3
	6	1	1	0	1	9

Instrumentation
This study examined the self directed learning readiness and perceptions of school culture of school instructional faculty and leadership, including teacher leadership. The *Self-Directed Learning Readiness Scale (SDLRS)* and the *School Professional Staff as Learning Community (SPSLC)* were the instruments selected to examine the variables.

Self-Directed Learning Readiness Scale

The *Self-Directed Learning Readiness Scale* (Guglielmino, 1977, 1978) is a 58-item, Likert-type instrument designed to assess individual attitudes, values, skills and personality characteristics supportive of self-direction in learning. Expert judgment was used to ensure the content and construct validity of the instrument. Based on input from a Delphi panel of 14 experts in the field of self-directed learning, a list of characteristics of individuals with high levels of readiness for self-direction in learning was created. In a three-round process, the panel arrived at consensus on the characteristics they deemed important for self-direction in learning, including attitudes, values, abilities, and personality characteristics. Those items emerging from the Delphi panel with a rating of *desirable, necessary* or *essential* were used as a basis for the construction of the *SDLRS* items.

An internal reliability of .87 (Cronbach alpha) was reported for the pilot instrument as well as the 58 item version used today. Most published studies on populations over twenty years old report similar reliability figures that fall within a range of .72–.92. In addition to internal reliability estimates, Finestone (1984) and Wiley (1981) reported test-retest reliability coefficients of .82 and .79 respectively. Based on a population of 3,151 individuals from the United States and Canada, a split-half Pearson product moment correlation with a Spearman-Brown correction produced the highest reliability figure of .94 (Guglielmino, 1997).

Although there have been some criticisms of the SDLRS, (Brockett, 1987; Field, 1989; Straka & Hinz, 1996), the vast majority of studies have supported the reliability and validity of the instrument (See, for example, Delahaye & Smith, 1995; Durr, 1992; Finestone, 1984; Graeve, 1987; Hassan, 1982; Guglielmino, 1989; Kasworm, 1982; Long, 1989, 1993; Long & Ageykum, 1984; McCune, 1989; McCune & Guglielmino, 1991). The *SDLRS,* with its self-scoring form, *The Learning Preference Assessment* (Guglielmino & Guglielmino, 1991), is by far the most widely used quantitative instrument in the study of self-directed learning (Merriam & Caffarella, 1999). Overviews of research using the instrument can be found in Brockett and Hiemstra (1992), Guglielmino (1997) and Merriam and Caffarella (1999).

School Professional Staff as Learning Community
The *School Professional Staff as Learning Community (SPSLC)* (Hord, 1997) is a self-report survey designed to measure perceptions of school culture. Each of the 17 items is grouped under one of five subscales. Respondents are asked to read a trio of indicators and select the one that best describes their school. The instrument is described fully in *Field Test of an Instrument Measuring the Concept of Professional Learning Communities in Schools* (Meehan, Orletsky, and Sattes, 1997).

Validity and reliability were assessed by testing the instrument on a sample of 21 schools chosen from a pool of elementary, middle, and high schools identified as learning organizations. The sample schools were drawn from four states. Internal reliability (Cronbach's alpha) was .94 for the overall instrument and ranged from .83 to .87 for the subscales. A test-retest reliability of .61 was reported for a small sample (23) (Meehan, et al., 1997).

Content validity was addressed in the design stage through a literature review and Hord's experience with schools operating as learning communities. Concurrent validity was examined in a correlational study between the total *SPSLC* and the Manning, Curtis, and McMillen's School Climate Questionnaire (.7489, p<.001) (Meehan, et al, 1997). A t-test of the difference between the means of a known group sample of 18 and the full sample of 595 resulted in a t-value 16.29 (p<.0001).\

Procedures

Data Collection
Letters of invitation to participate in the study were mailed to each school category, offering a report of findings in exchange for participating. The appropriate number of research packets was sent to the contact persons for responding schools.

The research packets included a cover sheet containing directions, a demographic questionnaire, a bubble sheet, and the two research instruments. The testing environment was not controlled; participants were directed in writing to complete the survey in a comfortable atmosphere. To ensure anonymity, each research packet was in an envelope that participants were asked to seal before returning the completed materials to the school contact. The school contact was given a date to return the surveys and a postage paid envelope in which to return them. When the data were returned to the researchers, a school code number was added to each bubble sheet before processing.

Data Analysis
The research questions were explored using Pearson correlations and analyses of variance; the Scheffe was used when post hoc analyses were warranted. Statistical significance was set at p<.05 for all statistical treatments. The SPSS–SPO statistical software was used.

LIMITATIONS

Several limitations were inherent in the research design. Since the sample was drawn from members of a professional development organization, caution must be used in generalizing the results to other groups outside of this type of organization. In addition, the sample was not chosen randomly, but was self-selected. Furthermore, the respondents who participated from each school by completing the instruments did so voluntarily. Therefore, even though the school leadership of administrators and teacher leaders may have chosen to participate in this study, individual faculty members were not required to respond to the surveys. Because the instruments concealed the participants' identities, knowledge of the basic demographic information about those who did or did not respond is not available. Finally, since the schoolwide action research component had been in operation for less than six months at the time of data collection and total school involvement had not yet begun, it is likely that there will be no differentiation between the two types of schools as yet; however, the data can provide a valuable baseline for future research.

FINDINGS

Two hundred forty seven people from the nine participating schools responded to the instruments. An overview of the demographic variables of all participants is represented in Table 19.2, followed by the findings related to each research question.

The majority of respondents (81%) came from the schools that are involved in both extensive professional development and schoolwide action research (EPD+SAR). Nineteen percent of the responses were from schools which are engaged in extensive professional development only (EPD). Of the staff, teachers represented the largest response group (73%), followed by teacher leaders (21%) and administrators (6%). Forty one percent of all respondents reported having between 4 and 8 years of experience at their current schools. The next largest group, 25%, reported having served at their schools for nine to fourteen years; and 16% reported working at their schools for fifteen or more years. Finally, 17% reported two years or less of experience at their schools.
Ninety percent of respondents identified themselves as female and 61% as European American. Thirty nine percent of the respondents indicated an ethnicity other than European American: Asian American (1%), African American (6%), Hispanic American (4%) or other (28%).

Findings related to specific research questions are presented in order.

Table 19.2.   Sample Demographic Variables

	Variable	
	Count	Percent
School Type		
Learning Organizations (EPD+SAR)	199	81%
Professional Development Organizations (EPD)	48	19%
Total	247	100%
Position		
Administrator	16	6%
Teacher Leader	51	21%
Teacher	180	73%
Total	247	100%
Years at School		
2 or less years	43	17%
3 to 8 years	101	41%
9 to 14 years	62	25%
More than 14 years	39	16%
Invalid response	1	0%
Total	246	100%
Gender		
Female	219	90%
Male	25	10%
Total	244	100%
Ethnicity		
African American	14	6%
Asian American	2	1%
European American	147	61%
Hispanic American	9	4%
Other	69	28%
Total	241	100%

Research Question 1: Analysis of variance revealed no significant relationship between individuals' levels of readiness for self-directed learning and their perceptions of school culture.

Research Question 2: No statistically significant relationship between mean levels of readiness for self-directed learning and mean school culture scores was found among personnel of the participating schools.

Research Question 3: Levels of readiness for self-directed learning were not found to be significantly different for personnel in the schools which had or had not committed to adding a schoolwide action research component to their existing involvement in extensive professional development.

Research Question 4: Perceptions of school culture did not differ significantly among personnel in the schools which had or had not committed to adding a schoolwide action research component to their existing involvement in extensive professional development.

Research Question 5: There was a statistically significant difference in SDLRS scores by position (df 2, F=3.6, p< .029). Tables 19.3 and 19.4 reflect the descriptive statistics and ANOVA results related to this finding.

Table 19.3.   Descriptive Statistics: SDLRS Score by Position

Position	N	Mean	S.D.	S.E.
Administrator	16	254.19	21.49	5.37
Teacher Leader	51	237.29	25.41	3.56
Teacher	174	237.61	23.79	1.80
Total	241	238.65	24.26	1.56

Table 19.4.   ANOVA of SDLRS Score by Position

SDLRS	Sum of Squares	df	Mean Square	F	Sig.
Between Groups	4142.79	2	2071.40	3.595	.029
Within Groups	137140.2	238	576.22		
Total	141283.0	240			

Additional analyses revealed no difference in SDLRS scores or school culture scores by sex, ethnicity, or years at the school.

DISCUSSION, CONCLUSIONS, AND IMPLICATIONS

Examined as a whole, the findings provided no surprises. The two groups of schools had been involved in the same types of extensive staff development for several years as members of the South Florida Center for Educational Leaders, and one group had only recently made a commitment to expanding their efforts to include a schoolwide action research component. The one significant finding is independent of school type and reflective of earlier findings related to the SDLRS.

Congruence of Findings Related to SDLRS
with Findings of Prior Studies

Three findings related to the SDLRS are aligned with those found in prior studies:

- Mean SDLRS scores of teachers, teacher leaders, and administrators were in the high range, as has been the case in prior studies of these groups (Guglielmino, Alligood, & Nowocien, 1999; Guglielmino & Nowocien, 1998; Guglielmino & Urban, 1997).
- As in previous studies, SDLRS scores did not differ significantly by sex or ethnicity. In addition, there was no significant relationship between SDLRS scores and years at the school or school culture scores.
- Mean SDLRS scores of administrators were significantly higher than those of teachers and teacher leaders. Similar findings linking SDLRS score and position have been reported by Durr (1992) and Roberts (1986), among others.

Lack of a Relationship Between School Culture,
SDL Readiness and Type of Organization

While the lack of a significant relationship between school culture and SDLRS scores is not reflective of what one might expect based on the literature (Guglielmino & Guglielmino, 1997; Kops, 1997; Senge, 1990; Watkins & Marsick, 1993), this finding is understandable for this study in light of the fact that the nine participating schools did not differ significantly in either SDLRS scores or school culture scores. In fact, all had been participating for a number of years in the same program of extensive professional development, as their schools were members of the South Florida Center for Educational Leaders.

Those schools that had chosen to participate in the schoolwide action research had just begun the process, with only administrators and teachers leaders involved in orientation and planning in preparation for schoolwide implementation. Therefore, this study provides valuable baseline data reflective of the similar prior experiences of the schools related to their commitment to school reform and their involvement with the SFCEL.

Suggestions for Further Research

A number of additional studies could contribute valuable information on the interrelationships of school culture, self-direction in learning, and differing school reform initiatives. Obviously, it would be valuable to again gather data from the same schools as the schoolwide action research component is implemented. In addition, data similar to that collected in this study could be gathered from schools which have not been involved in identifiable school reform initiatives. Another productive approach would be to gather qualitative data to inform and complement the quantitative data.

In our continuously changing society, it is of utmost importance that we thoughtfully examine the approaches to school improvement that are being implemented in order to ensure that students are being adequately prepared for the future they will face. Their interactions with and impact on school culture and teacher and administrator characteristics can provide valuable information for decision-making.

REFERENCES

Brockett, R.G. (1987). Life satisfaction and learner self-direction: Enhancing quality of life during the later years. Educational Gerontology, 13, pp.225-237.

Brockett, R.G., & Hiemstra, R. Self-direction in adult learning: Perspectives on theory, research, and practice. London: Routledge, 1991.

Dale, J.D. (1997). The new American school system.: A learning organization. International Journal of Educational Reform, 6 (1), pp.34-39.

Delahaye, B.L., & Smith, H.E. (1995). The validity of the Learning Preference Assessment. Adult Education Quarterly, 45, pp.159-173.

Durr, R.E. (1992). An examination of readiness for self-directed learning and selected personnel variables at a large midwestern electronics development and manufacturing corporation (Doctoral dissertation, Florida Atlantic University, 1992). Dissertation Abstracts International, 53, 1825p.

Field, L. (1989). An investigation into the structure, validity, and reliability of Guglielmino's Self-Directed Learning Readiness Scale. Adult Education Quarterly, 39, pp.125-39. (See also responses by Guglielmino, Long, and McCune).

Finestone, P. (1984). A construct validation of the Self-Directed Learning Readiness Scale with labor education participants (Doctoral dissertation, University of Toronto, 1994). Dissertation Abstracts International, 46, 5A.

Graeve, E.A. (1987). Patterns of self-directed learning of registered nurses (Doctoral dissertation, University of Minnesota, 1987). Dissertation Abstracts International, 48, 820p.

Guglielmino, L.M. (1977). Self-Directed Learning Readiness Scale. Boca Raton, FL: Guglielmino & Associates.

Guglielmino, L.M. (1978). Development of the self-directed learning readiness scale. (Doctoral dissertation, University of Georgia, 1977). Dissertation Abstracts International, 38, 6467A.

Guglielmino, L.M. (1989). Reactions to Field's investigation into the SDLRS. Adult Education Quarterly, 39, pp.235-240.

Guglielmino, L.M. (1996). An examination of self-directed learning readiness and selected demographic variables of top female executives. In H.B. Long & Associates, Current developments in self-directed learning (pp.11-22). Norman, OK: Public Managers Center, University of Oklahoma.

Guglielmino, L.M. (1997). Reliability and validity of the Self-Directed Learning Readiness Scale and the Learning Preference Assessment. In H.B. Long & Associates, Expanding horizons in self-directed learning (pp.209-222). Norman, OK: Public Managers Center, College of Education, University of Oklahoma.

Guglielmino, L.M., Alligood, C., & Nowocien, D. (1999). Restructuring a professional orientation program for teachers to promote continuous, self-directed learning. In H.B. Long & Associates, Contemporary ideas and practices in self-directed learning (pp.17-29). Norman, OK: Public Managers Center, College of Education, University of Oklahoma.

Guglielmino, L.M., & Guglielmino, P.J. (1988). Self-directed learning in business and industry: An information age imperative. In H.B. Long & Associates, Self-directed learning: Application and theory (125-148). Lifelong Learning Research/Publication Project, Department of Adult Education, University of Georgia.

Guglielmino, L.M., & Guglielmino, P.J. (1991). Learning Preference Assessment facilitator guide. King of Prussia, PA: Organization Design and Development.

Guglielmino, L.M., & Nowocien, D. (1998). Self-directed learning and teachers' professional development. In H.B. Long & Associates, Developing paradigms for self-directed learning (pp.91-106). Norman, OK: Public Managers Center, College of Education, University of Oklahoma.

Guglielmino, L.M., & Urban, V. (1997, February). Relationship of teacher readiness for self-directed learning to classroom practices and beliefs. Referred presentation at the International Symposium on Self-Directed Learning, Kissimmee, FL.

Guglielmino, P.J., & Guglielmino, L.M. (1982). An examination of the relationship between self-directed learning readiness and job performance in a major utility. Unpublished research report. See Guglielmino, Guglielmino, & Long for selected findings.

Guglielmino, P.J., & Guglielmino, L.M. (1997, September). Self-directed learning and the learning organization. Invited paper presented at The First World Conference on Self-Directed Learning, Montreal, Canada.

Guglielmino, P.J., & Guglielmino, L.M. (1998). Three studies of self-directed learning readiness in the People's Republic of China. In H. B. Long & Associates, Developing paradigms for self-directed learning (pp.61-74). Norman, OK: Public Managers Center, College of Education, University of Oklahoma.

Guglielmino, P.J., & Klatt, L.A. (1994). Self-directed learning readiness as a characteristic of the entrepreneur. In H.B. Long & Associates, New ideas about self-directed learning (pp.161-174) Norman, OK: Oklahoma Research Center for Continuing Professional and Higher Education of the University of Oklahoma.

Hassan, A.J. (1981). An investigation of the learning projects of adults of high and low readiness for self-direction learning (Doctoral dissertation, Iowa State University, 1981). Dissertation Abstracts International, 42, 3838A-3839A.

Hodges, H.L. (1996). Using research to inform practice in urban schools: Ten key strategies for success. Educational Policy, 10(2), pp.223-252.

Hord, S. (1997). Professional learning communities: Communities of continuous inquiry and improvement. Unpublished manuscript.

Kasworm, C. (1982). An exploratory study of the development of self-directed learning as an instructional curriculum strategy. In Whaples, G., & Rivera, W. (eds.) Lifelong Learning Research Conference Proceedings, College Park: University of Maryland.

Kops, W. (1997). Managers as self-directed learners: Comparing findings of studies in private and public-sector organizations. In H.B. Long & Associates, Expanding horizons in self-directed learning (pp.71-86). Norman, OK: Public Managers Center, College of Education, University of Oklahoma.

Leithwood, K., Leonard, L. & Sharratt, L. (in press). Conditions fostering organizational learning in schools. Educational Administration Quarterly.

Long, H.B. (1989). Some additional criticisms of Field's investigation. Adult Education Quarterly, 39, pp.240-243.

Long, H.B. (1993). Self-directed learning knowledge: Some important issues. In H.B. Long & Associates, Emerging perspectives of self-directed learning. Norman, OK: Oklahoma Research Center for Continuing Professional and Higher Education.

Long, H.B., & Agyekum, S.K. (1984). Multitrait-multi-method validation of Guglielmino's Self-Directed Learning Readiness Scale. Proceedings of the Twenty-fifth Annual Adult Education Research Conference.

McCune, S.K. (1989). A statistical critique of Field's investigation. Adult Education Quarterly, 39, pp.243-246.

McCune, S.K., & Guglielmino, L.M. (1991). Validity generalization of the Self-Directed Learning Readiness Scale. In H.B. Long & Associates, Self-directed learning: Consensus and conflict (pp.147-154) Norman, OK: Oklahoma Research Center for Continuing Professional and Higher Education.

Meehan, M.L., Orletsky, S.R., & Sattes, B. (1997). Field test of an instrument measuring the concept of professional learning communities in schools. Unpublished manuscript

Merriam, S., & Caffarella , R. (1999). Learning in adulthood. San Francisco: Jossey-Bass.

O'Neil, J. (1995). On schools as learning organizations: A conversation with Peter Senge. Educational Leadership, 52(7), pp.20-23.

Posner, F.G. (1991). Self-directed learning: The missing ingredient for school reform. Changing Schools, 19(1), pp.1-4 & 8.

Roberts, D.G. (1986). A study of the use of the Self-Directed Learning Readiness Scale as related to selected organizational variables (Doctoral dissertation, George Washington University, 1986). Dissertation Abstracts International, 47, 1218A.

Senge, P. (1990). The fifth discipline: The art and practice of the learning organization. NY: Doubleday.

Straka, G.A., & Hinz, I.M. (1996, May). Problems of measuring readiness for self-directed learning. Paper presented at the 10th International Symposium on Self-Directed Learning, West Palm Beach, FL.

Watkins, K., & Marsick, V. (1993). Sculpting the learning organization. San Francisco: Jossey-Bass.

Wiley, K. (1981). Effects of a self-directed learning project and preference for structure on self-directed learning readiness of baccalaureate nursing students (Doctoral dissertation, Northern Illinois University, 1981). Dissertation Abstracts International, 43, 1A.

York, D.J. (1991, February). Learning in the workplace: Organizational learning climate, self-directed learners, and performance at work. Paper presented at the Fifth International Symposium on Adult Self-Directed Learning. University of Oklahoma, Norman, OK.

CHAPTER TWENTY

SELF–DIRECTED LEARNING IN A DIGITAL AGE: WHERE NEXT TO BROWSE IS INFORMED BY REFLECTION

Robert J. Bulik & Joan Hanor

Over the last few years the World Wide Web has proven to be a valuable tool for education in terms of connecting students to an enormous fund of information and delivering various multimedia learning materials. There can be no doubt that computers and allied technologies have meant that huge quantities of data are available to students. Access to the Web, CD-ROM and other systems, means that there are sufficient reading and associated learning materials to meet everyone's needs.

The hypertext and hypermedia format used by the Web has received wide acclaim and its potential as an educational tool is derived from the nature of the learning that it supports. It has the potential to facilitate student-centered approaches, thus creating a motivating and active learning environment (Becker & Dwyer, 1994). It also supports and encourages browsing and exploration, student behaviors that are frequently associated with higher-order learning. Additionally, hypertext and hypermedia facilitate a very natural and efficient form for linking to and retrieval of information (Dimitroff & Wolfram, 1995). Further, the *Report to the President on the Use of Technology to Strengthen K-12 Education in the United States* (1997), argues that Web-based learning incorporates a constructivist approach to education that is self-directed *and* "quick."

These and other advantages offered by the medium have created considerable enthusiasm among learning theorists and teachers toward the Web and hypermedia as a learning tool. However, as with all instructional technologies, potential and reality are frequently not synonymous. For example, while the *Report to the President* specifically refers to self-directed learning in conjunction with distance learning, it is in the context of using the Web to complete a student project and only links this set of skills with the ability to "…quickly gain greater familiarity with the particular subject area…." (p.37). If self-directed learning and distance learning become connected in the literature <u>primarily</u> because there is an advantage in speed (or efficiency) for independent learning, and not on more educationally grounded issues, then the field regresses to the kind of reform Tyler suggested in 1949. Tyler's work, which spawned the *efficiency movement*, has lead to a linear perspective on classroom planning that supports technical implementation of curriculum over conceptual intentionality (Connelly & Clandinin, 1988).

How the dialogue is framed *now* between self-directed and distance learning will determine the impact of *future* reform. In educational discourse, language (and interpretation of language) is important. The way that *expert* or *authoritative* agencies or individuals use language to formulate concepts not only creates assertions, but in terms of educational practice, makes recommendations, advises, exhorts, hints, or suggests that certain outcomes must be followed and other results are less important.

A second example of *potential vs. reality* centers on the tendency to see the Web as a convenient, valuable, efficient, and inexpensive medium over which to conduct learning. While it can provide the means and resources for learners to think about the information that is presented, their own and others' practices, and to question their own assumptions in a given domain, educators cannot presuppose that learners will actively process given information in these ways. There is considerable doubt that the availability of information is always an advantage; simply acquiring or accessing data must be only a first step. Even educational technology tools for Web instruction, such as hypermedia technology that provides structure and links information nodes, is not necessarily the answer. In an article that examines findings from experimental studies of hypermedia technology, Dillon and Gabbard (1998) report:

> So what are we to conclude from the studies reviewed in this article? Clearly, the benefits gained from the use of hypermedia technology in learning scenarios appear to be very limited and not in keeping with the generally euphoric reaction to this technology in the professional arena. (p.345)

In other words, the Web (through Web-based courses and computer-assisted learning), only has the *potential* to support constructivist-oriented, self-directed learning. Likewise, hypermedia technology only has the *potential* to encourage self-directed learning. Consequently, faculty who design Web-based courses must take the total "virtual" learning environment into account, and not just provide access to educational resources; equating access to educational resources with self-directed learning is insufficient.

This paper will look specifically at two elements that can enhance or inhibit self-directed learning in a Web-based educational environment. In particular, we will argue that faculty have the responsibility for creating Web-based learning environments that encourage, not inhibit, self-directed learning.

RELATIONSHIP OF SDL TO THE WWW

A problem facing faculty who develop Web-based courses is the choice of strategy that should be employed to organize the material. While hypertext and hypermedia describe a particular type of learning environment, there are several forms of representations that assume these titles (Gillingham, 1993). The different forms of hypertext and hypermedia can be described through a continuum that depicts the nature of the linking involved. At one end of the continuum, the links are minimal and simply act to connect nodes in a specified sequence. This form of hypermedia closely resembles conventional text and is referred to as linear—a teacher-directed approach to learning that can be characterized as inhibiting self-directed learning. Web-based courses at this end of the continuum not only encourage, but also compel a student to follow an instructional sequence planned by the instructor.

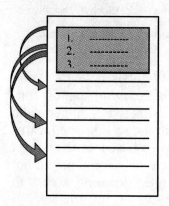

Example 1

Topic Buttons lead to vertically layered, sequential pieces of information.

Example 2

Forward/Backward Buttons link pages
in a horizontal, linear sequence.

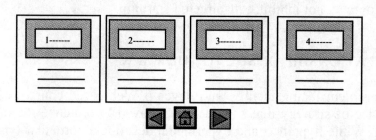

Further along the continuum, the links tend to form a hierarchical structure, giving learners more freedom in the choice of paths through the materials. At the far extreme, hypertext and hypermedia can provide a totally unstructured learning environment with multiple links between associated nodes. In this environment, learners are free to move between associated nodes through referential links and very little structures is imposed (or in evidence)—a learner-directed approach that can be characterized as enhancing self-directed learning.

Learning Modules

Module 1　Module 2　Module 3　Module 4　Module 5　Module 6　Module 7

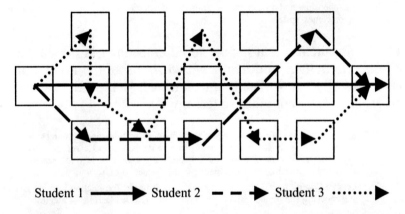

Student 1 ⟶ Student 2 − − ▶ Student 3 ┈┈┈▶

How students engage in learning (which path they select through the instructional material in a Web-based course environment), is determined by many variables. Providing students with opportunities to engage the learning material in a variety of ways is simply good teaching.

We agree with Hrimech and Bouchard (1998), when they indicate that computer-assisted learning is situated along a continuum between self-directed learning at one extreme and teacher-directed learning at the other end. However, we disagree with these authors when they suggest that "...computers place limitations on overall learner autonomy." (p.32)

Rather than centering the discussion on the machine (or the "tool"), or even focusing on hypermedia technology, we argue that it is faculty responsibility for creating a self-directed learning environment—again, in the academic classroom, in a business training setting, or in the computer-assisted/Web-based "virtual" class-room.

We feel it is necessary for faculty to focus on the principles and practices associated with self-directed learning. A definition of self-directed learning by Malcolm Knowles (1975), has become the most accepted description of this process in which:

> ...individuals take the initiative, with or without the help of others, in diagnosing their learning needs, formulating learning goals, identifying human and material resources for learning, choosing and implementing appropriate learning strategies, and evaluating learning outcomes. (p.18)

Two major themes that appear to be embedded in the above definition, *interactivity* and *learner control*, dispel the myth that SDL is necessarily an isolated, unconnected, self-sufficient, autonomous, or solitary approach to learning:

1. Interactivity—initiating an engagement or dialogue with learning resources (human or text-based), that allows for an active role on the part of the learner in constructing the set of conceptual structures that constitutes a personal learning base (a constructivist approach); and, participating in the evaluation of learning outcomes.

2. Learner Control—reflecting on personal learning needs, formulating learning goals, and choosing and implementing appropriate and preferred learning strategies.

These two themes, developed from the SDL literature, help cultivate a common ground for discourse with the distance learning community. For example, Garrison and Shale (1990) have considered the concept of learner-control as more useful than learner-independence in planning distance learning environments. They have argued that two-way communication is an essential component of the student-teacher transaction, and a necessary ingredient for learner control of "education at a distance" (p.133). A key aspect of Garrison's (1992) view is that control must be shared and realized through continuous and critical dialogue between the student and teacher.

INTERACTIVITY — CREATING A DIALOGUE

The term, *interactivity*, describes the forms of communication that a medium supports. Interactivity enables dialogue between the learner and the faculty, the learner and other learners, and the learner and the text, and should be an integral attribute of technology-supported educational environments. In relation to a Web-based course, simply clicking on paths and navigating through a Web instructional sequence is not representative of interactivity. Likewise, simply accessing a database or node through hypertext connectivity, does not equal *active* learning (Laurillard, 1993).

The most effective learning environments ensure that educational resources are used in a social context with students working in groups, discussing the issues, reporting back, presenting findings, interviewing, and debating the issues to ensure that the students have the opportunity to articulate, negotiate, and defend their knowledge—dialogue is fundamental to learning (Lave & Wenger, 1991). This form of active participation is a function of how well the learning environment is structured—once again, in the adult academic classroom, in a business training setting, or in the computer-assisted/Web-based "virtual" classroom.

A second element of interactivity involves deliberate action by the learner. Embedding a conversational framework in Web-based courses enhances a constructivist approach to learning. *Constructivism* is a learning theory that emphasizes the importance of the knowledge, beliefs, and skills an individual brings to the educational experience. It relies on the belief that knowledge cannot be transferred intact from the head of a teacher to the heads of students; rather, learners construct their own knowledge by combining new information with prior understanding and previous experience.

The dialogue can occur in various ways—between the learner and faculty, and between the learner and other learners, through chat-rooms, threaded discussions, or email.

Interaction, through discussion and collaboration, has become an essential component of any Web-based course (Hedberg,

Brown, & Arrighi, 1997). The literature supports a common argument—social interaction among distance learners plays an important part on learning outcomes (Jonassen, et al. 1995; Eastmond & Ziegahn, 1995; and Berge, 1995). Further, a dialogue can also be created between the learner and the subject matter. However, students need to do more than simply access information.

Creating opportunities for students to adapt the information on the Web site by adding to it, reflecting about it, or changing it, creates a dialogue with the content. The learner must not only have access to the major concepts being explained or advanced, but also be able to act on these explanations, to obtain feedback on their own thoughts on the same or different information, and to adapt the Web materials as a result of reflection (Laurillard, 1993).

LEARNER CONTROL — GOALS AND STRATEGIES

Many benefits have been postulated for Web-based education. While distance learning has been explored in the narrow arena of transmission of knowledge, representative of a behaviorist classroom setting (Hirschbuhl, Jackson, & Bishop, 1995), the larger issue of "learning" is not well addressed in the literature. Perhaps the most significant aspect of Web-based learning—who directs the learning encounter (teacher-directed or self-directed), has received relatively little attention. While we may argue for learner autonomy, control, and self-directedness, the structure of the learning environment often dictates the manner in which faculty wish to have learners engage "their" materials through hypertext and hypermedia.

These digital (or virtual) learning environments are characterized by the way in which they convey space (Murray, 1997). While books and film portray space through verbal or graphic descriptions, digital media presents space through navigational or dimensional descriptions. This spatial property is independent of graphical representations, pictures, or models, but rather results from the interactive process of navigation. We change locations by entering commands, and moves can be verified and relationships between spaces can be established by retracing our steps. The navigational space can elicit automatic or intuitive responses or it may require increasingly complex and challenging actions. How much the learner feels in control depends a great deal on his/her ability to maneuver through this space.

Many Web sites use hypertext and hypermedia links to create navigational pathways, and corresponding documents, that allow the learner to follow a sequence that is often unique to the course. The reasoning is based on the idea that an expert's (faculty-directed) sequencing and linking of nodes, provides a knowledge structure which reflects the way learning *typically* takes place in the content area. The sequencing of the material and the links are fixed, and not dependent on the individual learner's control, responses, or actions. Further, Web-based courses frequently subdivide skills into small sections that are then taught systematically in a logical order. This often results in the processes requiring little thought as the learner can deduce the answers correctly from the preceding section without a real understanding of the subject. Learners conclude that information must be relevant because it is in the same section (or *follows* the previous "page" in a linear fashion as the examples in the previous section depict), and that precludes the need for reflection.

A fundamental limitation of this faculty-directed approach is, first, not all students are *typical*. Second, the extent to which it is possible for students to acquire the original author's structure, and map it into their own existing structures, is questionable. Learners develop individual interpretations of information and hence, construct their own meaning. Since it is rare for two people to construct the same semantic structure, it is therefore unreasonable to expect that a learner could easily adopt the author's structure and meaning. Third, information that is accessed is not changed in any way by the student; simply accessing the information through a hypertext link is not interactive learning. The hypertext and hypermedia links in documents simply enable the learner to follow paths that are pre-determined by faculty, and this activity is not useful for providing interactivity or for receiving feedback. Finally, in order to solve the problem or complete the task, the student should be required to reflect upon the whole activity by predicting, hypothesizing, or experimenting to produce a solution.

Well designed links, based on faculty knowledge of what is important to know and why—not just structural links—can provide an opportunity for self-directed learning. These links can provide a motivation to the learner to understand the topic being studied. They are characterized by a tendency on the part of the learner to penetrate the subject matter, and to explore and integrate the knowledge gained into the learner's larger field of knowledge. Well-designed links enable learners to control their learning environment, and to explore the information in a manner that is relevant and useful to them at the time of their reading. The links created in a hypertext learning environment should be used to imply a relationship between two or more pieces of information, as well as to make explicit a pathway between them (Horney, 1993).

CONCLUSION

Hypertext–based systems are most often static, non-adaptive learning mediums. They do not "teach," but instead provide a linear path through the subject material. There is, inherent in the organization of hypermedia courseware, an author/expert defined structure to the material. To overcome the constraints imposed on the learning environment by the structure of the medium, faculty must actively build in opportunities for dialogue and for learner control. Olgren (1998) argues for the use of flexible course designs that use modular units, optional exercises, and modifiable instructional strategies to accommodate the differing knowledge level of students. Other solutions include using collaborative activities including peer teaching or work-study teams.

The opportunity now exists, with the increased development of Web-based communication tools and more sophisticated ways of presenting content, for faculty to create learning environments that can support the two global themes of self-directed learning identified in this paper. Within the context of Knowles's (1975) definition, the two themes provide an organization for thinking about incorporating the principles and practices of self-directed learning into the "virtual" classroom.

Interactivity—with the teacher, other learners, or with the text itself:

- Diagnosing learning needs
- Identifying resources
- Evaluating learning

Learner Control—within the "virtual" classroom created by faculty:

- Contributing to learning goals
- Choosing and implementing learning strategies

We argue that faculty must take on the responsibility for not only providing traditional reference-related links to information within the context of their Web-based course, but also for activities that encourage reflection through increased levels of learner control that assist students in focusing more attention on constructing their own knowledge.

REFERENCES

Becker, D., & Dwyer, M. (1994). Using hypermedia to provide learner control. Journal of Educational Multimedia and Hypermedia, 3(2), pp.155-172.

Berge, Z.L. (1995). Facilitating computer conferencing: Recommendations from the field. Educational Technology, 35(1), pp.22-30.

Boshier, R., Mohapi, M., Moulton, G., Qayyum, A., Sadownik, L., & Wilson, M. (1997). Best and worst dressed web courses: Strutting into the 21st Century in comfort and style. In I. Mitchell (Ed.). Distance Education, 18(2), pp.327-349.

Dillon, A., & Gabbard, R. (1998). Hypermedia as an educational technology: A review of the quantitative research literature on learner comprehension, control, and style. Review of Educational Research, 68(3), pp.322-349.

Dimitroff, A., & Wolfram, D. (1995). Searcher response in a hypertext-based bibliographic information retrieval system. Journal of the American Society for Information Science, 46(1), pp.22-29.

Eastmond, D., & Ziegahn, J. (1995). Instructional design for the online classroom. In Z.L. Berge & M.P. Collins (Eds.). Computer mediated communication and the online classroom, Volume Three: Distance learning (pp.29-36). New Jersey: Hampton Press.

Garrison, D.R., & Shale, D. (1990). A new framework and perspective. In D.R. Garrison & D. Shale (Eds.), Education at a distance: from issues to practice (pp.123-133). Malabar, FL: Robert E. Krieger Publishing Company.

Garrison, D.R. (1992). Critical thinking and self-directed learning in adult education: an analysis of responsibility and control issues. Adult Education Quarterly, 42(3), pp.136-148.

Gibson, Chere (Ed.). (1998). The Distance Learner's Academic Self-Concept. In Distance Learners in Higher Education: Institutional Responses for Quality Outcomes (pp.65-76). Madison, WI: Atwood Publishing, Madison, WI.

Gillingham, M. (1993). Effects of question complexity and reader strategies on adults' hypertext comprehension. Journal of Research on Computing in Education, 26(1), pp.1-15.

Gunawardena, C., & Boverie, P.L. (1993) Impact of learning styles on instructional design for distance education. Paper presented at the World Conference of the International Council of Distance Education.

Hedberg, J.G., Brown, C., & Arrighi, M. (1997). Interactive multimedia and web-based learning: Similarities and Differences. In B. Khan (Ed.). Web-based instruction. Englewood Cliffs, NJ: Educational Technology Publications.

Horney, M. (1993). Case studies of navigational patterns in constructive hypertext. Computers and Education, 20(30), pp.257-270.

Jonassen, D., Davidson, M., Collins, C., Campbell, J., & Haag, B.B. (1995). Constructivism and computer-mediated communication in distance education. The American Journal of Distance Education, 9(2), pp.7-26.

Jonassen, D.H. (1988). Designing structured hypertext, and structuring access to hypertext. Educational Technology 28(11), pp.13-16.

Kearsley, G. (1988). Authoring considerations for hypertext. Educational Technology 28(11), pp.21-24.

Laurillard, D. (1993). Rethinking university teaching: A framework for the effective use of educational technology. London: Routledge.

Lave, J., & Wenger, E. (1991). Situated learning: Legitimate peripheral participation. Cambridge: Cambridge University Press.

Murray, J. (1997). Hamlet on the holodeck: The future of narrative in cyberspace. NY: Simon & Schuster.

Olgren, C. (1998). Improving Learning outcomes: the effects of learning strategies and motivation. In C. Gibson (Ed.). Distance Learners in Higher Education (pp.77-95). Madison, WI: Atwood Publishing.

Panel on Educational Technology. (1997). Report to the President on the use of technology to strengthen K-12 education in the United States. Washington, D.C.: President's Committee of Advisors on Science and Technology.

CHAPTER TWENTY–ONE

A CONCEPTUAL FRAMEWORK FOR DEVELOPING A HOLISTIC ASSESSMENT INSTRUMENT FOR SELF–DIRECTED READINESS, MOTIVATION AND SUPPORTIVE ENVIRONMENT (SDRMSE)

Asghar Zomorrodian

Higher education institutions have realized in the past 15 years that the traditional educational format is not successful with all learners, especially adults. As an increasing number of post-secondary institutions are searching and experimenting with new modes of delivery for adult learners, often, there is a lack of tools to properly predict and assess the success of adult applicants and learners. This paper will try to explore the necessity of developing a multi-dimensional measurement instrument that can be applies for a holistic assessment of applicants and participants in adult-oriented learning programs. The proposed instrument intends to assess self-directed readiness of both prospects and learners, to depict their motivational profile, and identify the type of environment that can be more conducive to the success and enhancement of the learning process and achieving the learning results in the most efficient and effective way.

Although the paper does not intend to dig into the factors and parameters to be included in such an instrument, nonetheless, it will address a few major philosophical and conceptual issues related to the specific characteristics of adult and self-directed learning and objectives to be attained through such programs. References also will be made to a few attempts made by researchers and scholars to develop assessment instruments related to certain aspects of adult and self-directed learning, some of which can be used as a baseline for the proposed assessment system.

A NEED FOR A HOLISTIC ASSESSMENT INSTRUMENT

An increasing number of working adults are returning to college. According to the Department of Labor, 49% of the undergraduate student body by the year 2005 will be in the 35-54 age bracket. As colleges begin to provide education for working adults it becomes necessary to modify the conventional models of education in such a way that they accommodate the specific needs of the new student population. Among new features of a typical adult oriented program are flexibility of schedule, use of distance learning technology, and most important of all, new designs and delivery systems that are student-centered and tailored to individual needs. Such new modes of educational design and delivery need reliable measurement tools as they adopt a "foreign" educational methodology for which the existing educational system is not totally prepared. To help educational institutions and to secure the success of the newly designed programs, developing a comprehensive measurement tool as a vehicle for predicting the learners' success and providing an ongoing feedback to them as well as those who are responsible for program delivery and administration seems to be an essential requirement. Such an instrument must be capable of measuring at least three major dimensions of any adult-oriented learning program in an integrated and holistic manner:

- The level of self-directedness of the learners since most of the new program will be designed based on this specific parameter.
- The baseline motivation of the student and how it can be enhanced and maintained throughout the students' educational program.
- Factors affecting a learning environment that is conductive to the success of adult and learner centered educational program.

278

The instrument, if designed properly, can be of a tremendous help to educational advisors, faculty, administrators, others who are involved in the program design and delivery, and most important of all to the learners.

Although the instrument will have a great significance for all types of educational and training programs, nonetheless, mostly it will be instrumental in the success of a typical adult education program at the college and professional training in the following ways:

1. Help colleges to assess success probability/rates for adult applicants.

2. Identify cost effective learning opportunities for a larger and diversified population that are under-served due to constraints of an adult lifestyle.

3. Provide successful completion of academic programs particularly for the older, more mature and experienced working adults who seek college education for present and future advancement.

4. Impact directly on greater access to higher education and possibility of success for the less privileged, under-represented older and working population.

5. Improve the retention rate of those older working students who, in spite of other personal and family responsibilities, will devote their time, money and energy in furthering their education in a more appropriate and effective setting (Zomorrodian, 1998a).

ADULT LEARNING: A PHILOSOPHICAL BACKGROUND

Paulo Freire observed: "only the student can name the moment of the death of the professor." This story focuses on the clear role of the professor and the transformation of that role demanded by this effort at problem-based learning (Vella, 1994).

Freire's <u>Pedagogy of the oppressed</u>, called attention to the problem-based approach in teaching, which today comes very close to the concept of the student-centered learning. The whole issue has to do with making teaching and learning the way that prepares learners for the complex reality of the life.

Freire's and later Carl Rogers' philosophies and approaches called for giving students more space and freedom in their educational endeavor. The idea gradually led to the advent of different learning approaches, particularly in the area of adult education, and eventually to what is known today as *self-directed learning* or SDL.

There have been different interpretations of SDL. They range from total autonomy of the learners in pursuing their learning to a limited participation in curriculum design and delivery. The essence of the argument has to do with replacing the traditional, teacher-centered approach with one that is student- or learner-centered, and that allows the learner to become involved in decisions regarding both the content and the process of the learning.

THE ROLE OF THE ADULT LEARNER

Due to the student-centered nature of adult and self-directed and problem-oriented learning, the role of the learner (or traditionally speaking, the student) will be very different in the learning process and assessment of learning. Vella refers to a few examples of different designs and shows how, with proper training, professors internalized the meaning of problem-based designs using small group work and a kind of modular structure. They utilized a kind of interdisciplinary team approach and integrated the three concepts of designing learning tasks, demonstrating concern for safety, learners as subjects of learning, and an inductive approach to the learning into the process.

Looking at learners as the main subject of learning, as opposed to focusing on the subject matter, is the main issue in SDL. Thus, self-directedness will naturally start with a change in the perception of the students. This is the single most important effort in the beginning of the learning process and confirms what Gibson (1951) said, "We see things not as they are but as we are," meaning that the behavior of the learners does not change unless their perceptions are changed. This is true with the SDL due to its developmental process. The learner can improve her tendency, skills and mastery to become more self-directed progressively, thus perceptual changes become vital to this kind of developmental process. A student is usually willing to change his perceptions in situations that are not working and, with some encouragement from the teacher/facilitator, to work on those situations. Areglado and others refer to some 20 perceptions that relate to understanding of students about defining themselves, and use them as a vehicle for helping them to become more self-directed. Some of these perceptions relate to staying in control, helping others, holding more power over oneself, need for practice, and to be truthful to oneself among others. (1996)

Baguer and Revans also refer to a similar concept that comes very close to SDL. Their argument suggests that whatever we pursue, some ways of saying or doing fresh things can be gotten from others. Much of what is picked up in this way has already long existed. They call these "Programmed" in contrast to knowledge, ideas, attitudes, skills, and new perceptions of what goes on that are all new to the person. After the shock of finding out from one's own experience that some hallowed belief is no longer true, a learning occurs that by this nature comes from questioning insight. Moriss argues that simplistically we may say the fresh learning is the sum of programmed instruction and questioning insight (1991). His argument builds on the ideas of Revans, who formulated *Action Learning*, and who suggests that education and training have placed far too much dependence on Programmed learning, taught by accredited experts, rather than initiated by people questioning their own direct experience.(Revans, 1991).

Assessing learners needs become more and more complex for a variety of reasons. Major differences in learners expectations, professional situations, and most important of all the dynamic changes in the external environment places greater reliance on learner's own judgement and evaluation of his or her needs becomes more essential. Consequently even some traditional education programs, particularly those related to professional areas, are increasingly adopting student-centered methods that allow for more participation of the learners in the educational process (Zomorrodian, 1999a).

At a more formal level, the same argument can be made as why concepts like Action Learning (AL) that incorporate SDL as well as converting the changes in the external environment to the realities internal to both organizational and individual settings have become so appealing. McGill and Beaty refers to AL as "A continuous process of learning and reflection, supported by colleagues, with the intention of getting things done" (1995). Inglis refers to a similar definition, AL as "a process which brings people together to find solutions to problems and, in doing so, develops both the individual and the organizations" (1994). We have to take an important note here though. The definitions referred to for Action Learning are mostly directed toward the context of organizational learning which makes it somehow different from a more traditional concept of SDL which focuses on individual autonomy as will be discussed in the later part of this paper. Group learning which has become the core issue in today's organizational environment, applies the SDL concept and its learning methodology at both group and individual levels.

EVALUATION OF LEARNING

Regardless of the type and approaches to learning, evaluation has always been an integral part of the learning process. More traditional approaches normally focus on the amount of learning obtained by the learner. Recent approaches, particularly those related to Action Learning, SDL, and similar methods go a few steps beyond that and look at the outcome in terms of application, meaningfulness, and impact of the learning. As an example, Kerka refers to an assessment approach called Authentic Assessment (AA), which incorporates a wide variety of techniques designed to correspond, as closely as possible, to "real world" student experiences. Such assessments focus on high-performance workplace demands including critical thinking, self-directedness, and enhancing individual capability (1995).

Authentic Assessments have meaning in themselves, the learning they measure has value beyond the classroom and is meaningful to the learner. Aas address the skills and abilities needed to perform actual tasks and utilize a host of tools like checklists on learners' goals, writing, reading, simulations, essays and other demonstrations of performance, intake and progress interviews, oral presentations, informal and formal observations by instructors, peers, and others, self-assessments, and constructed-response questions. A most widely used technique in a typical AA is *Portfolio Assessment*. Portfolios are a collection of learner's work over time. They may include research papers, book reports, journals, logs, photographs, videos… group project, softwares, slides, and test results. The hallmark of a portfolio used for assessment is that the contents are selected by the learner (Hayse et al. 1994). The items are chosen according to a set of standards of objectives connected to the curriculum or learning events. Portfolios can serve as a catalyst for reflection on one's growth as a learner and as a means of identifying areas for improvement.

Authentic Assessments and other similar approaches all encompass elements of SDL both in their designs and implementations. Although most evaluation examples in the literature focus on the use of SDL in training in which trainees master packages of predetermined material, at their own pace, without the aid of an instructor, nonetheless these evaluation models have a few important things to offer for a broader SDL approaches such as a college program.

Generally speaking, evaluation of SDL can be broken down into two types. The first is evaluation of the trainees or learners, which is often termed user evaluation and is based on the analysis of the trainee, job, facilitator, and the format. The second is a package or system evaluation. This is evaluation of the SDL process which might involve a single package or an entire system, depending on the size of the structure. Two authors suggest that evaluation has two main components: cognitive and performance evaluations (Nadler and Nadler, 1993). Cognitive evaluation focuses on test development, in which each question is normally related to an objective. This method often is described as criterion-referenced or criterion-based questions. Criterion referencing and matching questions to objectives, is considered as a major component of a good SDL design and development

The second type of user evaluation common in SDL is performance evaluation. The term used by the authors to refer to an instrument other than a paper and pencil test. Performance test measures the ability to perform the task intended by the learning. They are planned for the trainee/learner to exhibit something that has to be demonstrated.

Garland proposes a group oriented approach to assessment. He suggests that for helping students to learn about the processes of working small groups, as well as helping the staff (and naturally faculty) to make effective use of group work, the outcomes of group learning must be assessed. His prescribed format consists of two components of assessing individual performances of group members, and the use of peer and self appraisal (Garland, 1992). A few important elements would be perception of educational benefits of the group work and the concern for reliability and validity of the method employed. Two major issues have to do with:

- What should be assessed: Product/Outcome?, Process, or both, and..
- Who should assess? Student self-assessment, peer group, instructor, combination, etc.

Long raises several interesting questions with regard to the effectiveness of the independent learning. Although, SDL, at least within the context of this paper, is not equated to an independent learning, since the learners will interact with faculty, advisor, peers, and receive as much guidance as they need, some of those questions are very relevant to the tenet of this inquiry:

a. How can independent learning be evaluated?
b. How does the independent learner determine the best resources?
c. How do the intentions of the learner affect the process(es)?
d. What kind of things do participants in learning projects do to encourage their activity?
e. What practical strategies are useful? (Long, 1998)

EXAMPLE OF A FEW SDL ORIENTED ASSESSMENT TOOLS

The literature contains a few specific examples of assessment tools developed by researches and academicians for evaluating different aspects of the adult and SDL oriented learning. Although, these tools, at least in some cases, might be in the infancy stage and have yet to be subject to rigorous validation, each may serve as a baseline for a particular aspect of a comprehensive assessment instrument for a typical SDL program.

Self-Directed Learning Readiness Score (SDLRS)
This is a Likert scale with five response options, was originally developed and field-tested in 1977 by Lucy Guglielmino. The Instrument was subsequently expanded to 58 items, and has been widely used for the assessment of readiness for self-directed learning. Based on compilation of more than 3000 respondents to the instrument, the Pearson split-half reliability is reported to be at 94 (P. & L, Guglielmino, 1998).

Learning Profiles Questionnaire (LPQ) and
Learner Orientation Instrument
Learning Profiles Questionnaire (LPQ) was developed by Confessore in 1994 as an instrument designed to identify various characteristics of self-directed learners. The questionnaire was based on the responses of the learners about the learning projects they have been involved in, if they were related to other projects they have had before, if they have been initiated by the learner, and a few assessments about basic learning skills, and perception of self as a life-long learner (Confessore & Confessore, 1998)

In discussing the development of a Learner Orientation Instrument the authors give a good overview of several decades of development in studying the participation and self-directed orientations of the learners.

They use Houle's typology of three types of learners, i.e. goal oriented, activity oriented and learning oriented as a baseline and present a comparison of his model with later developments made by Sheffield's 58 item instrument (1964), Boshier's 48 item Education Participation Scale (EPS) and the refinement made by Morstain and Smart (1974) using the EPS. They show the essence of their comparative analysis in the Table 21.1:

Table 21.1.   Comparison of Learner Orientation

Houle	Shefield	Boshier	Morstain & Smart
	Societal Goals (Houle's)		Social Welfare (identical)
Activity Oriented	Sociability	Social Contact	Social Relationships
Goal Oriented	Personal Goal	Other Directed and Inner Directed	Professional Advancement
Activity Oriented	Desire Activity	Intellectual Recreation	Escape/Simulation
Learning Oriented		Cognitive Interest	Cognitive Interest (identical)

Adopted from: Confessore & Confessore, 1998

Based on their conceptualization, the authors intend to develop an instrument for Learning Orientation assessment which they think will be added to the existing LPQ instrument. (1998)

Depending on how the instrument will come out eventually, it might be a useful instrument for assessing the learner's orientation based on what he is accustomed to. This can provide a baseline to look at the learner's present orientation and motivation. But as for the level of readiness and change, one needs to go further. We must also be aware of a problem with Houle's initial conceptualization since it is not geared toward self-directedness of the learners per se. Rather, it is centered on the (any) learner's general orientation.

Self-Directed Learning Perception Scale (SDLPS)

SDLPS is an instrument designed to investigate learners' perceptions of what helps them with the SDL process. The instrument focuses on the learning situation rather than the learner and is suggested to be a useful tool for instructors, trainers, committees and making decisions regarding SDL. This instrument is a 57 item self-report instrument developed over a seven years period is based on the SDL process model and investigates what helps learners with the self-directed learning. It is a Likert scale, and produces a profile showing what learners feel helps them with SDL in a specific setting and context (Pelling-Cormick, 1998).

SDRMSE: FRAMEWORK AND COMPONENTS

As discussed before, the purpose of SDRMSE is to build a comprehensive and multi-dimensional framework for assessing adult learners in an academic and professional program. The instrument focus is not only on the assessment of three major dimensions of learner's readiness, motivation and supporting environment, but it also looks at those dimensions as components of a unified body that can help in building an authentic learning program for an individual learner. The ultimate goal is to come up with the best fit between the program and each learner's specific needs, motivational profile, and readiness, using a series of pre, during and post assessments and feedback events on a continuous basis. Based on such assessments and feedback, and with the purpose to achieve the best fit between the individual and learning, curriculum and delivery method will be continuously changed and modified to reflect the changes in the individual and his or her needs. The assessments will be considered as an integral part of the continuous design-redesign and delivery of the curriculum for achieving an effective and efficient learning. The three major components (instruments) of SDRMSE assessment model along with a brief explanation about the nature and the scope of each one will follow:

1. ***Self-Directed Readiness Instrument (SDRI).*** Unlike similar tools, this particular aspect of the holistic assessment does not look at the absolute measure of self-directed readiness. Rather the intention will be to develop a qualitative oriented assessment that provides an initial profile of the potential learner in order to direct her to the best possible learning design and delivery system. Thus, theoretically, self-directedness is considered as a relative term that can range from minimum to the maximum in a continuum of being highly to partially self-directed. In the meantime, based on the initial assessment of the learner, he can be assisted in enhancing his level of self-directedness, if he chooses so. The key, however, is to assess the existing level of self-directedness so that the right match between learning and individual self-directed readiness can be achieved.

A relevant research question in this area would be "how the level of self-directedness in a potential college student can help her to successfully complete her educational program?" Once the answer to this question is established, the learner can be encouraged and assisted to enhance her self-directedness to the desired level that she feels comfortable with.

Although this component of SDRMSE is by nature different from the conventional type of testing and evaluation, nonetheless, as far as the mechanics of the process is concerned it is similar to the concept of Value-Added Testing. In VDT, students' achievements in academic subjects and life skills, such as analyzing a newspaper column, a mathematical table, or a television advertisement, are assessed before and after a certain period of formal education and study. The difference between pre-and post-course test scores is a measure of the value added by the educational experience (Alken, 1997).

In the SDR segment of the holistic assessment, the level of self-directedness before, during and after the learning experience will be assessed and then will be related to the level of outcome in term of knowledge, mental ability, critical thinking, problem solving and any other desired outcome. Then a correlation or covariance will be established between the degree of the self-directedness, delivery methods, and the outcome to assess the effectiveness of the model deployed for the learning.

2. *Motivational Level Instrument (MLI).* This component attempts to measure the relevant aspects of the learners' motivation that affect their learning in a typical adult and self-directed program. First, the existing motivations and motivational level as they may affect a SDL type program need to be assessed. Second, the focus will be on the potentials for enhancing the motivational level (above the existing baseline) as the learner progresses in her learning. Since different individuals may react differently toward different approaches of learning, it is crucial to pinpoint the characteristics of SDL mode of learning and to see if the potential learner has the actual or potential tendency for such a program.

3. *Supportive Environment Instrument (LEI).* By far this one might be considered as the most significant component in the process of holistic assessment Similar to the five basic elements of action learning that deal with the Problem, set, client, set advisor, and the process, the environment of an adult and SDL learning requires a different design and accommodation. The environment consists of a few crucial sub-environments which include physical, psychological, administrative, instructional and few others.

Among sub-environments, the psychological and instructional ones seem to have the most impact on the effectiveness of the learning. Creating autonomy, encouragement, freedom of action along with appropriate level of guidance and intervention (depending on the level of learners' self-directedness) are a few important considerations. In fact, any genuine adult and SDL program should have a built-in ability to empower learners. This is a feature so essential that without which the whole concept of SDL may totally fall apart:

Creating an encouraging environment, thus becomes essential for true SDL learning through the efforts the members of the learning community both individually and collectively, to allow the learners to be become self-directed and to get involved in the continuous process of self-empowerment (Zomorrodian, 1998c).

288

The LEI instrument will reveal that if the essential elements of the right environment for SDL do exist then to what extent can they help achieve the learning objectives. Since most learning environments are designed for traditional educational programs, assessing the mismatch between the existing environments with those required by the SDL learning is very important for the success of such programs. Based on the environmental assessment, major changes might be necessary in the administrative, support system, and the leadership of the college or institution offering such programs. LEI, in the final analysis, must look at both macro and micro levels of the learning environment. At the micro level, the attitude, training, knowledge, expertise, and orientation of the faculty, advisors and administrators of the educational program are addressed. At the macro level, overall leadership philosophy of the institution, organizational culture, and necessary infrastructure will be the targets of assessment.

OVERALL PROGRAM EVALUATION

Learning evaluation has a two-part objective: (1) to help learners find the best way of learning that can help them in achieving their stated objectives; and (2) address institutional outcomes of the program. The goal of program evaluation is to make judgements concerning the utility or value of educational, psychological and other social interventions programs. Various guides or models of program evaluations have been proposed for this purpose, including the CIPP (context, input, process, product) model, discrepancy evaluation, and adversary evaluation (Alken 1997).

Rossi and Freeman (1993) offer a comprehensive model characterizing the overall process of program evaluation in terms of four successive stages: planning, monitoring, impact assessment, and economic efficiency assessment. In the first stage, the extent of the problem or the goals, and the target population are identified. The second stage has to do with program monitoring which deals with making sure the designated resources and services are provided to the target population. At the stage three, the actual outcomes are evaluated to see if the goals of the program have been met. Various statistical and non-statistical procedures are applied to determine whether the outcomes are significant and in the predicted direction. Other unintended or unexpected outcomes are evaluated, but even when statistically significant, they may not be of sufficient practical significance. Consequently, it is the purpose of the fourth stage-economic efficiency assessment to determine whether the results of a program are worth the costs incurred in implementing it.

These models may not suit the objective of every single college or educational program. They definitely can provide a basis for any given institution or program to develop a holistic assessment system. Also, they can inform an implementation plan that can incorporate relevant situational factors and parameters.

REFERENCES

Alken, L.R. (1997). Psychological testing and assessment. Boston: Allyn and Bacon

Areglado, R., Bradley, R., & Lane, P. (1996). Learning for life: Creating classrooms for self-directed learning. Thousand Oaks, CA: Corwin press, Inc.

Confessore, G., & Confessore, P. (1998) Developing an instrument to establish learner orientation: using Houle's typology to understand learning events. Presented to the 12th. International Symposium of Self-directed Learning. Orlando, FL. February 1998

Garland, D. (1992). Assessment issues in group work. In H.C. Foot., et.al. (Ed.) Group and Interactive Learning. Boston: Computational Mechanics Publications.

Gibson. J. (1951). Theories of perceptions. In Wayne Dennis (Ed.) Current trends in psychological theory. Pittsburgh: University of Pittsburgh Press.

Guglielmino P., & Guglielmino N. (1998). Three studies of self-directed learning readiness in the People's Republic of China. In H.B. Long & Associates (Eds.), Developing paradigms for self directed learning (pp.61-71). University of Oklahoma, College of Education.

Hayse, E.R., Kretschmann, K., & Berry, M. (1994). Portfolio assessment in adult basic skills education. Madison: Madison Area Technical College. (ED 351 365)

Inglis, S. (1994). Making the most of action learning. Aldershot: England: Gower.

Kerka, S. (1997). Techniques for authentic assessment. ERIC: Practice and Application Briefs. Http://www.ericacve.org/auth,collab.hltm

Long, H. (1998). Theoretical and practical implications of selected paradigms of self-directed learning. In H.B. Long & Associates (Eds.), Developing paradigms for self directed learning (pp.1-14). University of Oklahoma, College of Education.

McGill,, I, & Beaty, L. (1995). Action Learning. 2nd. ed. London: Kogan Page.

Morris, J. (1991). "Minding our Ps and Qs." In M. Pedler (Ed.), Action learning in practice. Vermont: Gower Publishing Company.

Nadler, L., & Nadler, Z. (1993). Self-directed learning: A practical guide to design, development, and implementation. San Francisco: Jossey-Bass Publishers.

Pilling-Cormick, J. (1998). The self-directed learning perception scale: A step toward a toolbox approach to instrumentation proposed for self-directed learning. In H.B. Long & Associates (Ed.), Developing paradigms for self directed learning (pp.159-168). University of Oklahoma, College of Education. Chp. 12.

Revans, R. (1991). Action learning: Its origins and nature. In M. Pedler (Ed.), Action learning in practice. Vermont: Gower Publishing Company.

Rossi, P.H., & Freeman, H.E. (1993). Evaluation: A systematic approach (5th. ed.) Beverly Hills, CA: Sage Publication.

Vella, J. (1994). Learning to listen, learning to teach: The power of dialogue in educating adults. San Francisco: Jossey-Bass Publishing.

Zomorrodian, A. (1998a). Developing a multidimensional instrument for assessing the self-directed readiness, motivation and supportive environment for adult college students. A proposal for Research Funding submitted to Department of Education (FEPSI), November.

Zomorrodian, A. (1998b). Self-directed learning: An emerging paradigm in higher and professional education: Practical examples. In H.B. Long & Associates (Ed.), Developing paradigms in self-directed learning (pp.239-252). University of Oklahoma.

Zomorrodian, A. (1998c). New trends in leadership and their impacts on strategic management. Journal of Business & Behavioral Sciences, 4, December.

Zomorrodian, A. (1999). New experimental approaches to management education at the college level. A paper presented to the annual national conference of American Society of Business & Behavioral Sciences. Las Vegas, NV. February 15-18